THE MEMOIRS CALLED GOSPELS

For the apostles, in the memoirs composed by them, which are called Gospels, have thus delivered unto us what was enjoined upon them . . . .

Justin Martyr (*c.* 150), *Apology* I, 66

The
Memoirs Called
Gospels

G. P. GILMOUR
President and Vice-Chancellor of McMaster University

HODDER AND STOUGHTON

Printed in Canada for
HODDER AND STOUGHTON LIMITED, LONDON, ENGLAND

To my father,
Rev. Joseph Leeming Gilmour (1864 - 1924),
who taught me to love the scriptures
and the fruits of scholarship.

CONTENTS

viii
CONTENTS

PREFACE

No book escapes completely from its first draft. This one is what it is because it grew out of the attempt to lecture on the gospels to university freshmen over a period of more than twenty-five years. From their attention and inattention, their intelligent questions and their howlers in answering examinations, I have learned much.

It has seemed natural to present these introductory studies in three sections. Readers of the gospels need to learn that the Bible is bound up with the nature of language, a philosophy of history, the life of the church, and a series of events in history. They should also think in general terms about the gospel record, which most people know at first hand only in small fragments.

Bibliographical help is supplied in the form of relatively non-technical supplementary reading for various chapters, and in an introductory statement about the tools of scholarship at the end of the book. This latter was added because so many beginners do not know a concordance from a commentary, and are ignorant about the wealth of good work available. Some are even inclined to read a religious novel as though it were a learned journal.

The footnote references are there because I have found it necessary to check my sources, and because I think of this as two books in one, a series of introductory chapters on basic themes and a more exacting guide for serious readers who want to get directly at the biblical material, whether as individuals or in groups. Many people cannot or will not use a concordance; and sometimes they are grateful to be able to turn up biblical references that tickle the memory or arouse curiosity. Some cannot even find the parable of the Good Samaritan unaided. I hope that this feature will make this handbook useful for college classes, for study groups, or for the interested layman.

Text and reference material were, like the Synoptic Gospels themselves, designed to serve the intelligent beginner. This may be a religiously illiterate generation, but the illiterate are not necessarily indifferent, lazy or stupid. They often need only to be told where to look for the material.

These chapters are intended to be objective; but it will be evident that the writer stands in the tradition of "orthodox dissent", and believes that in the Bible is to be found the Word of God and all truth necessary to salvation.

I am particularly indebted to my wife and to my colleague, Professor H. W. Lang, for helpful criticisms and suggestions, and to Miss Jean Montgomery and Mrs. Gordon Ludlow, who deciphered and typed the manuscript.

G. P. GILMOUR

McMaster University
April, 1959

THE MEMOIRS CALLED GOSPELS

AN APPROACH TO THE BIBLE

CHAPTER I

ALL THINGS CONSIDERED

What then shall we say to this?—Romans 8:31
Always be prepared to make a defense to any one who
calls you to account for the hope that is in you, yet do
it with gentleness and reverence.—I Peter 3:15

I. MAKING A PRONOUNCEMENT

Man is so constituted that he must formulate or adopt
a total view of the universe and of his own place in it.
He must pronounce a last judgment, as well as prepare
for the Last Judgment. His pronouncement is his
religion, whether or not it is Christian, and whether or
not he calls it a religion. We are all, therefore, engaged in
a great argument that deals with the theme, "all things
considered". This argument is the substance of the Bible,
and to some extent of all serious literature. It may lead
a man to Christian faith, or to other religions, or to the
repudiation of all formal religion.

Sooner or later each of us faces up to serious thought
about God and the Bible. Some may, like Robert Elsmere, come to it "disastrously early";[1] others, like Willie
Keith's father, "too late".[2] Actually, we come to such
thinking early and late, both because its influence is all
around us, in art and architecture, poetry and prose, music
and drama, law and morals, and because early childhood
impressions have to be revised and enriched by later
knowledge.

A man's total view, his pronouncement, shapes his

3

mind, character, and conduct. That is why G. K. Chesterton insisted that before renting a room, the first question one should ask a landlady is "What is your total view of the universe?" In order of importance it is the first question a man must ask himself, although he may be long in committing himself to an answer and may resent being queried on the subject. Whatever his answer, it will involve a venture of faith. The evidence compels no man to this or that conclusion; the only compulsion is that he must venture, must agree to walk by faith, and not by sight. If he later changes his conviction, he will have experienced a conversion from one pronouncement to another, but he will still be exercising faith. He may exercise it alone, or in the fellowship of a shared faith, a church.

The choice among total views is limited. It includes such alternatives as that the universe is meaningless, being a chance collocation of atoms; that it is physically significant but morally meaningless because the Power behind it is not personal in any moral sense; that it is evil or unfriendly because it is the product of dark powers or of a dark Power, some Demiurge of ancient speculation; or that it is friendly and meaningful because it is the product and province of a good God. Within this last broad view there are many gradations, chief among them the Christian view that God is good in such a way that in loving-kindness He is actively engaged in the redemption of sinful men.

The inevitable great argument proceeds on two fronts. There is the argument of conviction and, consequently, the argument of obedience. Adopting a total conviction, whatever it is, calls logically for self-committal to live totally as though it were true. No one, however, does this completely. On the first front a man faces doubts, and, on the second, failure of nerve, of loyalty, or of wisdom. Christians are not the only people to have doubts and to know the bitterness of inner condemnation. It may appear that they are uniquely vocal on the subject because in hymn and prayer they confess to their God that the Christian faith is too hard to be grasped or too good to be true, and that they have failed miserably to live up to their convictions. But every total view gives rise to doubts as to whether all the deep questions have been deeply enough put and answered, and as to whether inner peace would really result from paying the price of wholehearted obedience to the answers accepted. The argument of conviction and the argument of obedience affect everyone, not Christians only.

2. WORDS WITH MEANING

It is not enough to rattle off high-sounding words and call that a pronouncement. Serious words must convey serious meanings. All serious words have theological implications, whether the theology be Christian or not. Atheism is a theological position, as is agnosticism.

There are doubtless those who would be happy to settle for the closing words of the most pessimistic and modern-sounding of Old Testament books, "Fear God and keep his commandments, for this is the whole duty of man",[2] because this sounds like a plain, respectable statement with no nonsense or theology about it. But it is no such thing. Every word is big with theological questions, thus:

(a) Who is "God"? Some capricious and arbitrary Olympian deity, some vengeful demon, some distant and impersonal Force, some inscrutable and relentless Judge or Fate, or Someone whom Jesus called "your heavenly Father"?

(*b*) What is "fear"? A cringing before cosmic caprice or relentlessness, an unacknowledged terror that disintegrates the personality, a cosmic loneliness in the presence of the Unknown, a defiance such as Henley flung out in "Invictus", or a reverence for "the God and Father of our Lord Jesus Christ", at once abasing and exalting, that hurts yet heals?

(*c*) What are "his commandments"? A complex of ritual acts and irrational tabus, the sum of socially accepted mores, or moral principles that inhere in the nature of things and that must be discerned within the complexities and hard facts of human life?

(*d*) What is it to "keep" them? A slavish obedience to the letter that kills, or a discernment of their spirit that leads to true freedom? Is the will free to obey? Is divine assistance necessary and available?

(*e*) Why is this "the whole duty of man"? Because it leads to social integration or self-development or the good life, because it is a debt owed by the creature to the Creator, or because it brings man into communion with his Maker and makes him truly man?

(*f*) Does this "duty" carry any reward? Is reward thought of as a dividend on a long-term bargain with God, is virtue to be disinterested and its own reward, or is the reward a free gift of "sonship" to those who have learned the obedience of love?

(*g*) Why is it impossible to feel that one has kept the commandments honestly or feared God worthily, and why is this conviction of failure more acute the farther one goes in the understanding of goodness? Is the final result to be a feeling of blindness, futility, or unforgiven sin, or does self-condemnation lead to the threshold of deliverance?

(*h*) What can be said to those who acknowledge that they have failed, and cannot balance their account with God? Is there no real problem involved, since "He's a Good Fellow and 'twill all be well", is there no hope of forgiveness but only "a fearful prospect of judgment", or is there a "grace of God" that "gives the guilty conscience peace" and is revealed most compellingly and convincingly in Christ?

All religions have wrestled with such questions. It is vital to decide which formulation of faith has asked the questions with the greatest penetration and recommended the most satisfying answers. The Bible is the record of how in the Judeo-Christian tradition these questions were asked with increasing penetration and answered with increasing satisfaction to the conscience and the mind. Because Christians believe that all that went before the gospel story was preparation for it,[4] and all that has followed has been interpretation of it, the chapters that follow briefly introduce the Bible and the gospels and then present certain aspects of the gospel story.

There is theological thought in the Bible and in the gospels and it is necessary to take some notice of it. Religious experience, "the peace of God which passes all understanding",[5] makes men want to understand it, to present the argument of conviction to their own minds and to other people. The result is theology. But theology is not experience. It is possible to know the theological arguments and have no experience, and it is possible to have the experience without holding to all parts of the accepted theology. Both the experience and the theology are bigger than any one individual can know. No person or age has enjoyed the full experience,[6] or held with equal conviction or sense of need all the theological assertions.

The Christian argument of conviction must at many
points be presented in the spirit of the proverb, *La vérité
est dans les nuances*.   One recent British speaker has said,
"What we need just now is . . . a more intensive conversation between Christians and between them and the
philosophers, historians and scientists who are not Christians at all. . . . The Christians . . . can lose the argument
not only by what they say but also by the way they say it."[7]
But there must be substance as well as proportion in the
argument: one must study the biblical evidence intelli-
gently before any argument that makes use of it can
proceed.

3. HEIRS OF TWO CULTURES

Such study must be related to the fact that we in the
western world are the heirs of two sources of serious
thought, the Greek philosophy and the Judeo-Christian
Bible and Church.   As the inheritors of western culture
we look back to "two views of life, and only two, which
have won the allegiance of large masses of mankind in
the West.   One of these comes from Palestine, the other
from Greece."[8]   There may today appear to be a third
claimant for allegiance, dialectical materialism, which
holds that man is governed by economic and physical
forces he cannot escape or guide, and that morality is a
matter of expedience or custom, not of principle.   But
this was in essence known and rejected by Plato and
others, and in the Bible *Ecclesiastes*, although affected
by it, denied its ultimate validity.[9]

The Greek heritage is more akin to our own way of
thinking because of its emphasis on education, its rejection
of the immoral and childish myths of a primitive cosmology,[10] and its beginning of the scientific method.
Plato and Aristotle have usually been dear to Christian

thinkers, since they taught men to think reasonably. But it is important to give careful thought to the Palestinian heritage also. It has informed our spirit; it took over when Greece perished; it has preserved and been preserved by the Greek heritage. The Bible is singularly lacking in an interest in science or in second causes, the Hebrews being content to ascribe everything to the direct action of God once they had fought free of polytheism, or what is called henotheism. This does not mean, however, that the Hebrews were irrational. They thought in pictures more than in closeknit argument. Both Greeks and Hebrews became monotheists, but for the former it was often a speculative, rather impersonal argument about the Absolute, while for the latter it was always a warm and personal faith in the Father. Both strains persist among us, the Greek having the better of it with many at the moment.

The Palestinian heritage suffers among us because of the strangeness of its atmosphere and vocabulary, and because of its preoccupation with the religious ordering of life.[11] The striking outreach of its thinking is lost to view partly because it is not systematically presented in the Bible and partly because a first acquaintance with it is often acquired from amateurs. The Greek heritage escapes this latter danger. Not being encountered until maturity,[12] it is largely the preserve of an *élite*. Yet the fact that the Palestinian is first known in childhood—childhood impressions can be as poor as they can be rich— and that amateurs, including parents and Sunday school teachers, wrestle with it and pass on something of it, is significant. Here is truth that can enter in at lowly doors. It was and is for all men, not philosophers only: indeed, the least may understand what the greatest overlook.[13] But the heritage is not today confined to the amateur.

Those who read Dorothy Sayers, T. S. Eliot, Christophei Fry, and C. S. Lewis may even suspect that Christian conviction, having lost some of its hold on the masses, is today in danger of becoming the preserve of the intelligentsia.

4. ELECTION AND GRACE

Our vocabulary owes much to both heritages. To choose only two words characteristic of each that have affected us deeply, the Greek has given us "reason" and "virtue" (*areté*), the Palestinian "election" and "grace". From the one pair we derive an orderly idea of man, from the other an orderly idea of the purpose of God. The Greek words are easier to use in education and speech, whereas the Palestinian sound as though they belonged only in church. All four can be debased. "Reason" can become cold and impersonal and "virtue" a badge of self-satisfaction. But because these pages are about the Bible the danger of debasement will be illustrated only as it affects "election" and "grace".

The New Testament makes use of both "reason" and "virtue",[14] showing that from the beginning Christian thought used strong words supplied by Greece. "Man's wisdom", while regarded as ineffectual by itself, was not regarded as inherently evil any more than was the ineffectual Jewish law.[15] "Reason" and "virtue" have become part of the Christian vocabulary but "election" and "grace" have not become part of the non-Christian vocabulary. Without these latter two words, however, the reading of the Bible is meaningless.

"Election" is not a species of Divine favouritism, the granting of exclusive privilege, or "salvation". It refers rather to the method of God in fulfilling His purpose by using selected men or groups as instruments. The "chosen vessel" is not the possessor but the conveyor of the "treasure",[16] its means of transport to a wider circle. An "elect nation" or "chosen people" is not the exclusive interest of God[17] any more than the twelve apostles were made the exclusive heirs of Christ's benefits when they were "chosen".[18] Jesus was "the Chosen One",[19] but was for that very reason God's instrument to benefit all men. The elect are not the whole harvest, but only its "first fruits".[20] Election does not promise a reward so much as require a duty. It looks beyond the instrument, entailing a stern judgment if it should fail or grow proud.[21] But the word can with fatal facility seem to mean the exact opposite of this, as popular ribaldry about a "chosen people" shows, and as some sectarian propaganda insists. The mark of election is humility (and often silence about the conviction), not spiritual pride.

The other word, "grace", is also of complex meaning. There is no satisfactory definition of it any more than there is of many other common words, such as inspiration, revelation, prayer or authority; but its general import is clear. Its greatest meaning is that the favour of God is unmerited, given freely to all who "call upon him". It cannot be bought, earned, or demanded. It cannot be withheld by any human agent, or automatically conveyed. It is the undeserved love of God in action. God's eternal purpose is to be gracious; His election of human instruments is an "election of grace"; "redemption" is by God's grace alone.[22] It is the only power known in the Bible that can cure both the pride and the despair that arise from what Paul rather obscurely calls "works",[23] the striving after what is usually called "merit". But this word "grace" in its turn can be misunderstood, to the point where it suggests something insipid or sentimental. It can also be so twisted as to suggest that for "the elect" grace works in such a way that all moral endeavour, or even moral decency, is unnecessary. This is the ugly trap of "sinless perfection", and the uglier error called antinomianism, against which Paul had to fight.[24]

Since salvation is sometimes thought of only as a means of escaping from the wrath of God, an emphasis on "grace" is of extreme importance, for it teaches that, on the contrary, salvation is escape from self [25] and seeking refuge in God,[26] God being concerned less with punishment or with the preservation of His own dignity than with "redemption".

The ideas of election and grace run through the Bible. Abraham first,[27] then Israel,[28] then a "godly remnant" of Israel,[29] and at last Christ and his Church[30] are presented as the elect instruments of God's purpose of grace. If an elect instrument refuses its task or its work is accomplished, another is raised up;[31] for God is "not mocked". His grace is the same for all: His election may be different for each.

So slight a discussion of key words must suffice to illustrate that the basic emphases of the Bible differ from those of Greece. These biblical words indicate in what spirit the deep questions were put and answered. To the Christian it seems clear that the questions and answers went deeper in Palestine than in Greece. In his mind, therefore, the Palestinian can crown and absorb the Greek; but the Greek cannot absorb the Palestinian.

5. MAN THE PROBLEM:
NATURE ORDERLY AND GOOD

Both heritages have to endure the fire of criticism and the ice of indifference nowadays. Metaphysics is held by some to be meaningless; and it is suggested or implied by many that we can well afford to give the Bible a long rest, and would do better to concentrate instead on the known facts of science.[32] If we want a religion at all we can get what religious exaltation we need out of communing with Nature. But before writing down the two inheritances, it is well to remember that two of the most basic problems man faces are still what to do about man, the only problem-child in creation, and whether the created world (Nature) is our enemy or our friend. Both are essentially religious questions, requiring religious answers. It may be possible to live an interesting life, to advance far in culture and education, and for all practical purposes ignore both problems. But it is not possible to live a good life so.

Man is the problem-child,[33] and only with grave difficulty is human society kept tolerable or individual life worth living. Law supplies restraint, and culture, polish, but only grace gives hope and only goodness gives happiness. The Bible reminds us of this at every turn.

As to the second problem, at first glance it may seem unimportant now. Creation, in our minds, is at worst callous and at best friendly, but is never man's enemy. But this is so only because the Greek convinced men that creation was orderly, and the Bible, that it was good.[34] Nature-mysticism, such as we inherit from the preaching of Wordsworth, is possible only on these two assumptions. George Meredith, exalting the mystical assurance of God's goodness with the words,

> *Into the breast that gives the rose*
> *Shall I with shuddering fall?*[35]

was writing for a society that was the heir of classical and biblical thought. Of old, however, it was not so. To the savage Nature was never friendly, but a brooding terror to be placated or managed by magic. Even in such relatively high civilizations as the Mayan in Yucatan, the ugly cost in human sacrifice of such placation, such control, was incalculable. Cruelty and fear, not to mention the cultic sensuality of fertility rites, are what Nature used to inspire in men, and the Old Testament bears eloquent testimony to the battle against them.[36]

Men may repudiate the Christian faith, or some weird caricature of it, but they benefit from its legacy. The Bible is an important part of the evidence in every man's great argument on both of the two fronts of conviction and of obedience. A wise heir knows something of his inheritance.

CHAPTER II

THE SACRED BOOKS OF
AN HISTORICAL RELIGION

Whatever was written in former days was written for
our instruction, that by steadfastness and by the encouragement of the scriptures we might have hope.

—Romans 15:4

I. THE THEME OF REDEMPTION

Christianity claims to be based on revealed truth; this
truth is imbedded in history (the Heilsgeschichte, or history of salvation); this history is recorded and interpreted
in sacred books ("the Bible" simply means the books);
and these present a religion of redemption, asserting that
man is in peril and is impotent to heal his self-inflicted
wounds, but that he can have God's help and mercy freely
in his extremity. As an historical religion, Christianity
has some affinities with Judaism and Islam. All the above
characteristics of Christianity are missing from certain
forms of religion, notably the emphasis on history and
the possession of sacred books.

Some people would prefer a form of religion, a total
view of the universe, that would not have any of the
four: a religion of speculation or ratiocination, independent of history, without records to which is ascribed
peculiar sanctity, and without the humbling insistence
that salvation is needed and comes by the grace of God.
But such a religion, however much it shares with, borrows
from, or professes to improve on it, is not Christianity.
Any attempt to understand the Christian faith must in-

volve an appreciation of these four immense claims; and care is needed in examining all four.

One must, for example, approach the Bible without any preconceived notions as to how a sacred literature ought to have been composed and preserved;[1] one must avoid the idea that because the Bible is "true" all other sacred books are wholly false or deliberately misleading; and one must recognize that none of the authors of biblical books was consciously aware that his writing would be included in a sacred canon.[2] The books of the Bible were books long before they were "bible"; they were given their place of special authority not by some magical formula but by the testing of long use. Nor can the Bible be expected to give guidance on themes outside its field. "Truth as it is in Jesus"[3] is not information about astrophysics or atomic fission. The scriptures are "able to instruct . . . for salvation through faith in Jesus Christ",[4] and however much incidental historical and archaeological interest they may arouse, such instruction is their only purpose and their limitation.

2. REVELATION AND DISCOVERY

Revelation is a word never exactly defined in the Bible or in Christian history.[5] But at least two things are clear in the record: that "revelation" did not come by automatic writing or dictation, without men as its conscious amanuenses and mouthpieces (although they uttered greater things than they fully realized);[6] and that revealed truth is not contrary to reason. The gift of reason is presupposed in the discernment of a revelation, since revelation is an inference from, or illumination of, things seen and weighed.

Truth came in the Bible by stages.[7] It was mediated through inspired men[8] who nevertheless shared the thought-forms, the cosmology, and even the moral myopia of their times. The truth they were shown they had to accept by faith, often unwillingly,[9] and that truth has still to be accepted by faith. But faith does not involve intellectual suicide. Biblical truth is not sanctified nonsense, mumbo-jumbo contrary to all reason. In some things revelation runs ahead of reason and can be confirmed later, and at other points it is beyond the ultimate reach of reason. That God's thoughts and way are not ours[10] does not mean that they are irrational or unintelligible: they are "higher" than man's,[11] not inherently contrary to what a man can accept. God "hides" himself, but gives man light enough to walk by.[12]

Discovery and revelation are not mutually exclusive. Admittedly, God's way of bringing men to redemption through Christ is not something that men discovered or could discover unaided.[13] But much that concerns the power and methods of God's working can be discovered and has been left to discovery.[14] Truth may be revealed as a "given" element after faithful efforts at discovery. This consideration is familiar enough outside the Bible. Scientific and other discoveries have been made by men who have testified that the truth was "given" to them, not found by them unaided, that they felt they were thinking God's thoughts after Him. Men in the Bible thought this way too. Truth was a "burden" thrust upon them. Peter faced a new and unwelcome idea at Joppa and Caesarea, and afterwards said, "I perceive".[15] There is an element of reasonable appreciation, as well as faith, in Paul's "I am persuaded".[16]

Revelation also had to wait for its appointed time: truth is meaningless to men lacking some preparatory discipline.[17] Nor is it ever promised in the Bible that everything has been, will be, need be, or can be revealed:

the word is "sufficient" rather than "complete".[18] To be led into "all the truth",[19] for example, does not mean to be given all the facts but to be enabled to understand the full meaning of what has been revealed. Truth once revealed can never again have the freshness of revelation about it, but such truth may lie forgotten or neglected, and its rediscovery will have something of the quality of fresh revelation to the individual or generation involved.

3. HISTORY AS A VEHICLE OF REVELATION

Christians hold that eternal truth is revealed and is to be discerned in certain events in time,[20] culminating in the work of Jesus. What is involved is not revealed history but revealing history. Events are not revealed: they happen.[21] But to men with eyes to see, they reveal something beyond themselves. It may be that all history is a vehicle of revelation, but no man can or need master all history. The Bible claims that there was a series of events and experiences that constituted a special vehicle, a small canvas upon which the essential features of a universal and timeless picture were presented.[22]

That history should be so regarded appears indefensible to those who contend that absolute truth cannot depend on contingent events. In certain activities, all of us feel that way. When we are engaged as philosophers or experimental scientists, for example, we are looking not at what is unique, as every historical event is unique, but at what is constant or repeatable. But when we are engaged as readers of the Bible, we must appreciate the viewpoint that certain events are regarded as uniquely significant, that is, an unrepeated sign of something beyond themselves. The "Lamb of God" who walked in Palestine once, and never before or again, is taken to be a revelation in time of something eternal.[23] Truth shadowed forth in traditional and repeated cultic sacrifices was given substance in the significant and unique sacrifice offered by Christ "through the eternal Spirit".[24]   This single sacrifice was the historic act of an historical Person; but this "blood of Christ" is significant of God's eternal purpose.   The important element here is the words "of Christ", which both root the act in time and interpret the ancient symbolism of "blood", with its associations of life, terror, and peace.

The relation between history and revelation is a topic with which theological thought has dealt repeatedly in recent years.   It calls for three qualifying considerations: (a) that history is not the sole vehicle of revelation; (b) that the "once for all" quality of certain events demands a certain view of the significance of time; and (c) that the revelation is discerned through an inspired interpretation of the events.

(a) There are at least three vehicles of revelation known in the Bible: Nature (the created universe), the Inner Life of man (including the exercise of reason), and a series of events in History.   (i) Nature is emphasized in many passages,[25] being regarded as essentially good and not the work of some alien or vindictive Power.   Man is physically part of Nature, dust from the dust, yet potentially greater than Nature.   "Natural religion" is not necessarily opposed to "revealed religion": the distinction is that between religious implications revealed through Nature and religious implications revealed in History. (ii) In the second place, the Bible puts much emphasis on man's endowments that make him capable of discerning revelation.   Man still bears "the image of God",[26] however gravely it is defaced by evil, and this gives him his unique endowment of self-consciousness, reason, moral judgment, spiritual discernment, and the capacity for shame. This alone makes revelation to man possible. Although the beasts may help to reveal, they cannot see the revelation. But not even man can see a revelation until he has been disciplined, until "the time has fully come."[27] Man may act as though he were blind, but he can be taught to see. He can sin against light, as beasts cannot, but he can be led to walk in the light.[28] (*iii*) The emphasis on History has already been referred to, and is involved below.

(*b*) Time, or History, is regarded as a vehicle of revelation. History is not a repeatable thing, as are cultic sacrifices, scientific experiments, natural processes, psychological reactions, and philosophical arguments. No New Testament reader can miss the emphasis on "once for all",[29] the unique importance of a stage in the time-process. To many among the Greeks, including the Stoics, the time-process could have no great significance: it was an endless repetition of equally futile cycles.[30] The Hebrew, however, held that time marches on to a goal under the hand of God. "The kingdom of God" is so much part of our thinking, though it may be secularized as "progress" or but faintly anticipated as a "far off divine event", that we scarcely realize that we owe our basic optimism about time to the Bible.

(*c*) The "Bible story" is not a mere chronicle or diary, a succession of bare events. It is a history plus an interpretation, and in the interpretation lies the inspired revelation. Thus to emphasize interpretation is nothing strange. Philosophies of history are as inevitable as they are controversial, and without interpretation history has no abiding value, is not a guide-post to anything. All history, sacred or profane, is written by interpreters. The interpretation, in fact, can become more important than the

event, more effective for good or evil. Lincoln's "Gettysburg Address" has been more influential than the battle
it recalled and interpreted in 1863. Tennyson's "The
Charge of the Light Brigade" has been more influential
than the futile and misdirected manœuvre at Balaklava in
1854. The Hebrew prophets[31] and psalmists were interpreters of events, and so were the New Testament writers.
So is A. J. Toynbee, and so are those who disagree with
him.

The problem, of course, is whether a particular interpretation truly reveals the truth inherent in the event.
There can be no dispute that Jesus was "crucified . . . under
Pontius Pilate"; that was an event. But there can be
dispute as to whether he was "crucified for us under
Pontius Pilate", whether in that event sinful men killed
"the Author of life", whether in it "God was in Christ
reconciling the world to himself".[32]

4. THE DOCUMENTS OF EXPERIENCE

There can be no intelligent acceptance or rejection of
a proposed interpretation until men have learned about
the event, its circumstances, its actors, and its issues. Information must precede thought. So there can be no thinking about Jesus until one has learned what is in the
records to be thought about. The evangelists or gospel-
writers who recorded what Jesus said, did, and suffered,
did so because the events had caused them to think, and
think again. They did not record everything,[33] or even
try to interpret everything they recorded. They wrote
out of experience. Thinking on the basis of their information may not produce any satisfactory conclusion or
experience for the modern reader for a long time, since
the Bible, in which events and interpretation are presented,

cannot in itself be "religious experience" for any man. It is the documentary record of ancient experience and helps to reproduce it in us if we are willing.

The books of the Bible are sixty-six in number, of varying dates over a period possibly as long as 1600 years, of many literary types (some of which are quite strange to modern readers), and of varying importance now. How these books came to be gathered into a "canon", by what means their text has been preserved and edited, whether every part of them can be said to be "inspired" (genealogical tables and estimates of casualties in battle, for example, are not inspired but compiled), and why some are more completely and lastingly important than others are demanding subjects of study not undertaken here.

It is noteworthy, however, that the history and its interpretation have come down to us not as oral tradition but in written form. It is therefore held by those who regard the scriptures as the basic objective authority that all offices, institutions, doctrines, and practices among Christians must be "agreeable to the Word of God", because the Church, from within which the books emerged, has, by its very recognition of them as sacred, bound itself to be judged by them. The relation of "scripture" and "tradition" is one of the thorniest of problems, dividing Roman and non-Roman churches deeply. To hold that "scripture" is supreme and "tradition" secondary and derivative is characteristic of Protestants, however much they may differ as to whether their emphasis in interpretation is to be Bible-centred, Church-centred, individual-centred, or Spirit-centred. They regard the Church as the guardian and not the proprietor of Scripture, its servant and not its master, set to interpret and apply but not to supersede "the Word". There has been a marked revival of interest in biblical theology recently, in both Roman and non-Roman circles.

5. TWO COVENANTS

The Bible is divided into two "covenants" (testament is now a misleading term), one being spoken of by Christians as old, the other as new. These adjectives are based on Jeremiah 31:31-34, "I will make a new covenant . . . not like the covenant which I made with their fathers . . . which they broke."[34]

"Covenant" is a complex and baffling word, as are other important words such as time, love, good, evil, science, number, reality, right, wrong, sin, nature, soul, mind, cause, effect, truth and salvation; but the simplest explanation is that it denotes an agreement or arrangement between two parties. Usually a covenant is between parties roughly equal, but in this case it is between God and man, and the initiative is God's. God makes "promises", on condition that man observes obligations.[35] To contrast these obligations as "works" under the "old" and "faith" under the "new" is an over-simplification, but an important one. It emphasizes man's growing appreciation (or capacity to discern revelation) of God's unchanging character and purpose of grace, which He adapted for a time to man's "ignorance" and "hardness of heart".[36] The New Covenant (New Testament) is called "the covenant of grace", not because grace was then first intended or extended, but because it was then clearly revealed. The basic truth about grace was dimly foreseen by Abraham, "the father" of all "men of faith",[37] but it was tragically obscured in later years and was at last made plain to all men in Christ. "The law" existed, according to Paul, to be the tutor to bring the child or heir to Christ, who as the mediator of the new covenant enacts "better promises"[38] and grants "adoption as sons".[39]

The above paragraph is written in a kind of shorthand, compressed almost as mathematical formulae are. To follow this formula through the Old Testament and New Testament is an exacting and controversial study, seldom attempted by the average reader. It is mentioned here only to explain why the Bible is divided into two parts, and to indicate that there is a technical vocabulary (distinct from the figurative vocabulary of the next chapter) involved in any intensive biblical study, just as a technical vocabulary supplies the shorthand of mathematics, physics, or psychology. Technical terms sound meaningless on the lips of people who delight in using catchwords and shibboleths, whatever the field of study. The vocabulary is as international as is that of science, and involves such words as justification, redemption, pardon, grace, incarnation, person and nature.

CHAPTER III

UTTERANCE IN ADEQUATE WORDS

To whom then will you liken God, or what likeness
compare to him?—Isaiah 40:18

I. BETWEEN TWO SILENCES

The speech of religion is an intermediate thing lying
between the brutish silence of ignorance, of having
nothing to say, and the eloquent silence of mutual understanding and communion, of needing to say nothing.
During the pilgrimage from the one to the other comes
the speech-making of worship, of argument, of exhortation, of penitence, and even of godly complaint,[1] punctu-
ated by the silence of moments when a man senses the
ineffable,[2] or keeps a stricken silence lest he "curse God".[3]

Words are not the only form of utterance. Music
speaks, and architecture, and art, and the ritual movements of dance, procession, sacrifice, and festival.[4] But
because the Bible is a written document, its speech is that
of words, employing verbal images with variety and exub-
erance, with rich symbolism and allusiveness. That the
speech of religion should be thus figurative is not surprising. It can be argued that all the words men use are only
symbols. At least, whenever speech passes beyond the
pedestrian work of giving simple information words grow
the wings of poetry. This is as true of science as of the
religious expression of love and faith. The scientist has
to use analogy to describe things invisible and known only
by their effects: his sticks and beads that represent complex

molecules, his likening of atoms to planetary systems, are
not equivalents but analogies. It is hard to speak at all
about anything that matters.

Every area of high speech has its own vocabulary, that
must be learned almost as a separate language. So religion
has its own vocabulary, and that of biblical religion falls
strangely on untutored ears, partly because it is often
uttered in archaic English, but chiefly because in origin
it is not English at all. Those who originated these words
neither spoke nor thought as we do. Even their geogra-
phy is ancient and foreign and must be translated in the
mind. But "Zion", "Jordan" and "the holy hill" have
come to have for us other than local significance. Paul
can say, "Jerusalem above is free, and she is our mother",[5]
and we sing of "Jerusalem the golden" as a "dear, dear
country". The symbolism is more demanding when
one goes on to speak of "washed their robes and made
them white in the blood of the Lamb",[6] or "my flesh is
food indeed",[7] or "we are members of his body".[8]

Many people prefer not to talk about religion, feeling
either that it is bad form to do so or that there is nothing
to be said. Religious people prefer to talk little because
faith eludes speech and is not established by argument.
But there must be speech if there is to be worship and
communication. The rich associations of the words, however, are never apparent at the first time of asking. Words
are richest when they proceed from enriched minds and
stored memories.

2. THE INEVITABILITY
   OF FIGURATIVE SPEECH

The Hebrew, from whom we borrow so much, was
more adept at "picture-language", concrete in allusion but
symbolic in meaning, than at abstract reasoning about

reality, process or values. Picture-language uses pictures and does so deliberately. There never was or can be, for example, literally such a thing as a "tree of life", but we can learn much from early references to the plucking of forbidden fruit and later references to permitted plucking.[9] Neither was there ever, for that matter, literally a "man who stood at the gate of the year", and none who heard George VI quote these words of M. Louise Haskins thought there was. Yet some people are inclined to think that biblical language must be literal or it cannot be "true". No one takes literally the graceful and true compliment to a beloved woman,

Where'er you walk, cool gales shall fan the glade,
Trees where you sit shall crowd into a shade;

and neither should anyone suppose that when God is said to make the hills skip or the trees clap their hands it must be meant literally.[10]

Symbolic language is always difficult, but it presents special difficulty to people with humourless minds or a narrow conception of truth. Some have therefore anticipated that when "the stars shall fall from heaven"[11] it will be a cosmic catastrophe rather than an overwhelming experience that changes the face of the universe for a man; or have insisted that when it is said concerning the safety of Israel in the wilderness, "thy raiment waxed not old",[12] it means that no clothes wore out; or have feared that "white robes", "harps", and "crowns"[13] promise a literal eternity of such things; or have imagined, in the supposed interests of reverence, that laws written by "the finger of God" involved God in physical incisions on rock.[14] Truth is something greater than information. That "God is true"[15] is not a matter of the fact of His existence but of

His character; and "truth as it is in Jesus"[16] has little reference to factual information.

Symbolic language has no set pattern,[17] and is as baffling as it is necessary. It abounds in the Scriptures with a frequency and vehemence startling to people who suspect the use of imagination, and think that religion should be dull and prosy. Imaginative utterance (not the same as imaginary) raises many difficulties of interpretation, as the long history of allegorical, analogical, and typical systems testifies; but it cannot be avoided if ideas are to live. The point is not whether language is to be figurative, but whether it is to present true analogies and express them adequately.

Once a vocabulary worthy of its great theme has been built up, nothing is gained by trying to create a new one. The available words are rich in themselves, and ennobled by long and godly use. They retain their strength and delicacy in liturgical speech: they lose both strength and delicacy when roughly handled by prosy people, whether they be religious or irreligious.

3. THE ACCENT OF THE MIDDLE EAST

Behind the English words of our translations of the Bible appear Middle Eastern idioms and metaphors, and references to far away and long ago. The un-English quality of many of these figures of speech can be suggested in such illustrations as the following. Some passages illustrate more than one of the seven categories listed.

(a) Hebrew metaphors increase in intensity as the importance of the analogy increases. To phlegmatic Anglo-Saxons, the ancient Hebrew sometimes sounds emotionally crude;[18] but at least he was never mawkish or sweetly sentimental. This increase in hyperbole under pressure is nowhere better seen than in certain uses of those two rich sources of analogy, human relations, including sexual, and the starry heavens.

(*i*) The exuberant analogies between religious and marital faithfulness can astonish and repel the English reader (particularly if he is reading aloud). We never quite get used to idolatry being called "whoring after other gods",[19] however much we know of the cultic prostitution at ancient fertility shrines and groves. Nor do the frank metaphors of betrothal, marriage, childbirth, and adultery[20] come naturally to our lips, although we see what Jesus meant by an "evil and adulterous" generation.[21] Circumcision has become for us only a surgical correction, and we have difficulty in appreciating why this ancient religious rite was so controversial a matter for the early Church, and why it is used as a telling analogy by the Apostle Paul.[22] But the equally sexual idea of the Church as "the bride of Christ" appeals instantly.[23]

(*ii*) The same is true of references to the heavenly bodies. The sun is to be heated sevenfold,[24] the moon is to be confounded,[25] and the stars to fall,[26] not in some distant catastrophe, but when the Lord heals the hurt of his people,[27] or when the Christian apostles are endowed with the Spirit.[28] As for the earth, it sings and applauds.[29] Our own poetic use of the pathetic fallacy pales into insignificance before this kind of thing. But there is one significant omission in Hebrew usage: the Hebrew does not use the imagery of astrology that credits the heavenly bodies with a will or influence of their own. The poetic phrase, "the stars fought against Sisera",[30] does not alter the plain evidence that the Old Testament is full of warnings against worshipping or fearing the heavenly bodies, since it is God who calls them by name and leads them out.[31] But neither was the Hebrew an astronomer. He

saw the heavenly bodies as the orderly works of God's
hands, witnessing to His power. He was not interested
in tracing their orbits or their constellations.

(*b*) There is frequent resort to hyperbole, apart from
the themes already mentioned. This sometimes appears
in the use of the unreal negative (where we would say
"not only", rather than "not"),[32] but usually in the form
of imaginative overstatement, such as cities "walled up to
heaven".[33] "For ever", which to us suggests eternity,
was often used by the Hebrew to mean a lifetime or a
very long period.[34] Such use of hyperbole makes sayings
piquant and memorable, and it was frequently used by
Jesus. The Old Testament sometimes gives us two
accounts of the same phenomenon, one in prose and the
other in poetry, as in the case of the exodus from Egypt.[35]
Had Hollywood realized that "wall" is a frequent metaphor for a barrier or defence,[36] it might have produced
a different film of the Red Sea crossing. Another example
of hyperbole can be seen in that although the New Testament states that "all Judea" went out to be baptized by
John the context shows that what is meant is widespread
enthusiasm and not the literal involvement of everyone.[37]

(*c*) There is generous use also of meiosis (litotes or
understatement). That the bruised reed will not be
broken[38] really means that it will be restored, and not
just spared; that Tarsus was "no mean city"[39] suggests
that it was very great; and that God does "not despise"
the contrite spirit[40] means that He values it highly. Bethlehem being "not least"[41] is really the greatest. As for "a
thousand hills",[42] God's cattle are on numberless slopes;
and that 12,000 are sealed from each tribe[43] is not a
limiting count but a suggestion of ideal numbers. That
a man is said to be of more value than many sparrows[44]
is intended not to cheapen but to magnify him, since one

does not ask how many is many. We use meiosis in our own speech. "He is no better than he ought to be" is a damning indictment and, from a Scot, "It's no' bad" is high praise.

(d) The Hebrew had a way, foreign to us, of expressing a result in terms of a purpose. "Lest they be converted" seems a strange way of stating that men's hard hearts prevented their conversion. We would not say, as Jesus did, "Thou hast hid these things from the wise",[45] or state that God had sent prophets in order that a later generation might pay up for their rejection.[46] Nothing can make this idiom sound natural on English lips, and even English ears have difficulty with it.

(e) There are idiomatic peculiarities that cannot, and should not, always be translated out. Sometimes, of course, they can be and should be, as is the case with the polysyndeton or frequent use of connective particles common in Greek. The Authorized Version retains this frequent use of "and" with the consequence that in Mark 12:12-35 one meets 17 out of 24 verses, plus 7 other clauses, that begin with "and". Later translations have edited this out with no violence to the original. But there are other instances where the foreign idiom must stand or much is lost.

This can be seen in what is known as the Hebrew construct form, which is to be literally translated into English (and Greek) as "son of" or "children of". We can and do translate "sons of the flame"[47] as sparks, and "sons of death"[48] as men about to die, and, in recent versions, "children of the bridechamber" as wedding guests.[49] But we keep "children" of wrath, of wisdom, of light, of God, of the devil, of Israel, of men,[50] and "sons" of the prophets, of affliction, of the living God, and of thunder,[51] because "child of" or "son of" implies a relationship of purpose or character. One gains nothing by turning a "son of perdition"[52] into a lost soul, or "sons of Belial"[53] into evil men, or "the daughter of Zion"[54] into the people of Jerusalem. Even if we let these go, there would remain the complex terms "son of man" and "son of God", of which a literal translation is unavoidable because no English words will quite do. "Son of man" sometimes means simply man,[55] but after the Exile there grew up the idea of the expected "Son of man"[56] who sums up in himself human nature and human destiny. "Sons of God" in one place means humble believers,[57] and in another "the Son of God" is One who shares the character and nature of God and is His agent of revelation and redemption.[58]

(*f*) It is possible to conceive of certain events, but not to describe them, since no man has been through them. Two such events, if one dare use so crude a term, are the creation and consummation of all things. The mind cannot really form any idea of such a beginning or such an end, yet must use both as reference points.[59] The Bible often refers to them, but always in the language of symbolism, involving interpretation of purpose rather than details of fact. They are called, for example, a spreading-out and a rolling-up.[60] It may be that the two creation stories are deliberately set side by side with mutually contradictory details[61] to forbid us to take either of them as literal descriptions. Later, Paul uses yet a third frame of reference for his interpretation of creation and the battle of moral order against chaos.[62]

(*g*) Very striking in Hebrew symbolism is the unhesitating use of anthropomorphism, that is, the ascription to God of parts of the human body and of human emotions. It is vital to recognize that such terms were treasured among a people who vehemently asserted that

God had never been seen,[63] that there must be no visible images, since there is no adequate likeness to which to compare Him,[64] that any comparison is dangerous,[65] and that it would be as fatal for a man to look upon God[66] as it would be to the eye to look upon the sun. But it seems as though the prohibition of graven images involved no curb on verbal images. So, man is said to bear "the image of God";[67] God is our "Father";[68] and His arm, eyes, face, footstool, throne, voice, hand, finger, wrath, and love are referred to in human terms.[69] Sometimes the metaphor is so startling that it seems irreverent.[70] Only occasionally are such phrases as "in a figure" or "as it were" introduced;[71] but none of this language is to be taken literally.

Two considerations can help us to understand the purpose and even necessity of anthropomorphic language.

(*i*) One is the insistence that God is "the living God", in contrast to the dead or doomed gods of the heathen or to a philosophic hypothesis.[72] To meet this God "face to face"[73] is, as the Old Testament testifies, to encounter Him in a vital experience, not to construct some abstract philosophic concept that lacks the sense of an awful, living Presence. True, anthropomorphism later became a source of embarrassment when picture-thinking Jew met philosophic Greek, as the writings of Philo show and as can be seen in the works of Jewish medieval philosophers; but nothing can quite equal this sense of a real encounter that the Bible conveys. For the Christian the awful yet gracious Presence of God is realized in the Incarnation of God in Christ.

(*ii*) The other consideration is that the Hebrew and the Christian refused to think on any plane lower in analogy or in moral dignity than the anthropomorphic. It is not possible to go higher, within the bounds of analogy and symbol. The Hebrew had no dog-headed deities: he repudiated golden bulls and all animal gods,[74] and particularly he fought against the phallic worship associated with sacred groves.[75] True, he occasionally pictured impossible hybrid creatures as symbols of the presence and power of God;[76] and he used the metaphor of wings as a symbol of protection.[77] But God was not literally a bird-like creature to him, any more than He was One who carried a literal sword or had one physically protruding from His mouth.[78]

Some untrained readers of the Bible may be misled at first by such anthropomorphic terms, and may even suppose that mature religious people today think of God as some bearded potentate on a golden throne. Other readers may feel that they would prefer mathematical or chemical analogies to human ones. Such analogies are quite justifiable, although not used in the Bible. Its writers were not mathematicians or chemists. But impersonal analogies of this type lack the connotations of personal intelligence and conscious purpose that make God an experience rather than an object of study, and that transform speculation about the order and power of God into a conviction of His Presence and His grace.

4. ARE ANALOGIES TRUE AND WORTHILY EXPRESSED?

It is neither necessary nor accurate to say that there is a separate language of religion. Its speech has much in common with all poetry. Perhaps it has too little in common with science, but poetry and science talk of many of the same things from different angles. Thus, to say "It is bitterly cold", using an analogy drawn from taste to express a feeling and an experience, is poetic, whereas to say "It is zero" is scientific, but hardly a record of experi-

ence. If there is for religion no separate language, however, there is a special vocabulary with an ancient and
foreign air about it. The important question is not
whether figurative language is legitimate but whether the
analogies used are true analogies, expressed memorably
and worthily. Seeing "in a glass darkly" we can perceive
spiritual truth only indirectly, not directly. But that is not
the same as seeing the phantasies of nightmare or the
delusive visions of a diseased imagination. What is
known "in part" is recommended as true knowledge as
far as it goes.[79] Language cannot say everything, certainly
not everything at once.

In this discussion we have dealt with figurative language and not with the growth of ideas that the metaphors express. It must suffice to emphasize that the
language of Christian worship is drawn from the maturer
parts of the Old Testament and from the New Testament.
The progressive nature of the revelation of truth means
that some earlier ideas are outgrown or disciplined, and
that some figurative expressions drop out of use. The
New Testament conceptions of God are built on the
noblest Old Testament vision; and both Christian and
Jewish worship are obviously on a higher plane than is
suggested by the theological perceptions of Jephthah,[80]
or by Samuel's ritual killing of Agag.[81] Chiefly from the
Psalms, the Prophets and the New Testament are the
Christian vocabulary of worship and the imagery of its
thought drawn.

CHAPTER IV

FROM ANCIENT TEXT
TO MODERN VERNACULAR

Which is to say, being interpreted. . . —John 1:38

I. THE BIBLE IN ENGLISH

Although the Authorized Version has the best claim to be called "the English Bible" because of its profound effect on both the English language and religion, such a title can belong to no one translation. It is more accurate to speak of "the Bible in English".

In common use are the King James Version of 1611 (for rather obscure reasons called "the Authorized Version"), the Roman Catholic Douay Version of 1582-1609, the English Revised Version, 1881-5, the American Standard Version, 1901, and most recently the Revised Standard Version, 1946-52, as well as individual translations by Moffatt, Ronald Knox and others. A revision of Douay is in progress, as is also a new British translation, expected to depart more radically from the Authorized Version than does the Revised Standard Version. In addition, fragments from some older versions linger in use. Our most familiar ritual form of the Lord's Prayer, for example, is from the "Great Bible" translation of 1539, as are also the Psalms in the Anglican Book of Common Prayer.

The various translations, notably those from 1525 to 1611, provide a historical study of immense interest, but to do more than acknowledge our debt to the vigorous

Anglo-Saxon words of William Tyndale, to the formal
Latinism of the Douay Version, or to the strong Puritan
request that preceded the Authorized Version cannot be
attempted in a chapter devoted rather to basic problems
of translation. The Bible in English supplies an English
dress, often old-fashioned, to clothe a body of Middle
East breeding, which body in turn is a fleshly tabernacle
(that is, tent) or "earthen vessel" for the eternal Spirit.

2. INCIDENTAL PROBLEMS OF TRANSLATION

Translation is never easy and never perfect. Some of
its difficulties are not really those of translation as such.
One is the resentment that greets any change; another is
the use of modern printer's devices.

Every new translation has been greeted by opposition
because an earlier version has furnished a passionately
loved form of sound words. Even the Authorized Version, which people have long regarded with special reverence, had to outlive half a century of opposition. Its
translators anticipated bitter criticism when they wrote
in their "The Translator to the Reader", "Whosoever
attempteth . . . the opening and closing of the word of
God . . . casteth himself upon pikes, to be gored by every
sharp tongue."

Printer's decisions are numerous but as a rule have
no religious implications. Mechanically, to compress
three-quarters of a million words into a single manageable
volume requires special paper, special type, the sacrifice
of margins, and the use of double columns, with the
result that the Bible is at once the best-printed and the
worst-printed book we use. The inclusion of a ready-
reference system of chapters and verses (no such divisions exist in ancient manuscripts) may, as in the Auth-

orized Version, result in a serious error in emphasis
through printing verses as paragraphs. The addition of
punctuation, relatively unknown to the ancients, who
above all knew nothing of the modern device of quotation marks, involves few religious problems but many
editorial decisions. The use of capitals and the introduction of quotation marks do, however, raise problems
for the translator as well as printer.[1]

3. BASIC DECISIONS
INVOLVED IN TRANSLATION

The most important problems are not those of the
printer but of the scholar who must be rigidly faithful to
the documents, even though his translation does not
always satisfy the ill-informed who may prefer the familiar
to the correct. Sometimes even the scholar is baffled,
although the Bible lends itself to translation more readily
than do many other ancient religious documents.[2] He
may not always be right, but he must be a devout steward
of truth. Accurate translation from an accurate text is
of particular importance for those Christians who regard
the Bible as the supreme authority by which doctrine and
practice are to be judged.[3] After the scholar's work is
done, every man has to undertake the further task of
translating ancient truth into terms of his own needs and
duties. In this task he usually seeks the guidance of
scholarly and devotional leaders. But he must be persuaded in his own mind,[4] and is not subject to bare
authority.

The average reader is scarcely aware of the complex
decisions that lie behind the finished printed book put into
his hands. These decisions can be typified as: whether to
translate, what to translate, how to translate, and why to
revise translations from time to time.

4. CIRCULATION OF SCRIPTURE
IN THE VERNACULAR

The decision to put the scriptures into the tongue of the common man was made early in the Christian era and is taken for granted now. Indeed, translation began before the gospels were written, since they present at least some of the words of Jesus already in a translation out of Aramaic into Greek.[5] Translations into Latin, Gothic and Syriac were made in the early centuries. But when in the sixteenth century it was desired to substitute for Latin, the universal tongue of the learned, the English tongue of the common man, there was, as is well known, strong opposition, resulting in martyrdoms, persecution, and heated debate.[6]

To translate is an important decision, by no means to be taken for granted. The Koran cannot yet be officially used in translation. The heritage of the Greek and Latin classics has not been available to the common man as readily as has the Bible, since it was assumed until relatively lately that translations were chiefly for those who had at least some first-hand knowledge of the ancient languages involved. Christians have not felt thus about the Bible. Translation has been most vehemently desired since the day when the Renaissance, the Reformation and the invention of printing made possible the wide circulation of the Bible in the vernacular. Such enthusiasm was based on at least two typical convictions: that the Church must be brought under the judgment of "the Word" so that only institutions and observances clearly justified by or "agreeable to" the Word of God will be recognized; and that the "perspicuity" of scripture is such that, aided by the inner witness of the Spirit, the humblest as well as the greatest may hear the voice of God sufficiently. Possession of a private copy of the Bible was, of course, made possible only by the invention of printing. No early Christian, except some such prominent man as Theophilus,[7] could hope to own a copy. The rest were dependent on "the reader" in church.[8]

Such confidence in the capacity of the common man is the more remarkable in that the Bible is almost the only "primary source" the average person ever reads. It brings him face to face with antiquity and trains him to trace the progress of ideas, to judge between the lasting and the temporary,[9] and to exercise his own judgment in submitting to ecclesiastical authority. The careful reader of the Bible has a sense of history that others often lack. His speech, moreover, is influenced by the noblest English style and vocabulary that exist.

5. THE DETERMINATION OF THE TEXT OF SCRIPTURE

To arrive at the text to be translated is an exacting scholarly task, involving the examination of manuscripts, ancient translations and patristic quotations. This task is never quite completed, and the extent of it and its scientific methods can become familiar only to scholars. It is, however, hinted at in occasional footnotes in the Revised Standard Version. Fortunately, the recovery of the exact text can be accomplished with almost complete assurance, since the store of manuscripts is large, much larger than that available for Greek and Latin classics. The original manuscripts, of course, have long since perished.

One curious phenomenon that alert readers may notice is that New Testament quotations do not always coincide exactly with the Old Testament passages referred to.[10] This is partly accounted for by the fact that the New Testament writers were quoting from memory, but more often by the fact that the New Testament writers usually used the Septuagint translation of the Old Testament into Greek, whereas we use the Old Testament in a translation made directly from the Hebrew. Other well-known phenomena are the "lost ending" of *Mark* (see Chapter V), and the variable placing of the passage about the woman taken in adultery. This latter passage appears in some ancient manuscripts after Luke 21:38 or after John 7:36 or 7:44, instead of after John 7:53. It is generally not regarded, therefore, as an original part of St. John's Gospel, although it is manifestly a genuine part of the words of Jesus.

6. THE TASK OF TRANSLATION

Translation is difficult for such reasons as: (*a*) that our knowledge of the Hebrew and Greek involved is still imperfect, although greatly superior to that of the Authorized Version translators, and (*b*) that English words cannot always convey the complex meaning of the terms to be translated. Some words are simply transliterated rather than translated, such as cherubim, seraphim and baptize;[11] but a baffling problem arises when an English word has to be used that cannot do the work assigned to it. Sometimes new words are coined and put into circulation; Tyndale added dozens of such words, including "lovingkindness". But at other times no device is sufficient. Another translator's problem is (*c*) whether always to change an inaccurate traditional rendering. Illustrations of these three follow.

(*a*) The Hebrew verb form is the same for "he shall" and "may he" (or let him), and the Authorized Version translators sometimes used the future tense in the wrong place. Psalm 72 in the Authorized Version uses "he shall", whereas the Revised Standard Version has "may he", with heightened effect because the psalm is a prayer.

(*b*) The word we translate "save" means both heal and deliver,[12] a double sense that Greek, Latin and Romance languages can convey, but not English. No one has found a really good English word to translate the Hebrew term that the Authorized Version usually calls "mercy" and the Revised Standard Version "steadfast love". There is no real English equivalent for *pisteuo*, a Greek word meaning not only believe but assent to and trust in. If we could say, "Abraham faithed God",[13] we might convey the subtle combination of intellectual assent, personal trust, and act of will involved. "The Word"[14] is a poor equivalent for the Greek *logos* which suggests thought, reason, mind in action, speech, and the bridging of a gap, as speech does if intelligence is at work in both parties. Neither "charity" nor "love" will really do justice to the Christian term *agapé*.[15] "Everlasting life" is not as good a translation as "eternal life", but neither is very good.[16] The "kingdom" of God is a poor equivalent for a word that means realm, rule and authority. Neither "trespass" nor "debts" is good enough to catch the sense of the Lord's Prayer, but "sins" (although used in Luke 11:4) is not an accurate translation of Matt. 6:12, and neither is "offences".

Incidentally, some words that people think are in the Bible are not. The "apple" in Eden is always "fruit" in the Bible;[17] "the Fall" is not so named in Genesis 3, although the New Testament uses such a metaphor for each man's sin;[18] and the term "original sin" appears first in the Latin of Tertullian after 200 A.D., even though the idea is drawn from Psalm 51:5.[19]

(*c*) Sometimes an older translation is continued because little would be gained and much lost if a familiar rendering were changed. "Daily bread" remains in the Lord's Prayer,[20] although "bread for the morrow" is more accurate; "the shadow of death" remains in Psalm 23, although "deep darkness" is meant; and "carpenter" is not changed to "artisan",[21] or "Servant" to "Slave".[22] But "child" is changed to "servant" where it is used misleadingly in the Authorized Version.[23]

7. THE NEED FOR REVISION OF TRANSLATIONS

Everyone knows that revised translations appear from time to time in the interests of accuracy and intelligibility. Even the Authorized Version itself, although this is not generally known by those who resent changes from it now, underwent revisions between 1611 and 1769. The marginal notes and Ussher's dates, for example, were added in 1701. In the references to approved changes in sections (*a*) to (*d*) below, the Authorized Version and the Revised Standard Version should be compared in every instance.

Revision is necessary on the following grounds:

(*a*) Since 1611 important manuscripts have been discovered that shed light on obscure readings, and on "spurious" verses,[24] which are not deliberate falsifications, of course, but insertions by later hands, glosses that have been copied into the text, a thing easy to do and hard to undo.

(*b*) The Authorized Version renderings, in spite of the magnificence of the work, are sometimes of poor quality. "Bottle" should have been wineskin,[25] and "glass" is a bad description of a metal mirror.[26] The definite article, important in Greek but missing in Latin, is carelessly treated in the Authorized Version, although it is important to know whether one is reading about "faith" or "the faith",[27] about "Christ" or "the Christ".[28] Some of the Authorized Version renderings are at least questionable,[29] and in other cases alternate renderings should have been made the first rather than second choice.[30] That the spelling and syntax of the Authorized Version strike us occasionally as wrong is not important, but today no one would be allowed to say, "Let each esteem other better than themselves."[31]

(*c*) Suitable printing is a continuing problem, and the Authorized Version used many devices that obscured the sense. Poetry must therefore no longer appear as prose (as in Joshua 10:12-13, the *Psalms* and *Job*), even though it is difficult to decide how many utterances of the prophets are poems. The peculiar use of italics in the Authorized Version (first used in the Genevan Version of 1560) to indicate words supplied by the translator might be justified if people knew why it is employed, but italics are now misleading, since they suggest emphasis. Ussher's marginal dates are often inaccurate and must be dropped. Verse-divisions must be un-emphasized and paragraphing given proper prominence.

(*d*) Of greater interest to most readers is the constant changing of the English language, which has been so great since 1611 that most people find that many words in the Authorized Version have become unintelligible and even misleading. It is desirable that when revision is undertaken the majestic English style of the Bible be retained; but the vocabulary, though conservative, should be such as is "understanded of the people".

Many words in the Authorized Version represent meanings that still linger on in use in one form or another. "Ear" no longer means "plough",[32] but we still talk of arable (or earable) land; "let" no longer suggests "hinder",[33] but we still use it for a let ball in tennis; "prevent" does not now mean anticipate or go before,[34] but it lingers on in "prevenient"; "harness" does not now mean armour,[35] except possibly on a football player; and "strange" is not quite the same as "foreign",[36] although we still distrust strangers. "Witty" might, to some, suggest wise;[37] but "by and by" almost never means immediately.[38] "Fetch a compass" scarcely suggests make a circuit,[39] although encompass can mean surround; and "peculiar" now carries its old and noble meaning of something very dear[40] only when we speak of a man's peculiar treasure. "Comprehend" can still suggest swallow up or take in[41] when the reference is to a comprehensive statement, but it usually means only to understand. "Quick" can still mean alive[42] but usually means swift. The list of fascinating archaisms could go on to include "unicorn", an ancient rendering of "wild ox",[43] "garnished", which used to mean "furnished",[44] and many more. But it would not include, from the Authorized Version, "learn" in the sense of teach, although this was once quite respectable, and is to be found in The Book of Common Prayer.[45]

The worst trouble comes when words that have changed their meaning have doctrinal significance or involve our emotions. Important words get hardening of the arteries as they age and become narrower in their reference. "I will" no longer is as emphatic as "It is my will".[46] "Want" no longer suggests lack so much as desire, but it cannot be allowed to mean desire in Psalm 23:1 or 34:9. "Bishop" now connotes a definite officer, and this is misleading if one is talking simply of an overseer or guardian, as the New Testament does.[47] "Master" should suggest teacher,[48] but scarcely does to people who think of a headmaster as a petty overlord. "Bowels" is now an anatomical term, not a reference to the seat of the emotions:[49] we talk, equally inaccurately, of the heart. "Comfort" does not now readily mean counsel, exhort and strengthen, and "the Comforter" has therefore to be rescued from the connotation of cosiness.[50] "Ghost", which means spirit (ghostly counsel once meant advice on religious subjects), has gone downhill, although "give up the ghost" still suggests death.

Among the best examples are "hell" and "atone". In the seventeenth century, "hell" could still mean the abode of all the dead, without penal significance or moral distinction, and the Authorized Version used it in this sense; but the Revised Standard Version quite properly substitutes "hades", "Sheol", the "grave" or the "pit",[51] except where the idea of rampant wickedness is intended.[52] To atone, in the early seventeenth century, meant to produce peace or at-one-ment, as when it was said that an officer was sent to atone a brawl, and so it should be thought of in connection with Christ "who is our peace" and who "made peace".[53] But it has come to suggest, at first glance, the placation of wrath or ritual expiation, an idea that may be proper in some Old Testament passages.[54] For this reason, the Revised Standard Version always speaks of reconciliation rather than atonement in the New Testament.

8. A TASK NEVER COMPLETED

For manifold reasons the revision of translations must go on, although English people are probably better served by translation than are men of any other language. We must remember that certain complex associations take centuries to grow up around key words such as "God" and "Saviour". It is hard to select a word for "God" if one is translating the Bible into the language of people who have no such complex associations.[55] Even climate raises problems; when one attempts to use such familiar symbols as shepherd, bread, and wine among Eskimos there are no words to use or associations to recall. The annals of translation by modern missionaries are full of such problems. The work is never perfect: no translation is final. Neither is there an end to the languages into which the Bible is to be translated. Many of them are given written form for the first time by missionaries intent on supplying men with the Bible.

AN INTRODUCTION TO THE GOSPELS

CHAPTER V

THE GOSPELS AND THE EARLY CHURCHES

That you may know the truth concerning the things
of which you have been informed.—Luke 1:4

I. THE FOUR GOSPELS

The New Testament speaks often of "the gospel",[1] the
good news—a word not found in the Old Testament—
by which is meant a complex of confident assertions regarding the love of God and the restoration of man
based on the words and work of Jesus. Heading the
New Testament canon are four books called "gospels"
which, although not the first New Testament books to be
written, have pride of place. The first three are remarkably similar to one another and are called collectively the
Synoptic Gospels because they present a common view,
or synopsis. *John*, the Fourth Gospel, is strikingly different both in literary form and in its selection and treatment of material.

Modern books, by means of the printer's date, the
author's references to his sources, and the preface in which
he states why and for what readers he has written, usually
answer at once the question of what is technically called
"introduction". But in older works, such as those of
Chaucer or Shakespeare, no such information is supplied
and there is need for scholarly "introduction" if the
modern reader is to appreciate the special period, the
type of author, the circle of first readers and the reasons

why the author emphasizes or omits certain matters. Through similar information the gospels gain in clarity.[2]

2. THE PURPOSE
OF THE SYNOPTIC EVANGELISTS

Two characteristics of the Synoptic Gospels are their freedom from heavy preachment and their omission of the kind of information that would make them biographies in the strict sense. Such omission is evident in that they tell nothing of the physical appearance of Jesus, give no careful dates, largely neglect thirty years of his life, and do not follow him in his public work in order from place to place. Many of his sayings are associated with no identifiable place or ascertainable time. It is not possible, therefore, to write a "Life of Christ" as one would write a "Life of John Wesley". Nevertheless, the gospels paint a portrait more vivid than any biography could give. Through these brief and unadorned accounts, unspoiled by moralizing or homily, we receive an impression of Jesus more memorable than that of any other figure in human history. If they were not written as biographies (one early Christian father calls them "memoirs"), what was their purpose and why are they at once so much alike and so characteristically different from one another?

It is generally agreed that the Synoptic Gospels should be regarded as "catechetical manuals", books compiled for the training of catechumens, or learners, preparing for Christian baptism. One of them gives itself such a label, stating that it was primarily for the private use of a prominent convert, and remarking that many such books had been prepared.[3] A "gospel" was designed to pass on the elements of Christian morality and a knowledge of the ministry of Jesus, with special reference to his death, together with the conviction that this Galilean carpenter

was the promised Messiah, the Christ,[4] and the universal
Lord of men.[5] They were definitely not bare chronicles
but "gospels" that proclaimed the good news enunciated
and exemplified by Jesus in his Life, consummated in his
Passion and confirmed by God in his Resurrection. They
were not written for silent reading, a relatively modern
practice, but for public lection, probably in short sections
that the hearers would memorize.[6]

These three alone, out of the "many" mentioned by
Luke, have survived as "scripture". Undoubtedly they
survived on their merits, winning the confidence of the
churches by being associated with apostolic names and
by sounding the authentic note. If the modern reader
wishes to see how great their merits are, there are sur-
viving fragments of rejected gospels, often heretical, frequently childish, and uniformly inferior, brought together
in M. R. James' *The Apocryphal New Testament*. Significantly, each of the three represents the outlook of one
of three main "schools" of early Christian orthodoxy:
the Petrine (Peter), the Pauline (Paul), and the Jacobean
(James of Jerusalem).

They were not written, at least in final form, in the first
years of the Church. Most of the New Testament epistles
were written earlier than the gospels.[7] The "books and
parchments" mentioned in II Tim. 4:13 were either Old
Testament books, selections of Old Testament passages,
or collections of the sayings of Jesus, but not our gospels.

Little need for written records would be felt so long
as the voices of companions of Jesus[8] could still be heard.
But these voices fell silent, and because of the danger
from alien ideas that were being mingled with the Christian message, writing became necessary. The oral tradition was replaced by the written tradition.[9] It is difficult
for us to appreciate the tenacity and accuracy of men's

memories of the spoken word during a whole generation because dependence on books has weakened our power to memorize. But any who have told stories to children can testify to their exact memories and their insistence on verbal repetition, qualities that are soon lost after they learn to read easily. Regarding the transition from oral to written tradition, only two topics will be mentioned here: the pericope form, and the so-called Synoptic Problem.

3. THE RESEMBLANCES AMONG THE THREE

(a) *The Pericope.* The influence of the oral tradition can be seen in the preservation of short, easily memorized passages, such as catechumens could learn, and on which the teacher[10] could enlarge. These appear frequently in the Gospel of Mark and less frequently in the Gospels of Luke and Matthew, which were compiled later and with greater literary art. Each such short passage is technically called a pericope. It was a rabbinic device, resembling also a literary form in vogue among Greek rhetoricians. The Greeks called it a *chreia*, a concise and pointed account of something said or done, attributed to some particular person. Christian teachers still use the device of "a text", which a congregation can remember even if they forget the comments on it.

In the Gospel of Mark the subject changes rapidly and often, because the record is made up so largely of these relatively short and distinct passages; each contains a saying associated with an incident whose date and place are usually not noted. This pericope method can be seen in such short passages as Mark 4:30-32, 35-41; 8:11-12, 13-21, 22-26, 27-30, 31-33, 34-38. For this reason, public lessons are more frequently read in Christian services from *Matthew* or *Luke*, the listener's thoughts being less frequently interrupted by abrupt changes of topic.

This type of oral teaching was evidently used side by side with another type, the narrative tradition, notably the continuous Passion narrative of Mark 11:1-16:8. Such a narrative is also readily remembered.

(b) *Documentary Possibilities*. The possibility amounting to strong probability, exists that in addition to access to the store of common or regional oral traditions the Synoptic evangelists had access to some written sources. Minute similarities, particularly in the narrative sections, suggest this. It is called "the Synoptic Problem". Careful study (which involves purely literary considerations and raises no religious problem)[11] has given wide acceptance to the hypotheses: (i) that *Mark*, the earliest of the three, was used as a basis for the composition of both *Luke* and *Matthew*, since they follow its chronological order[12] and since all but about thirty verses of *Mark*[13] are substantially reproduced in both or one of them; and (ii) that the further close resemblance between *Luke* and *Matthew*, in selecting and quoting numerous sayings of Jesus[14] (Mark records relatively few of Jesus' words) suggests that these two used also some compilation of Jesus' sayings, a "teaching document". The existence of such a document is purely hypothetical, but among scholars it is referred to as "Q" (from the German word *Quelle*, source).

4. THE DISTINCTIVE CHARACTERISTICS OF THE THREE

If there are striking resemblances, there are also important and characteristic differences among the three Synoptics.

(a) The Gospel of Mark was, according to a statement of Papias of Hierapolis (about 130 A.D.), composed by John Mark from his memory of Peter's preaching, presumably mainly in Rome.[15] This gospel is largely narrative and such explanations as "for the Jews do not eat unless they wash their hands"[16] indicate chiefly Gentile readers. It preserves vivid details, often omitted by the others, that draw attention to the human difficulties of Jesus' work.[17] The relative absence of Jesus' sayings and parables accounts for the comparative neglect of this gospel among early Christians (Papias sounds almost apologetic about it) but it has an important significance just because it omits so many sayings. We are too easily persuaded that the earliest Christian emphasis was chiefly on Jesus as a great moral teacher. That this was far from being the case is indicated by *Mark*: the chief basis of apostolic preaching was not the morality inculcated by Jesus, but the faith that he was man's Benefactor, or God's "mighty act" with Divine authority and significance. He was "Saviour" as well as "Teacher" from the earliest days of the faith.

There is added interest because of the "lost ending" of this gospel. Apparently all our copies of *Mark* descend from a slightly damaged copy, ending at 16:8, possibly in the middle of a sentence. Two endings have been supplied by later hands. The longer of the two is familiar through the Authorized Version; the Revised Standard Version supplies both; some ancient manuscripts have neither.

(*b*) *Luke*, together with *Acts*, is to be associated with the circle of Paul, and with the "beloved physician".[18] Easier to read than *Mark*, because of its superior style, it is the gospel from which the average English reader's conception of Jesus is chiefly drawn. It emphasizes the universality of the work of Jesus and his place as Someone even greater than the expected Messiah. Jesus is often called "the Lord",[19] a title constantly used by Paul. Luke refers seldom to the Jewish law, but often to the universal compassion of God,[20] and to the place of women and children.

In this gospel appears a long section[21] dealing with Jesus' last journey to Jerusalem with a fullness not found in the others. In *Luke* alone are found several of the best-known parables, notably the Prodigal Son, the Good Samaritan and the Rich Fool.[22]

(*c*) *Matthew* has a different atmosphere and emphasizes the fulfilment of Old Testament hopes in Jesus. Where Mark and Luke refer seldom to the Old Testament, Matthew constantly does so with emphasis on the fulfilment of Old Testament expectations in Jesus.[23] Probably, therefore, it was composed primarily for use among Christians who had formerly been Jews, the type represented by their most notable leader, James of Jerusalem, who succeeded Peter in that locality.[24] Its Jewish emphasis is as evident as *Luke*'s universality and, because its material is arranged as a Jewish rabbi might have arranged it, it is pre-eminently the "teaching gospel".

In addition to certain incidental signs of Jewish interest and emphasis, such as the reverential use of "kingdom of heaven" instead of "kingdom of God",[25] and the careful preservation of sayings that emphasize Jesus' earthly mission as first to and thereafter through the Jews,[26] this gospel is characterized by the deliberate grouping of topical material in large blocks, such as the "kingdom sayings" of the so-called "Sermon on the Mount",[27] Sabbath incidents,[28] and denunciations of scribal hypocrisy.[29] These blocks are constructed with great literary care.

Like *Luke*, *Matthew* gives much space to the teachings of Jesus, and this gospel alone preserves some of the greatest parables, notably, The Sheep and the Goats, the Labourers in the Vineyard, and the Wise and Foolish Virgins.[30] There is in this gospel an occasional "doubling", substituting two figures for one in *Mark*,[31] for which curious (and often unnoticed) variation there is no satisfactory explanation.

The same Papias who spoke of *Mark* says that "Matthew recorded the oracles [of the Lord] in the Hebrew tongue".[32] Since our present gospel appears to have been composed in, not translated into, Greek, the literary and historical problem as to whether the apostle Matthew[33] is directly or only indirectly the author of this gospel in its present form must remain open.

5. THE FOURTH GOSPEL

John views the work of Jesus not so much against the background of first-century Palestine as against the background of eternity, *sub specie aeternitatis*. Far from stressing the occasional human weakness and the constant struggle, as does *Mark*, it emphasizes the awful, though veiled, majesty of "the Word made flesh".[34] While the chapters that follow here are based chiefly on the Synoptic Gospels (the Fourth Gospel being given further notice in a concluding chapter), much that is of value for filling out the synoptic narrative is in *John*.

For such matters as the earliest work of Jesus before he preached in Galilee, the overlapping of his work for a time with that of John the Baptist, and the length of his ministry, we are indebted to this gospel. Most readers are unaware that had we only the Synoptics it could be asserted that the ministry of Jesus must have taken place during a single year. But John mentions a number of Passover feasts and visits,[35] and Jesus' public ministry is therefore taken to have been two and a half or three years in length. The frequency of his visits to Jerusalem, established by *John* (the Synoptics mention only his final visit), accounts for the presence of old and trusted disciples in or near Jerusalem at the end of Jesus' ministry, such as the owners of the Ass of the Triumph, of the Garden, and of the Upper Room.[36] Further, only the Johannine account of the Feeding of the Five Thousand clearly indicates the crisis that it precipitated, the eagerness of the populace to force Jesus to be their king, and his deep anxiety lest all, and not only some, of his disciples succumb to the popular fever and, disappointed at his refusal, desert him.[37]

6. THE GOSPELS AND THE GREAT CHURCHES

The question of the dates of the gospels is complicated, and scholarly opinion varies. *Mark* is usually associated with about 65 A.D., partly because of hints that Jerusalem was still standing, partly because that date is close to Peter's martyrdom. The other two synoptists are thought to have written later, their gospels assuming their present form nearer 85 A.D.[38] *John* may well be slightly later again.

Questions of date and authorship have no essential bearing on the confidence of the Christian reader in the record. The story gets its authority from itself, and from the approval of the early churches, not from the workmanship of individuals. The books were produced within the churches, and convey respectively the emphases of the circles of Peter, Paul, James of Jerusalem, and John. If places can be assigned, they would probably be Rome (Peter, *Mark*), Corinth (Paul, *Luke*), Antioch (James, *Matthew*), and Ephesus (John, *John*).

7. THE STUDY OF THE THREE
OR FOUR TOGETHER

Our memories tend to combine into one story the accounts appearing in all four gospels or in three or two of them. Sometimes such a conflation has been attempted in written form. This was done by an early Christian writer named Tatian, in his *Diatesseron* (about 160), and in our time has been attempted in *The Dartmouth Bible* and in Komroff, *The One Story*. But it is doubtful whether this is really satisfying. Nevertheless, detailed comparison is important. To facilitate this, the gospels are sometimes printed in parallel columns, in volumes called harmonies. Of this type are *A Harmony of the Synoptic Gospels for Historical and Critical Study*, Burton and Goodspeed, and more recent, a harmony of the Revised Standard Version translation entitled *Gospel Parallels*.

If we wish to study the contrasting methods of Matthew and Luke in presenting the words of Jesus, it is necessary to be able to see at a glance how the evangelists have selected and arranged their material. Matthew, like "a scribe who has been trained for the kingdom of heaven",[39] gathers related material into continuous prose, because some striking occasion brings up a particular topic, whereas Luke scatters the same material throughout his pages as various occasions involve it.[40] That the wording is not always identical may be because of slight variations in the oral tradition, but may also be because Jesus, like every skilled teacher, undoubtedly said the same thing repeatedly, not always necessarily in exactly identical form.

CHAPTER VI

FROM THE PERSIAN TO THE ROMAN

Cyrus the king made a decree that this house of God
should be rebuilt.—Ezra 5:13
Is it lawful to pay taxes to Caesar, or not?—Mark 12:14

1. THE HISTORICAL BACKGROUND OF THE GOSPELS

The gospel story was lived in a definite period of history. How the historical setting differed from that existing at the close of the Old Testament can be seen in the historical questions suggested by various phrases in Matthew 2:1-8. "Jesus was born"; why is the name in the Greek form instead of its Hebrew equivalent, Joshua or Hosea?[1] "Judea"; why the name of a Roman province instead of the old tribal "Judah"? "Herod the king"; who is he, and how a king? "Wise men from the East"; why this apparent interest of Persian magi in a Jewish hope? "King of the Jews"; why are the Hebrews now called Jews? "Chief priests and scribes"; why are scribes important? "The Christ"; why this Greek form for the Hebrew term Messiah or Anointed One? "It is written"; why consult sacred books? "Come and worship"; why is such a pretence of king-worship on Herod's lips? All this grows out of relatively new political and religious conditions; and still other new words such as "synagogue", "Pharisee", "Sadducee", "lawyer" and "doctor" (teacher) soon dot the record.

Such changes had come because after the Babylonian

Exile the country had been successively governed by Persians, Greeks, a ruling Jewish family, and Romans; and because during the same period Hebrew religion had developed into what is known as Judaism. With the capture of Jerusalem by the Babylonians in 586 B.C.,[2] the old ways had gone; and the later restoration of Jewish institutions, made possible after the fall of Babylon to Persia (about 538 B.C.), involved important changes. The baffling and fragmentary records of the succeeding centuries, for example, in *Ezra* and *Nehemiah*, make possible only a general outline; but it is plain that throughout the post-exilic period political and religious developments were closely related.

2. THE RISE OF JUDAISM

"Judaism" denotes the later form of Hebrew religion, to be differentiated from earlier phases which may be referred to as the "Mosaic" and "Prophetic". Moses and Elijah had been their typical figures;[3] Ezra, "the scribe",[4] typifies this third phase. The three divisions of the Hebrew canon of the Old Testament, the Law, the Prophets, and the Writings,[5] suggest these three stages. Judaism was a religion possessing sacred books, with great weight given to the written law,[6] and consequently to a "tradition" of commentary thereon,[7] to holy scriptures (the canonizing of the Old Testament books was still not complete in Jesus' day), and to institutions and office-holders required for the use, copying and explanation of books (for example, the synagogue, a combination of local church and school in contrast to the centralized sacerdotal system of the single Jerusalem Temple, and such people as scribes, lawyers and doctors).

Where the priest, administering a somewhat fluid law, had been characteristic of the days prior to 800 B.C., and the prophet, preaching on his own God-given authority (and often highly critical of the priestly tradition), had been prominent in the golden age prior to about 450 B.C., the scribe was important in Judaism. The danger of the first had been the abuse of power by venal priests, of the second, the irresponsible, fanatical or time-serving "false prophet", that of the third was the hidebound traditionalist destroying the spirit of the law through bondage to the letter. But all three periods produced noble ideals and noble leaders.

The nobility of Judaism lay in its warm and personal monotheism, differing from the coldness of much Greek monotheistic speculation, its lofty ethics, its regimented moral life, its broad interest in education and its aniconic worship: its tragic flaw lay in its bigotry, its bitter nationalism, and the introversion produced or intensified by political helplessness. This same praise and this same devastating criticism can, of course, often be applied to the Christian Church of later times. Judaism's influence beyond its own community can be seen in the broad spiritual preparation of many Gentiles who were swiftly to adopt the Christian faith,[8] and in the existence of synagogues abroad, many of whose members were probably not Semitic in blood.

3. THE SUCCESSION OF CONQUERORS

A few dates will serve to relate Jewish history of this period to other events and people: the battle of Marathon, 490 B.C.; the battle of Salamis, 480 B.C.; Plato, died 347 B.C.; Aristotle, tutor of Alexander the Great, died 322 B.C.

(a) *The Persian Period* (about 538 to about 333 B.C.). The colonial policy of these new masters of the East differed from that of Babylon and permitted the return of captives to Palestine. A few thousand from among the upper class minority that had been exiled sacrificed their newfound comfort for their ancestral faith and went back; their famous leaders, from 538 to about 440, were Zerubbabel, Ezra and Nehemiah. These men founded the Returned Community, a relatively small and ill-defined area centring in Jerusalem; and in it, because of Persian indulgence, they were able to develop a church-state. In these years, the synagogue, the legal code, and an emphatic sabbatarianism became characteristic. The rigorous reform carried out by Ezra in the interests of a supposed racial purity both expressed and served to harden a frame of mind against which the implied protest of liberal-minded books such as *Ruth* and *Jonah* was largely futile.[9]

(*b*) *The Greek Period* (about 333 to about 167 B.C.). In 334 Persia crumbled before Alexander the Great, and by 332 Jerusalem was in Greek hands. The Returned Community was submerged in this new Greek civilization; Greek language and customs swiftly infiltrated society, and Jewish settlement in Alexandria developed on a large scale. In the second century B.C. these influences were to give place to a deliberate attempt to extirpate Jewish religion as something preventing assimilation and loyalty. During most of this period Palestine was disputed territory between Egypt and Syria, two of the four divisions into which Alexander's empire split under the successor-kings, the Diadochoi, after 320.

(*i*) *Egyptian Rule* (320 to 198 B.C.). Under the Ptolemies, Jewish settlement flourished in Egypt. There the Septuagint translation of the Hebrew scriptures into Greek was made after 250 B.C. There a more liberal, Greek-speaking Jewish type developed, represented by the famous Philo. Some early Christian Jews were of this type, called Hellenists or Grecians in the New Testament.[10]

(ii) *Syrian Rule* (198 to 167 B.C.). In 198 the Syrian monarchs, the Seleucids (with their capital at Antioch, founded in 300 B.C.), conquered Palestine and strove to lure Jewish loyalty northward. This accounts in part for the large Jewish settlements in Asia Minor in New Testament days. The Syrians strove to hasten assimilation by persecution. Seleucus IV (187—175) plundered the Temple, and his brother and successor, Antiochus Epiphanes (175—164), attempted in 170 to blot out the Jewish religion, capturing Jerusalem, slaying and enslaving thousands, burning the sacred scriptures (a policy that hastened the definition of the canon of at least "the law and the prophets"), and forcing many into apostasy. Of this time *I Maccabees* is a record; and *Daniel*, in its present form, appears to have been written to interpret the crisis and encourage resistance to this gigantic paganism that embodied, as in a great image, the vices of Babylon, Persia, Media and Greece (the latter now "a kingdom divided", with clay in its feet), but that was doomed to fall before the godly, and give way to the kingdom of the "Son of man".[11] Many Jews gladly surrendered—the old purity of the Returned Community was no more— but a hard core of resistance emerged, finding leadership in a great family, whose influence was to remain for over a century.

(c) *The Asmonean Kingdom* (167—63 B.C.). The priestly Asmonean family, headed by Mattathias, resisted the Syrians at Modin in 167, precipitating the Maccabean War and rallying the Chasidim (Hasideans) to the support of the ancestral faith and customs. Judas Maccabeus ("the Hammer"), the greatest soldier in Hebrew history, led a brilliant and largely guerrilla campaign. Jerusalem was recaptured, and the temple was rededicated in 165.[12] Judas died in 161 but his brothers continued the struggle until Simon, the last of them, achieved Jewish independence in 141, thanks partly to recognition by Rome.[13]

Simon's son, John Hyrcanus (135—106), brought Jewish political power to its peak, but sowed seeds of future bitterness by conquering and forcibly converting the Idumeans (from among whom the Herods were to arise), and by destroying the Samaritan temple at Mt. Gerizim.[14] After him decline was rapid. The noble ideal of the union of political and priestly power was dishonoured when Aristobulus I (104—103) took the title of king; and his attempt to extend his rule over Galilee outraged the Pharisees, who opposed any such secularizing expansion that threatened the religious purity for which heroes had fought. Thereafter, the High Priesthood became a political football.

The precarious independence of this Jewish state ended in 63, when Pompey came to Jerusalem, the Romans having been invited in 65 to resolve a dispute involving Aristobulus II (king and High Priest, leader of the Sadducees) and the Idumean Antipater. Pompey did so by taking Judea for the Roman Republic. The High Priest was never thereafter a king, though he remained a potent political figure. The hope that someone would "restore the kingdom to Israel" lingered on.[15]

(d) *The Romans* (from 63 B.C.). The Asmoneans declined, as a new ruling family emerged, the Herods, who were to dominate Palestine for a further century, the last of them sitting in judgment on Paul.[16] Antipater became the real power under Rome; his son, Herod I (the Great), continued his shrewd opportunism and so ingratiated himself with the Romans that he was made king of Judea ("King of the Jews") in 40 B.C. He established himself in Jerusalem in 37, thus ending Asmonean rule. Before Herod's death in 4 B.C., Jesus had been born.

Herod the Great attempted to reconcile all parties, and at the same time advance Greek culture and consolidate Roman power. His architectural genius resulted in the building of Caesarea and of the new Temple in Jerusalem, the third on the site, which was begun about 20 B.C. and was still being finished in Jesus' day.[17] Its significantly magnificent Court of the Gentiles was typical of Herod. His personal cruelty, which became a scourge from 13—4 B.C., and his political strength combined to embitter Jewish life. Such an act as the "slaughter of the innocents"[18] is typical of his record.

The country was prosperous and safe, but the Roman yoke galled. Never patient subjects, the Jews revolted in vain, until at last Jerusalem was trampled under foot by the Romans in 70 A.D. Such political restlessness was worsened by religious hopes of direct, imminent and forcible interference on the part of God. This affected the Messianic hope. Whatever the ideals and demands of the great prophets had been, the hope that the Christ would appear became a material and military hope among many. Jesus had therefore to reshape the idea before he dared use it openly: he had to redeem words as well as men.

The Romans were not oppressive, but they were firm and contemptuous. The resultant tension embittered everything: the end came in the war that broke out in 66 A.D., and the Jews perished as a nation. Even before the days of Jesus, the vanishing hope of independence and power had produced widespread frustration and introversion; national pride had become embittered; and those small requirements of the law which people could observe no matter who was master had been magnified for many into dogmatic necessities.

Such bitterness is not uniquely Jewish: it is human. It must never be overlooked that while the historical setting and religious background of Jesus' ministry were Jewish, its psychology and issues are universal. There is no justification for anti-Semitism on religious grounds.

4. DIVISIONS ON THE MAP

The map, or successive maps, of Palestine reflected these changes. From the holy island of the Returned Community, Jewish traditions spread out (involving as they spread the large substratum of the population whose forebears had not been carried away captive) until they invaded Galilee, through pioneering settlements, by Herod I's day. When the latter died, he divided his kingdom among three of his sons. Archelaus[19] was to have the kingly title and half the kingdom; but Jewish protests caused the title to be changed to ethnarch, and ten years of misrule led Rome to replace him with a procurator. The fifth of these, Pontius Pilate, ruled Judea from 26 to 36 A.D., Idumea and Samaria being part of his province. The other sons were given one-quarter each, hence their title of tetrarch. Herod Antipas (usually called simply Herod in the gospels)[20] ruled over Galilee and Perea. Herod Philip had a poorer tetrarchy in Iturea and the lands to the northeast, Caesarea Philippi being its main city.[21] In addition, account must be taken of a league of independent towns of a Greek type known as the Decapolis,[22] and occupying an ill-defined territory south and east of the Sea of Galilee, with their capital at Scythopolis. These cities were not subject to the tetrarch, and, like Galilee, were predominantly Gentile.

5. SOCIAL CUSTOMS

Political and even cultural changes affect peasants and small townsfolk little and slowly, so far as local customs and social life are concerned. The public ministry of Jesus among such people scarcely called for references to the Greek and Roman presence and ways. From the relatively timeless life of these peasants many details in his parables are drawn: the patching of cloth, the replacing of worn wineskins, marriage customs, the tilling of the land and the one-roomed dwellings.[23]

Education and religion were under Jewish control. Jewish religion was tolerated by Rome, even though emperor-worship was normally required in the Empire. Criminal law was in Roman hands, religious jurisdiction, in Jewish.[24] The standard of literacy was relatively high because of the synagogue schools, where boys attended by compulsion from the age of six or seven to thirteen. Jewish women had more freedom than many of their Gentile sisters, and more education. Family life was fundamentally sound, though marred by too easy divorce.

Art and architecture were largely foreign, the Jews having then no developed gifts in that direction. Sanitation and medicine were primitive by our standards, though medical practice was influenced by Egyptian and Greek usages; filth and filth-diseases abounded, despite the elaborate sanitary precautions of the Old Testament law. So far as the populace at least was concerned, any disease involving mental disturbance, delirium or spasms was attributed to demons, believed to swarm in the air.

6. BUSINESS AND LANGUAGE

The Romans interfered little and were reasonably just overlords, even allowing the Jews a Jewish guard for the Temple;[25] but the influence of successive conquests appeared strongly in business and in language. Foreign merchants were common, and Greek was the language of commerce. Jews were often bilingual, speaking both Hebrew (or Aramaic, its late form) and Greek, particularly in "Galilee of the Gentiles", where the pioneer settlers spoke with an accent harsh to the ears[26] of those who lived in Jerusalem.

It is unlikely that Jesus spoke Latin, for it was not demanded that the subject peoples speak the official language; but it seems certain that he could speak the other two languages of the inscription on his Cross.[27] He probably spoke Aramaic most of the time, even though his sayings have come down to us only in Greek,[28] but that he could speak Greek is entirely likely, because of his easy contacts with Gentiles[29] and his final colloquy with Pilate, who would scarcely deign to speak the tongue of the conquered.

Early Christian missions beyond Judea were conducted in Greek, and the Greek Septuagint became the earliest Christian Bible, to which the New Testament books were gradually added. That Greek-speaking Christians needed a translation is illustrated in some gospel passages.[30] As noticed in Chapter IV, the use of the Septuagint accounts for most of the variations between New Testament citations and their form in the Hebrew Old Testament from which our English versions are translated.

CHAPTER VII

THE CLIMATE OF RELIGION
IN FIRST-CENTURY PALESTINE

The scribes and Pharisees sit in Moses' seat.—Matthew 23:1
Unless your righteousness exceeds that of the scribes and
Pharisees, you will never enter the kingdom of heaven.
—Matthew 5:20

I. THE GREAT TRADITION

The gospels must be read with some appreciation of
contemporary religious institutions, parties, sects, and attitudes of mind regarding religious duties and hopes.
Neither Judaism nor Christianity has remained as it was
in that day: indeed, although still closely related, they
are in some ways farther apart now than then. The study
of Jewish institutions and attitudes as reflected in the
gospels is in many ways a study of religious behaviour in
all places and at all times, for habits of mind do not
change. There is much to appreciate, for the Jewish was
the noblest religious tradition known, and the ministry
of Jesus would have been largely unintelligible in any
other setting.

Challenging as were the political and social conditions
referred to in the preceding chapter, and important as a
knowledge of them is for interpreting incidental references
in the gospels, it seems plain that Jesus was not primarily
concerned with them. Far from sharing the popular
unrest, he showed no animus against the Romans, and
such few of his recorded sayings as hint at their presence
are conciliatory in tone.[1] That he was at the last de-

71

nounced and executed as a seditionist[2] is a crowning irony. Nor was he, in any commonly accepted sense, a social reformer. He sought neither by economic formula nor by a social programme to unseat the government, level out society or dispossess the well-to-do. He insisted in all cases on the prior necessity of seeking God's kingdom,[3] and he refused to preach that kingdom as something to be established by force or enjoyed through material plenty.[4]

His consuming passion was religious: to purify and fulfil the hopes of Israel. So sharp were his rebukes of hypocrisy and other religious failings that one may fail to appreciate the fine quality of the Jewish tradition;[5] but the tragedy of his story must never obscure the greatness of the Old Testament preparation. Here as elsewhere, the Christian must beware of the temptation to compare the worst in other religions with the best in his own. Jesus had a great foundation on which to build.

2. INSTITUTIONS AND PARTIES

Religious and community life is always dependent on minorities of committed people; the majority are unsure or uncommitted to anything demanding. And minorities produce fringes of extremists, who mingle ugliness and venom with what should be beautiful and salutary. So it was in Judea.

Organized religious life was expressed chiefly in two institutions, the Temple and the synagogues, and in two parties, Sadducees and Pharisees. As politico-religious parties, these had existed formally only since the days of John Hyrcanus. As states of mind, however, they are timeless, and as tendencies within Judaism they were at least as old as Ezra's day, when the priestly families resented the reforms of the famous scribe.[6] The party names have obscure origins, Sadducee being possibly derived from the family name of the Zakodites and Pharisee from the anti-Gentile "pure ones" or Hasideans. These parties and some minor groups can be briefly described.

(*a*) *Sadducees.* Comparatively little is known about them, but essentially they were a body of aristocratic, rather secular-minded, priestly families, who dominated the Temple and the Jerusalem Sanhedrin and lived well on the perquisites of the sacrificial system. They favoured co-operation with Gentiles, and frowned on post-exilic developments such as the hope of a liberating Messiah and an elaborate angelology.[7] This is not to say that they were anti-Messianic, but their position was such that a political Messiah would not improve their lot and might displace them. Nor is it to say that they repudiated all idea of immortality: rather, they disliked extreme Pharisee expectations of fleshly reanimation and preferred the reserve of the "Books of Moses" on the subject. Since they were weak outside Jerusalem, they scarcely appear in the gospel story until the end; and since they lost importance in Judaism soon after Jerusalem fell, records concerning them are slight. But it is known that their strict views regarding vested authority led them not only to take the chief part in getting rid of Jesus but to persecute and kill some early Christian leaders as well. Authority rather than personal piety was their emphasis. Nevertheless, some of them were among the early converts to the Christian faith,[8] and it is to be remembered that John the Baptist was of priestly stock, and that Nicodemus and Joseph of Arimathea were members of the Sanhedrin.

(*b*) *Pharisees.* These inheritors of the strong anti-Gentile and exclusive attitude of the Maccabean martyrs were the noblest element in Judaism; their ideal was to bring the whole of life into obedience to the will of God. Such piety as theirs, however, readily produces literalists and hypocrites, and the presence of bad Pharisees is so prominently noted in the gospels that the reader must take extra care to appreciate that Jesus was very close to some types of Pharisee and that Paul had been a Pharisee. None feel the frustration of pious hopes as deeply, or see the fine details of moral duties as clearly (and as stupidly), as those who take them seriously, as the Pharisees did. The frustrated and scrupulous aspects of Pharisaism are very evident in the gospels. These aspects remained ugly when transferred to Christian circles. The "Judaisers", whom Paul had to fight, were almost certainly Christian Pharisees.[9]

Among the Pharisees there was a cleavage between those who lived more strictly than the priests and the more liberal who genuinely sought for master-principles amid the details of law and tradition. Among these liberal men were those who were friendly enough to warn Jesus of peril[10] and the inquiring lawyers whom he treated with genuine respect.[11]

The anti-Roman bias of the Pharisees gave them sympathy with apocalyptic hopes and schemes of rebellion; and it was probably from extremists among them that there arose, in the terrible days of Herod, the obscure and dangerous sect of the Zealots.

(c) *Zealots.* These fanatical revolutionaries believed in precipitating the intervention of God by acting as *agents provocateurs*, providing by acts of violence occasions when it would seem appropriate, even necessary, for God to act to fulfil His own promises. They were a lunatic fringe, and were probably more dangerous to the work of Jesus than is usually realized. Simon, one of the twelve, is called "the Zealot",[12] James and John are called "sons of thunder" (which may not refer to oratory, but to the desire for fire from heaven),[13] and it is likely that many people of this sort were readily attracted, at first, by Jesus' preaching. Possibly Barabbas was one of them,[14] and it is evident that Pilate was encouraged to feel that Jesus was one, too.[15] But nothing was farther from the spirit of Jesus than zealotry. His rebuke to his disciples, which certain ancient manuscripts elaborate with the words, "You do not know what manner of spirit you are of",[16] stands as a rebuke to all fanaticism.

(*d*) *Essenes.* Possibly descended from the same separatist stock as the Pharisees were the Essenes. They never appear directly in the gospels, and there is no reliable evidence that either Jesus or John the Baptist came in contact with them. But they are known to have been communities or cells of people who lived a strict, practically monastic and often vegetarian life apart from all other men, and who refused (as the Pharisees sought) all contact with politics. Undoubtedly, some of their tenets resemble Christian moral teachings, as parts of all serious moral codes do. The Dead Sea Scrolls contain evidence of communities of this type, but that evidence is still under review.

3. TYPES OF RELIGIOUS EMPHASIS

No religious system can be understood solely through its formal organization. Important as were groups such as the Pharisees, the religious thinking of the time must be judged also by the existence and mingling of strains of thought. The Old Testament books show, for example, how the priestly and prophetic traditions could exist side by side, sometimes in opposition but usually mingled together. In first-century Palestine, four distinguishable emphases existed.

(*a*) The priestly tradition, very old, but in its revised and elaborate form traceable largely to Ezekiel, had its visible centre in the Temple. The records do not show that Jesus had any personal interest in Temple sacrifices: he used the Temple only as a place for teaching.[17]   But there is no evidence that he disapproved, provided men offered their gifts on the altar after effective self-preparation.[18]   In fact, he ordered some men to fulfil their ritual obligations.[19]   His hesitation about paying the Temple tax was rooted elsewhere than in complete disapproval,[20] and his melancholy anticipation that the Temple would be destroyed arose from considerations that affected the whole of society.[21]   The strict attendance of the early Christians at the Temple prayers,[22] while it does not suggest that Jesus had ever permitted his own followers to offer sacrifices, does reflect disciplined reverence.   This priestly tradition has its greatest influence in the New Testament in providing Christian thought with the symbolism of sacrifice, in connection with which Jesus is both High Priest and Sacrificial Lamb.[23]

(*b*) The legalist tradition, also very old, received its greatest emphasis through the work of Ezra.   It was dominant in the synagogues and among Pharisees, and had to do with moral duties and with dietary, ritual and sabbatarian rules and prohibitions more than with altar-sacrifices.   The artificiality and hair-splitting that too often resulted angered Jesus, who denounced the spiritual sins of pride and of judgment by externals much more severely than he did the sins of the flesh.[24]   His deliberate challenging of an artificial sabbatarianism and other ritual niceties, however, must not be allowed to obscure the fact that he required severe self-discipline of his followers.[25] Nor should it lead us to suppose that a life disciplined by regulations is always unhappy or unworthy. The joy of a regimented life is plain in every verse of Psalm 119, and not all the sour bigotry that legalists could exhibit[26] can cancel that sweet joy. Although Jesus was not brought up in legalistic circles, he could admire lawyers whose discernment of principles made them "not far from the kingdom".[27]   He insisted that legal righteousness be freed from legalistic self-righteousness.[28]   Peter and Paul were later to translate this idea of self-discipline into new terms, and to insist that Gentile converts were under no obligation to accept Jewish ceremonial rules. They were obligated to produce "the fruit of the Spirit" and not "the works of the flesh".

(c) The prophetic tradition, largely influenced by the prophet who wrote Chapters 40-66 of the Book of Isaiah and expressed in many of the Psalms, could be seen in a type of religious life the characteristic emphasis of which was not on minute legal regulations or institutions so much as on "the consolation of Israel". Such unadorned piety, toward which some of the best Pharisee life tended, was largely to be found outside the organized religious parties, among "the quiet in the land", the "poor in spirit", as Jesus called them. It must not be concluded that such people opposed or neglected the synagogue and Temple, for Anna and Simeon,[29] who were presumably of this type, were found in the Temple. The point is that such people had a quiet joy in God, an expectation of His mercy, that contrasted strongly with the angry piety of many and the feverish Messianic hopes of others. In such an atmosphere Jesus himself and probably Peter and others of Jesus' disciples were reared. Peter was not a Pharisee, nor had he been a disciple of John the Baptist, as his brother Andrew had been; but he had never been irreligious, and his soul went out to Jesus as the type of leader for whom he had looked, perhaps unconsciously and certainly in vain.

It was this spirit that became most characteristic of the early Christianity of the New Testament. The Christians called themselves the true Israel, the spiritual children of Abraham.[30] One of their earliest themes in preaching was that Jesus was "the prophet" who was to complete and supersede the work of Moses.[31] As for the Temple, they came to emphasize God's independence of any house made with hands;[32] as for the Mosaic law, its ceremonial requirements were regarded as temporary preparatory discipline now made obsolete by the work of Christ.[33] Much of this can be found in Stephen's speech preceding his martyrdom.[34]

(d) The apocalyptic element in Jewish thought and writing cannot be overlooked, although it is difficult for most of us to appreciate. "Apocalypse", which means "unveiling", was a style of writing of which there are several Old Testament examples[35] and which in the New Testament appears in *Revelation* (The Apocalypse of John the Divine), in the "little apocalypse" included in the record of Holy Week,[36] and in many incidental phrases. It flourished richly in non-canonical Jewish literature in the generations immediately before Jesus' day. The apocalyptic style was never widely adopted as a literary mode by Christian writers, no doubt in part because it was a Jewish mode, whereas the Church soon became predominantly non-Jewish. A parallel illustration of the way fashions in literature can dominate a given period and then pass out of use is the way allegorical writing flourished in politics as well as religion in the seventeenth century. Yet Bunyan's *Pilgrim's Progress* is the only allegory of that age most people know today. Apocalyptic writing is therefore strange to our ears, even though some of our most vivid metaphors come from apocalyptic literature, including "the great white throne", the "four beasts", the white-robed throng with blood-washed robes, "the new Jerusalem", pillars of the church, the "book of life" and "feet of clay".[37]

Apocalyptic literature is both an expression and a source of what may be called the apocalyptic frame of mind. Characteristic of apocalyptic writing were its cryptic references, plain to the initiated reader but meaningless to outsiders, its elaborate and vehement imagery,[38] and its insistence that God's will would be imposed on mankind through some majestic irruption of His power, to destroy His enemies and vindicate His saints. It was born out of a sense of the helplessness of the godly before their pagan and "beastly" foes, and was a defiant profession of faith that God would triumph at last over His foes. But by "at last" apocalyptic writers tended to suggest "very soon now", and by God's "enemies" they usually meant their oppressors and people other than themselves.

In Judaism, apocalyptic expectation was not in the main stream of the tradition, but on the fringes it had immense popular appeal. The Zealots fed on apocalyptic hopes of a judgment to fall on all those, from Antiochus to Herod, who held Israel in thrall. The apostles were not untouched by the hope that the kingdom would be immediately restored. The early Christian church in turn looked at first for a swift and literal winding-up of earthly conditions.[39] Care must be taken, however, not to insist always on reading a literal or political meaning into Christian apocalyptic metaphors. The real emphasis in the "Benedictus", for example, is not on the destruction of enemies so much as on the opportunity to serve God "without fear".[40]

Most of us dislike apocalyptic literature because we distrust the fanatically apocalyptic mind. We point out that obedience to the will of God cannot be forced on any one, and that goodness can be established only through patient obedience. We have been taught not to identify God's "enemies" with people we hate or suffer under, not only because we are forbidden to "judge"[41] but because we know that the truly penitent man feels that he, too, is or has been God's enemy and needs pardon and reconciliation as truly as the worst tyrant.[42] What is most distasteful of all to us is to see apocalyptic hopes flourishing among fanatics now as they did among the Zealots long ago: we want none of it. We know that life itself is apocalyptic: at times whole nations are overwhelmed in one night by great catastrophes. But fanatics are always guilty of making caricatures out of great truths such as this.

Whatever interpretative difficulties may arise from Jesus' use of apocalyptic imagery, it is vital to notice that he stood firmly against the two favourite ideas of the fanatical apocalyptic mind, ancient or modern: first, the idea that God's "enemies" do not include oneself, and second, the idea of a foreknown timetable of events. He warned those who thought of themselves as God's "servants" to look first to their own stewardship, and he professed ignorance or maintained silence as to when certain judgments of God would fall.[43] To rob apocalyptic enthusiasts of these two ideas is as hard on them as John the Baptist's prohibition of looting and grumbling must have been on soldiers.[44]

4. THE PUBLICANS AND SINNERS

Not everyone was vitally interested in religion then, any more than now. The majority of the common people, especially in Galilee, lived without organized religious life. Neglecting the synagogue and the ceremonial law, they were lumped together as "sinners", a term which therefore does not always connote an openly reprobate life.[45] Among the sinners the most despised were the tax gatherers (publicans), frequently dishonest, and everywhere regarded as traitors because they served the hated overlord. Both with the neglectful and careless and with openly evil-living "sinners" Jesus purposely and unhesitatingly associated,[46] finding in them an honest need and an unprejudiced interest often lacking in "the righteous".[47] This does not mean that he regarded them as acceptable simply because they were unconventional. Sinners had to repent, as Zacchaeus did.[48] The story of the Prodigal Son does not suggest that the repentance of sinners occurred either easily or with great frequency; the point is that the harsher Pharisees were dubious about the propriety of promising anything even to repentant sinners.

A SURVEY OF THE GOSPEL RECORD

CHAPTER VIII

THE COMING OF EMMANUEL

His name shall be called Emmanuel, which means,
God with us.—Matthew 1:23

I. THE THREE MYSTERIES

The gospel story opens with a cradle mysteriously
filled, and ends with a cross mysteriously occupied and
a grave mysteriously emptied. Of these three mysteries,
only the second was a public event. The third was made
known only to "witnesses"; the first could have been
directly known only to one person, the mother of Jesus.[1]
All three are included in the Christian creeds, in affirmation of the belief that "God was in Christ, reconciling the
world unto himself."[2] All emphasize the high claim
that in Christ there was an inexplicable combining of
human obedience and Divine authority.

This union of human and Divine is the peculiar feature of Christianity, in contrast to religions that are based
on either human prophets or mythological theophanies.
Here is the claim that within history God became incarnate for the sake of man, that in Jesus there was an
embodiment of God as fully as this is possible within the
framework of humanity.[3] This is expressed in such
words as "in him dwells the whole fullness of deity
bodily", and "I am from above."[4]

The Christian faith, in company with other highly
developed religions, stresses the uniting of the believing
soul with God as the true goal of life. In certain forms
of mysticism, what is looked for is absorption into God

85

and cessation of individuality, but this is not a Christian emphasis. The New Testament speaks of this mystical union in such words as "you are God's temple and God's Spirit dwells in you", "Christ in you the hope of glory", "we are to grow up in every way into him who is the head", and "become partakers of the divine nature".[5]

How Incarnation and such union are to be finally distinguishable language cannot say. The crucial thing is that finality is not here yet,[6] and that until then Christ is the ordained first fruits of mankind. The Incarnation is the basis of the New Testament, for it leads to man's reconciliation with God. The story opens with a climactic movement of God toward man, for man's sake, in the Nativity.

2. EMMANUEL AND THE NATURE OF GOD

Much profound theology is sung every December, whether or not people appreciate what they are singing. Probably theology ought always to be sung, since it is a kind of poetry built on historic events, ancient longings and promises, and ineffable experience. At Christmas, the child who sings "Christ was born for us", is learning to express something essential to Christian faith,[7] that Jesus is God's Representative to man's consciousness, man's most adequate idea of God, and that he also represents us to ourselves as man's most adequate idea of man. He is "Christ the Lord", and he is "our childhood's pattern", "Son of God" and "Son of man". This early theological lesson is followed later by the assertion that "Christ died for us", or "for our sins", and that he is "a forerunner for us".[8] But the child is happily unaware how complex a word "for" is.

Such an early lesson has a salutary, a healing or saving influence. A feeling of insecurity is one of the most terrible ills of child and man, and a sense of cosmic insecurity, of man's unprotected loneliness in an unfeeling universe, is the deepest of religious perplexities. The conviction that God is "for us" and "with us" gives assurance and hope;[9] otherwise, hope does not abide.[10] The child senses that for the Christian the world is the Father's house and not a prison. Later, he can profitably learn that it is not only a home but a place of pilgrimage.[11]

The New Testament, of course, teaches that there is much to be known about God that is not revealed in Jesus, aspects of God's power that the physical universe proclaims by itself[12] and about which neither Manger nor Cross can tell us anything. The late Archbishop Temple's trenchant saying, that God has a lot more to do than attend meetings and listen to prayers and that much of His activity is not what we would call religious at all, cannot be too often recalled. But it is the character of God, His Name, rather than His laws of biology or astrophysics, that is of religious concern. That in God are found love, justice and mercy is more vital to the soul than a discovery of the rate of acceleration or the constitution of atoms. Science is properly and honourably concerned with the orderly working of God's laws; philosophy speculates as to whether God can be known at all; religion is concerned with whether His Name is worth knowing and what is the way of "saving knowledge".[13] The Bible asserts that God can be sufficiently, although never fully, known; and "the gospel", the good news, is that God's character and purpose may be seen plainly in Jesus. The true "glory" of God is evident.[14]

3. THE FESTIVAL,
   THE CALENDAR AND THE FAITH

Everyone in our society is annually made aware of the "coming" of Jesus because of a midwinter festival and the way we date years. Neither festival nor calendar is

known in the New Testament; indeed, it is surprising
how little is made of the birth of Jesus in the New
Testament as compared with our annual season of joy.
It is the "man Christ Jesus",[15] not the Holy Child, that is
significant in the New Testament; it is his death rather
than his birth that first led men to rejoice.

But the festival gradually emerged for many reasons
both symbolic and expedient;[16] and it has become a mixed
festival, gathering to itself and purifying many midwinter
festal customs, Scandinavian, Dutch and Mediterranean;
so it has become the richest and most complicated of all
our festivals. Although the New Testament gives no hint
as to the day or season of Jesus' birth, the old winter
solstice, December 25, with its rich symbolism of light
and darkness in combat, became almost universally
adopted in the West soon after the "conversion" of Con-
stantine early in the fourth century. The twelve days of
the old sun-cycle continued as the "twelve days of Christmas".

The calendar in its turn was to bear testimony to the
dominance of "the faith" in the Roman world. The
Roman Empire came officially under the sway of the
Christian faith in the fourth century, but it was not until
the sixth century that the years ceased to be reckoned
A. U. C., from the supposed date of the founding of Rome,[17]
and began to be reckoned A.D., "in the year of the Lord".
The Roman abbot, Dionysius Exiguus, who introduced
our reckoning about 532 A.D., mistakenly took 1 A.D. to
be 754 A.U.C., although Herod the Great died in 750 A.U.C.
Our calendar is therefore at least that much in error.
How much greater the error is depends on how long
before Herod's death Jesus was born; when it can be
considered likely that a census was held in Judea; and
what may be the date of the striking celestial phenomenon

known as "the Star of Bethlehem".[18]   No final answer
is possible, but the limits of calculation appear to lie
between 8 and 6 B.C.

All this is interesting, as are the considerations that
the annual festival of the holy birth has enriched family
life, disciplined and exalted marriage and sexual morality,
raised the status of women and children, and given men a
haunting conviction that all classes and races are equal
before God, as they were in the presence of the Child.
But the festival is also an annual reminder that, from the
earliest days, Christians have believed that the manner
of birth, like the Man born, was unique, and that the
Child was born of a Virgin Mother. The festival therefore has theological implications as well as historical and
folk associations.

4. THE ORDER OF FAITH

A child's first consciousness of Jesus is of him as a
Child. This does not involve any thought of Virgin
Birth (more accurately, virginal conception); nor does
it reflect the order of New Testament experience or
preaching, but reverses it. The apostles can have known
nothing about the Christ-child or his birth when they
were called, and no New Testament writer bases any
argument or exhortation on the Holy Infant. The first
and only contact was with the Man.

This is still the order of faith. There are numbers
of believers who would not want to be catechized closely
about their attitude to the Virgin Birth, and who feel
happy to be allowed to share the silence of most New
Testament writers. When with mature faith a Christian
accepts this particular doctrine from the heart it is as a
result of and not as a foundation of or introduction to his
faith in Jesus as "the Saviour of the world".[19]   He accepts

it as a conclusion from, or as being congruous with, his belief in Christ: he does not believe in Christ because of it. This order of faith was recognized by the late Bishop Charles Gore when he wrote,

> Nothing concerning [Jesus'] birth entered into the first preaching of the Gospel or the first knowledge of the Church. Certainly nothing concerning the birth of Christ was part of that assurance on the basis of which faith in Jesus was claimed. I may add that it ought not to this day to form part of the basis of the claim. . . . The question of the birth is secondary and not primary.[20]

The feeling of reserve among the devout is often inarticulate. It can have several causes. It may arise from a conviction that the Virgin Birth, while clearly intended to teach that the Spirit of God was uniquely active at the conception of this Child, is a poetic or symbolic affirmation and need not or should not be interpreted with biological literalism. It may stem from an unwillingness to consider that virginal conception is physically possible;[21] or from fear that this Christian story may have been influenced or inspired by heathen parallels.[22] Hesitation to commit oneself may also be traceable to the absence from the New Testament of any statement giving clear reasons for or results arising from it. This New Testament silence extends even into the theological argument of Paul,* which does not specifically mention the Virgin Birth, although it may presuppose it and in no way contradicts it.

Suggested reasons for and results from the Virgin Birth have, as is well known, been given considerable prominence in the course of Christian history. These are, typically, that the sinlessness of Jesus could have been

---

* Resumed in Section 5 below.

possible only through such a birth, that the entail of "original sin" was removed in this way,[23] and that "the Word" could have been "made flesh" in no other way. The New Testament's omission of any such suggestions may appear to leave the Nativity stories hanging loose. That they do not in fact hang completely loose is suggested below, but that considerations such as those above are nowhere clearly referred to in the New Testament must be recognized.

The careful reader cannot miss the fact that the virginal conception is mentioned in only two New Testament passages,[24] and never again; and that *Luke* does not scruple to speak of Jesus' "parents".[25] He need feel little difficulty, however, over the two genealogies,[26] which omit generations and follow different lines of descent, not only because genealogies are not inspired documents but compilations from human records, but because the tracing of Jesus legally to Joseph need give no difficulty in view of the inclusion of at least one adopted son in the list as a son and heir.[27] The absence of specific reference elsewhere in the New Testament does not remove all support from the two references to the Virgin Birth: the New Testament can always be interpreted in harmony with them. Of course, the phrase "born of a woman" is only the normal reference to human birth, as when Jesus speaks of "those born of women".[28] The reader should be aware that the point of the Nativity stories and of "born of a woman" is as much an insistence that Jesus was really born "in the flesh", being no phantom figure of spiritual power,[29] as it is that he had a unique birth. The New Testament anchors Jesus "in the flesh" as clearly as it anchors his life "within the veil".[30]

There are certain inferences that must never be drawn, or even entertained as devout suspicions. One is that the doctrine of the Virgin Birth means that there is something ineradicably unclean about marital sexual relations or that the unmarried state is intrinsically more holy than the married. The Bible's sustained respect for the marriage-bed forbids this; marriage is held in honour, only unfaithfulness being unclean.[31] Another improper inference is that Jesus was in consequence endowed with automatic and unassailable goodness, unable to sin, free from the hard necessity to exercise faith, untroubled by genuine moral conflict. Any such condition would make a mockery of the gospel record.[32] Whatever else Jesus was, he was not a play-actor pretending to feel a struggle from which he was by definition exempt. If any reader of the gospels feels that either of these inferences can or should be drawn from the birth stories, he had better forget about the Nativity and, like the earliest Christians, know nothing about it for a while.

It is unwise to claim that the Virgin Birth was emphatically anticipated and bound to occur because of certain Old Testament "prophecies", since the only Old Testament passages involved[33] do not by their context encourage interpretation as anticipations of Jesus and of no one else. It is more convincing to suggest that these passages were pressed into Christian use after the Birth doctrine became known, when the early Christians ransacked the Old Testament to find anticipatory hints of it. They did not construct the doctrine out of Old Testament hints, even though they adorned it with all the scriptural support they could find.[34]

5. THE THEOLOGICAL BASIS

The basic reason for holding the doctrine is theological. While it cannot be said that the Virgin Birth was a necessity for God, it is claimed by theologians that it was congruous, or fitting, that the union of Divine and human "natures" in the mystery of "Incarnation" should be accomplished through the direct and unique working of the Holy Spirit on Mary as a human agent or matrix.

This interplay of Divine and human in Jesus is a continuing mystery for Christian thought and devotion. It arose in the earliest Christian days, and is not peculiar to the Apostle Paul. It seems clear that Paul, in the passionate claim summarized below, does not feel that he is saying anything strange or novel. It may well be thought to represent in substance the common tradition about the "new creation" involved in the redemption of mankind.

That something of cosmic importance was involved in the coming of Jesus is taught in the New Testament. Although the Nativity stories announce only the advent of the expected Messiah, the cosmic drama, if one may call it that, is set forth later in the New Testament. Its master-theme is the twofold assertion that "God" has been savingly revealed in Jesus and that something has been savingly done for "man" through Jesus. Man (in the generic sense of mankind or humanity) has been reconstituted, given a new head, a new beginning, a second birth, as the result of the achievement by which human nature has, in Jesus, at last become what God intended it to be. Jesus is normal or true Man; sinful "Adam" had been abnormal. The first creation of man had resulted in tragic and endlessly repeated failure. There is now a "new creation", in which all men can share by being united by faith to Christ.

The birth of Jesus can therefore be thought of as resembling the beginning of creation, and as being, like the birth of "Adam", a direct act of God, a creation not accomplished through ordinary parentage. The similarity is that both were given a clean start: the difference is that whereas "Adam" failed, Jesus triumphed. Both results affected "man". Even as "Adam" dragged all men down to "death" by disobedience, Jesus lifts all men up to "life" by obedience.

This profound theological argument is most familiar through the tortured prose of the Apostle Paul in I Corinthians 15.[35] Admittedly, it is the Resurrection of Jesus rather than his Birth that is the immediate consideration, but the nature of the Person raised must be taken into account. Jesus is called "the last Adam", "the second man, the Lord from heaven", a "life-giving spirit" rather than simply "a living soul". He is the "firstborn of creation", the "first fruits of the dead", "the image of the invisible God". The "first Adam" died spiritually because of his sins; the "second Adam" died because of sinners, "to put away sin". As all have "died in Adam", even though their individual sins "were not like the transgression of Adam", "so also in Christ shall all be made alive".[36]

Many people find all this about "Adam" extremely puzzling, and well they may. They sing gladly with Charles Wesley about the "second Adam from above"; but who is "Adam"? No one can be certain, because this name, which appears remarkably seldom in the Old Testament, simply refers to "man".[37] It means "earthy" or "taken out of red earth", which is the point of "as we have borne the image of the man of dust, we shall also bear the image of the man of heaven".[38] Whether by "Adam" the biblical writers intend an individual, or a personification of all men as they have become through sin, is not made clear; but the New Testament certainly means by "the second Adam" an individual, who sums up in himself human nature as it was intended to be and in whom men are to have a second birth. If men resolutely and finally decline (and no man may judge as to who or how many these may be), they die a "second death".[39] There is "no other name given" by which men are to be saved (or healed).[40] From this assurance it follows that all who are saved (and again we are no judges) are saved by this "name", wherever they are and whenever they live, because this is the changeless character and purpose of God, which the New Testament message declares.

The preceding paragraphs are strong meat; but no one who has heard I Corinthians 15 read at funerals can miss the high poetic ecstasy (theology is as poetic as it is logical) of the confidence that man is not a hopeless and ruined animal but an object of God's mercy, and that the instrument of His mercy is Christ. If this were not so, something would be sadly missing from religious life. Christ's birth is an assurance that God is "with us" in our battle,[41] unlike gods who are out of reach or who must be bought off or evaded.

For some, it seems simpler to avoid the ecstasy of Paul and the puzzle of the Nativity stories, and to make only the highly theological affirmation of *John*, "the Word was made flesh and dwelt among us".[42] They place their faith there, and remain uncommitted to more specific explanations. No one has a right to quarrel with the way any man wins his faith, or with his honest inability to follow every New Testament writer at every step. There is no evidence that all New Testament writers thought alike at every point; and none of them makes an explicit affirmation of belief in the Virgin Birth a condition of salvation,[43] or of membership in the Church.

6. THE SURROUNDINGS
   OF THE YOUTH OF JESUS

Jesus grew up in Nazareth, but nothing can be known
of his early life except one glimpse of a twelve-year-old
boy in the Temple, eagerly questioning (not instructing)
the "doctors".[44]   Christ-child legends are for the most
part childish and unworthy. We can, however, know
something of his youthful surroundings. Nazareth was
in the hills of Galilee fairly close to a main artery of international traffic and within sight of the historic Plain of
Esdraelon. Thus, present and past were constantly before
the eyes of the youthful Jesus. Raised not in poverty but
in the scant comfort of a skilled workman's household, he
was a member of a pious but not meticulously ritualistic
household, akin to "the quiet in the land" rather than
to "the righteous". Educated at the synagogue school,
he had no formal rabbinic training, or "letters".[45]

Until his thirties, he remained at Nazareth, possibly as
the oldest of a family of children.[46]   His years were
evidently spent in constant meditation on religious faith
and on the deepest hopes of the Old Testament, until the
records were part of him and until he was sure what was
the real hope, the true will of God, for those days of
bitterness. This he believed to be bound up with his
own life; and when the preaching of John the Baptist
aroused wide "expectation", he left Nazareth and presented himself for baptism, in which act his God-given
call was confirmed and clarified.

CHAPTER IX

THE SPIRIT AND POWER OF ELIJAH

Thou shalt go before the Lord to prepare his ways.
Luke 1:76

Among those born of women there has risen no one
greater than John the Baptist. . . . He is Elijah who
is to come.—Matthew 11:11, 14

I. THE GREATNESS OF "THE BAPTIST"

On the threshold of the gospel story appears an un-
couth yet dominating figure, whom Jesus ranked as the
peer of any earlier prophet,[1] and who has the distinction
of being one of the few New Testament men whose name
is linked with a title. He was "the Baptizer", as Simon
was "Peter" (the Rock) and Jesus "the Christ" (Messiah).
His greatness is obscured for us by his proximity to Jesus
and by the fact that he represents a type of piety most of
us find unattractive. But his effectiveness can be gathered
from the popular speculation that he might be the expected
Messiah,[2] and from the evidence that traces of his work
appeared later as far afield as Ephesus.[3] It even seems
to have been necessary for one early Christian writer to
insist firmly that the work of Jesus had been the greater,
because "water and blood" (baptism and sacrifice) were
more effectual than "water only".[4] John's influence lived
on for long years in the East.

"The Baptist" is called "the Forerunner", and Jesus
regarded him as the true fulfilment of the hope that
Elijah would reappear before "the day of the Lord".[5]
But he stood so strongly in contrast to Jesus that the dif-

ference between them, as "children of wisdom", could best be expressed by the contrast between children playing funeral and children playing wedding.[6] We find some attraction at least in the wedding idea (the figure of the Bridegroom more than once refers to Jesus in the gospels);[7] but the condemnation pronounced on Jesus' contemporaries was that, cantankerously, they would not play either way.

2. OBEDIENCE THROUGH WITHDRAWAL

John belongs to the solitary, ascetic religious type exemplified by Elijah and Amos, who did their work from the outside of society, in contrast to the type exemplified by Elisha, Hosea, and Jesus, who were deeply involved in everyday life. He may have been influenced by the Essene movement, on which the Dead Sea Scrolls have shed some light; but it is more likely that he was inspired to adopt a special garb and solitude by the example of the old prophetic schools, or by the Nazirite tradition,[8] that saw in any complex civilized life the root of evil, and sought the remedy in either a partial and temporary or, as in his case, a complete, permanent and solitary return to the simple nomad ways of life before men tilled the ground or built cities.[9] This untenable but deadly serious Nazirite conviction, if it was the root of his thinking, throws light on John's refusal to wear woven cloth, eat or drink the products of agriculture, or dwell in a house,[10] let alone labour in the Jewish priesthood, to which he was by birth entitled, as Jesus was not.[11] His preaching was done on the edge of the settled community, and people had to come out to hear him. His message was of an axe at the roots of their way of life and of the need for salutary flight.[12] His training of disciples in ritual prayers and fasting,[13] a training which

Jesus apparently avoided in disciplining his own company, is one of the few things reminiscent of his family
connection with conventional religion.

This eccentricity of John, and our recognition, which
he apparently shared, that such work as his, that of
denouncing and awakening men, could produce little
that was positive or permanent,[14] must not blind us to the
widespread effects of his preaching,[15] the expectation he
aroused[16] but could not satisfy, and to the fact that some
of Jesus' apostles had first been followers of John.[17]
Indeed, John's preaching had much to do with the attention initially paid to Jesus, who even adopted John's
theme as the burden of his own earliest preaching on
repentance and the coming "kingdom".[18]

John died at the hands of Herod Antipas, tetrarch of
Galilee, whose life exemplified the evil John saw in man's
departure from primitive simplicity. There is a human
touch in the pathetic doubt that came in the dungeon to
this once free wanderer. Jesus' cryptic reassurance[19] must
not be taken as a further and unfair trial of John's faith,
but as part of Jesus' avoidance of any premature public
announcement that he claimed to be the Messiah, which
might have inflamed expectation to the point where his
remaking of the idea would have been even more difficult than it was.

3. THE RENEWAL OF "PROPHECY"

John's words had the quality of the old prophetic
utterances, a quality that had long died out. He revived
the conviction that prophecy was not a bygone phenomenon: that God could still speak through the living voice,
and not only through traditions, rites and written codes.
That conviction had been, and still is, the essence of
"prophecy". The ancient prophets, from Elijah to Mala-

chi, had been not so much foretellers of the future (although that was one part of their message) as men who spoke immediately from God, with "Thus saith the Lord." This immediacy of authority, as contrasted with authority fixed and traditional, was an unwelcome idea to the religious vested interests.[20]

Any claim to such authority must be examined and tested, but John's declarations had a self-authenticating note. He attacked and weakened such strong religious prejudices as that acceptance with God is dependent on or guaranteed by racial privilege, ancestral heritage or minute formalism.[21] Such prejudices unfortunately have never died out, but they can never again be regarded as justifiable. The other note, perhaps not so easily heard by us, was that one whom men "knew not" stood in their midst, one who had the true answer to man's sin.[22]

John's work touched the outcasts and "the quiet", as that of Jesus was to do, and brought him into contact with soldiers,[23] presumably Gentiles (that is, belonging to "the nations"). But he saw the futility of his own type of message unless something constructive and positive, such as the work of Jesus, came to complete it. Beyond his words of warning and anticipation, he had no message. He counselled men to do their plain and usually distasteful moral duty[24] until further light came, but he organized no church and "did no miracle".[25] He had that rare nobility of character that refuses to be jealous of another's success,[26] and concerning himself he had no delusions of Messianic grandeur.

4. THE BAPTISM OF REPENTANCE
AND PREPARATION

The most striking feature of John's ministry, and the practice for which he is chiefly remembered, was his administration of an initiatory rite of baptism. Little is known of baptism before John. Every serious religion employs the symbolism (or magic) of the cleansing power of water, and the Hebrew religion had long had many lustral or ablutionary rites.[27]   It seems certain, however, that after the Exile a rite of proselyte baptism grew up, in which converts from alien religions symbolized their cleansing from the defilement of their former heathenism by a ritual bath, which was self-administered, as John's apparently was not. This had been required only of former Gentiles: John adapted it to his conviction that all men are basically defiled with sin; all therefore, whether Jew or Gentile, require baptism. Such a requirement was an affront to established authority but men were afraid to challenge him openly, for he had, as has been noted, the old independent way of a prophet and immense popular influence. His baptism had another meaning also. In addition to repentance and forgiveness, it symbolized a man's personal preparation for the "new age"[28] and the mysterious privileges of "the kingdom".

Christian baptism is in its turn an adaptation of John's, but adds the idea of fulfilment, of baptism "into Christ", to ideas of repentance, forgiveness and preparation. In view of its later prominence in Christian practice, it is notable that Jesus is recorded as having laid little stress on it during his active ministry.[29]

5. THE PROBLEM OF DATE

"The fifteenth year of Tiberius Caesar",[30] the date attached to John's brief ministry, may be either of the years 26—27 or 28—29 A.D., according as one reckons from 12 A.D., the co-regency of Tiberius, or from 14, the death of Augustus. This accounts for the difference of two years in the dates commonly assigned to the crucifixion

of Jesus, 30 or 32 A.D. The year 33 is often assigned to
this latter event, the difference of a year being due to the
difficulty of deciding within a day the relationship of the
Crucifixion to the Passover.[31] This indifference to exact
dating, characteristic of both Old Testament and New
Testament writers, is unexpected by the average reader,
but is familiar to every student of biblical or non-biblical
ancient literature.

CHAPTER X

THE CALLING OF THE SERVANT

Taking the form of a servant.—Philippians 2:7
One who in every respect has been tempted as we
are, yet without sinning.—Hebrews 4:15

I. BRINGING ISSUES INTO FOCUS

The gospels compress much into little, nowhere more
evidently than in the accounts of the Baptism and Temptation of Jesus.[1] These offer a key to his thinking on
contemporary religious hopes and on his own dread vocation; and although the third person is used, it can be
suggested that these words must have been employed by
Jesus himself much later to interpret to his disciples the
governing decisions he had made in solitude at the beginning of his career. The consummate wisdom with which
issues are stripped to their essentials becomes more evident on successive readings.

As Jesus passed from his baptismal exaltation to the
perplexing task of obeying the vision, he faced choices
that were in the deepest sense peculiarly his own, but that
resemble the problems of choice that every serious man
faces. Such problems confront us particularly when it is
not a case of deciding between known good and recog-
nizable evil, but of searching for the unknown will of
God among alternatives that all appear to be good.

Both Baptism and Temptation involve experiences that
are almost impossible to put into words at all. In the
accounts of these, therefore, picture-language is employed:

the opened heavens,[2] the stones that look like loaves and the invitations to worship Satan and to stand on the Temple pinnacle are symbolic. Even the most casual reader recognizes that there is no physical mountain from which earth's kingdoms can all be seen, and that "took him to Jerusalem" need not suggest that Jesus travelled bodily from the wilderness.[3] Here also appears the first of many New Testament references to the "Servant of the Lord", the Suffering Servant of *Isaiah*, who is to set judgment (that is, justice) and truth in the earth.[4] The gospels were written in the conviction that Jesus had consciously identified his work with that of the expected "Servant" or "Son".

2. THE "SERVANT-SONGS"

It is unfortunate that the Authorized Version translation of these four difficult and important Old Testament passages[5] is sometimes unduly obscure, for no Old Testament material is more frequently on Christian lips. The passages themselves had not clearly identified the Servant; he could be interpreted as an ideal Israel, or the godly remnant after Exile, or some individual. But however variously the figure had been interpreted earlier, the gospels portray Jesus as identifying himself with the Servant and as identifying the Servant with the Messiah.[6] The baptismal vision meant that the ancient promise "I have put my spirit upon him"[7] was finally being fulfilled. The testing in the wilderness was to determine how and how not "the will of the Lord" was to "prosper in his hand".[8]

3. THE BAPTISM OF JESUS[9]

As though John's preaching were an awaited signal, and as though his own thoughts concerning his mission were now in essence clear, Jesus presented himself for baptism despite John's protest. In Jesus' action there was no evidence of personal repentance, such as John called for,[10] but rather of self-identification with the needs and condition of sinful men, and of self-dedication to the mission that years of reflection in Nazareth had convinced him was to be his. Either through inspiration of God or under a tragic delusion, Jesus from that moment acted as one who regarded himself as the Promised One, the Christ or Messiah. That he should until near the end have been silent about this in public, except that he used the mysterious title "Son of man",[11] may have been owing to the necessity of first revising the popular conceptions of the Messiah.

4. THE TEMPTATION IN THE WILDERNESS[12]

The word "tempt" means both to test and to entice,[13] and the essence of the most subtle temptation is always that it appears not as evil, but as a good suggestion. The subtlety, in the case of the tempting of Jesus, can be discerned not only in that the suggestions he saw to be Satanic delusions were regarded by many pious men of his day as being good, but because the modern reader's first reaction probably is that these are not temptations at all as we think of the word. Here was no suggestion of indulgence or fleshly excess, no selfish aiming at power at the expense of justice, no defiance of God. Here rather was the kind of thing many of us regard as both good and desirable. What could be better than the abolition of want, what more admirable than the concentration of political power in the hands of the Messiah, what more godly than an unquestioning trust in God? Yet Jesus refused them. Why the struggle?

The long fast, which is by no means unique in human

history, testifies to the intensity of Jesus' struggle, but is
of secondary importance. The simplified description of
the temptations may deceive the reader into supposing
that the issues were throughout as clear as the story makes
them seem; but such clarity was arrived at only after
"forty days" of intense examination of alternatives. If
it took Jesus so long, we must not suppose that the solu-
tions were obvious from the start, or that similar temptations will present themselves to us in simple, unmistakable form. Issues are never clear when they are important and involve the master-hopes of an individual or a
community. It is, for example, obvious in retrospect that
to throw oneself from a sacred height might move men
to wonder but would not move them to repentance. But
it took a long time to reduce a very complex problem to
so simple a pictorial form. Nor must we suppose that
once this temptation was over, Jesus had no further struggle. Temptations are never over and done with; they
appear in new forms. The New Testament states that
Jesus' struggle was continuous; and the sharpness of his
rebuke of Peter's well-meant protest at Caesarea Philippi,
as coming from Satan and not from God, suggests that
the pressure of temptation had not eased.[14]

The recorded order of the Temptation differs in *Luke*
and *Matthew*, but seems to be intended in both cases to
suggest an ascending order of difficulty. The order of
presentation in *Luke* is followed here. *Matthew's* identification of the worst temptation as the seizure of power
may be a warning to Jewish-Christian readers who would
feel most strongly the hope that Messiah would "restore
the kingdom", whereas Luke's readers and the modern
reader would feel a greater subtlety and urgency in the
temptation to presume on God's promises. The account

of the temptations in either order depicts Jesus as refusing Messianic careers of various types hoped for by good and pious men, and recommended in certain Old Testament passages and in religious books then circulating and familiar.[15] He chose to undertake a career at variance with pious hopes and not acceptable even to his closest followers.[16]

(a) The "stones into bread"[17] idea did not get its power from Jesus' physical hunger (his fast was voluntary, and John had lived for years in the wilderness without starving), but was an expression of the hope entertained by many people, and promised by some writers, that miraculous plenty would be the mark and result of Messiah's work. The "kingdom of God" would in that case involve "food and drink". Of course the poor did and still do need bread, but unearned plenty is no guarantee of piety, any more than poverty is.[18] Jesus refused to encourage any hope of bread without toil. To make Messiah's work primarily economic—and there are those among us who like to think that to abolish material poverty and physical hardship would result in the disappearance of evil—would be to concentrate on the one word of God, bread, and obscure the necessity of living by "every word" (or "everything") from the mouth of God.[19]

Food is one of the most gracious gifts of God. But it is only one of them, and it is one that men can live by safely only if they are set right in spirit. Comfort brings greed, and bread becomes man's undoing unless it is received as from God, and paid for at the price of toil that He has placed on it. This is the easiest of the temptations for us to appreciate.

(*b*) *The "worship of Satan"* through the seizing of political power is more difficult for us to grasp. But we realize that, in addition to our naïve confidence in the salutary results of material comfort, we cherish the equally naïve hope that if all power were concentrated in the best of hands, we could relax and be good or, what we suppose amounts to the same thing, be secure.

Grave misunderstanding would result if this passage were taken to mean that Jesus taught that earthly power is evil, and that the absence or abolishing of external authority would be a good thing. The point is not that all political power is inherently Satanic, but that the seizing of political power by the Messiah would be a betrayal of the will of God, a refusal of his true mission, and therefore a worshipping of Satan. This can be gathered from the many biblical references to the power of the civil ruler[20] as being God-given, not Satan-derived. Jesus nowhere condemned civil or military power as such; but, in his understanding of God's will, the Messiah was not to be directly involved in it. Coercion, the stern rule of law, has an important place in human life; but that place is at a level lower than that at which the Messiah is to operate. Coercion can be left to others. The Romans, for example, were exercising political authority better than any Jewish government had ever been able to do, and nothing would be gained by a mere transfer of earthly power at the top level. What men needed was not a collective change of masters but an individual change of heart. Messiah's "kingdom" was in this sense "not of this world".[21]

Power, whether of king, employer, parent or teacher, is a corrupting possession, and tragically often is genuinely a worship of Satan. Power has to be exercised at many levels, in the family, in industry and within the individual, but the basic problem is to acquire not power over others but power over one's self.

(c) *The sin of presumption*, in the Gospel of Luke the final and most subtle temptation, is the most difficult for us to analyze. When and how does faith become presumption? When and how does reliance on God's promises become a demand for "special providence", for exemption from the rules and hazards of life? When and how does a pious resolution to do the will of God get mixed up with a self-willed determination as to how God's promises must be fulfilled if we are to continue to believe in Him? The insistence that God must follow our particular interpretation of the rules, our understanding of His promises, so that we can act as the referee as well as the players in the game of life and death, is seen in the insistence of many that they will believe in God only on their own terms. They say to God, "stand and deliver", and quote His promises to back their claim. For purposes of such quotation, Psalm 91 is ideal, particularly in the case of One who has been assured that he dwells in the secret place of the Most High.

This temptation may have derived its particular symbolic form from Zealot hopes. It was not just any pinnacle but the pinnacle of the Temple that was involved, suggesting a professedly religious venture that would proceed in the absence of all normal precautions.[22] The Zealots would gladly have launched some hopeless rebellion in the name of God, relying on God's last-minute aid. Such a defiant and godly gesture would, they reasoned, necessitate God's interference to save His own reputation: otherwise He would stand condemned, unmasked as a God helpless, indifferent or forsworn. But Jesus refused thus to jog the elbow of God. God's promises of help are real, but man must fulfil the conditions before claiming the promises, and can in no case demand their fulfilment to order.[23]   No man dare snatch the initiative from God by putting God "on the spot" or "to the proof".   That is exactly what "you shall not tempt God" means.   Such presumption had been repeatedly forbidden in the Old Testament.[24]   It is repeatedly cropping up in religious circles and in individual hearts still. Familiar forms of it are, "If my child is spared, I will start going to church", or "If I get the promotion I want, I will believe in God."

There can be many applications of this temptation in addition to a rebuke of the Zealot hopes and programmes for the Messiah among Jesus' contemporaries.   But there is one popular interpretation that seems clearly ruled out, namely, that in resisting this temptation Jesus was refusing to invite approval or compel faith by means of miracles and signs.   He did refuse to do this,[25] but this temptation can scarcely have reference to it.   It has nothing to do with the impression Jesus might make on other people; it has everything to do with divinely promised personal safety in his times of personal peril.   The gospels insist that Jesus voluntarily forwent any such guarantee or hope of personal safety.[26]

It did not take him "forty days" to decide that jumping literally from a dangerous height would have no evidential value, no truly spiritual effect, or would not prove that the Son of man had authority to forgive sins.   That is something most of us can see in a moment.   It did take time to resign the pious expectation that Messiah would at all times be visibly approved by God before men, and to realize and accept the fact that the will of God is not something to be dictated by man to God or to be approved beforehand by those who are called to carry it out.

5. THE POSITIVE DECISION

The decisions in the wilderness were negative decisions. What was to be the positive decision? What was Messiah to aim at, apart from material security, political power, and personal safety? All of these are commonly desired by men above all else. None of them is evil in itself or forbidden. But none of them by itself is spiritually safe. Jesus had closed certain doors that pious men expected the Christ, if he ever came, to open. What doors was he to open? And how was he to enter them?

There could have been such doors as the grim and self-sufficient endurance of Stoicism, or the apathy of the Buddhist search for Nirvana, or the idea of flight and escape practised by the Essenes. But Jesus chose none of these, preferring to work close to men and to make their normal and difficult lives the pathway in which they were to seek and serve God. He did this at the risk of misunderstanding and malicious gossip.[27] He chose a type of Messianic career almost, if not completely, at variance with what everyone expected.[28]

He became a Teacher,[29] unlike John the Baptist; and the gospels record that he identified the Messiah (or the Son of man) with the Suffering Servant, who is the bringer of grace and the sin-bearer. Whether in the wilderness he saw the stark necessity of suffering as clearly as he did later we are not told. The wilderness narrative, as has been said, records only negative decisions. This Dominical identification of Messiah with Teacher and Sufferer became the theme of apostolic "preaching", along with the assertion that "the kingdom of God" was realized in the coming of this "Son of man".[30]

Granted that "the Servant" had a preordained and costly task to do, that task had to be performed in a way that would give it meaning. A framework must therefore be constructed for it. Jesus did not rush headlong upon suffering for its own sake, but came to it as the climax of his ministry. Sacrifice may be pathetically useless, however noble its motives; by no means all sacrifice is wise, necessary and salutary. Further, if all Jesus had to do for men was to die, as well-meaning people sometimes appear to suggest, it would surely have been salutary for mankind and easier had he died as a baby at the hands of Herod's soldiers. To state the suggestion thus baldly is to show its folly. To be salutary the death had to be at least such as to reveal the indefeasible love of God, and such as to move men to repentance and faith. It is blasphemous, of course, to suggest that it could in any way be parallel to ancient human sacrifices such as that of the king of Moab's son,[31] or that the shedding of blood could be a piece of superstitious placation or sympathetic magic.

That men proved unwilling to repent is a human, not a peculiarly Jewish fault. Jesus' fellow-countrymen would have been happy to see the Romans humiliated: few of them would have rejoiced to see them forgiven. Rigid Pharisees were not happy to see sinners forgiven, nor did they feel any need to repent themselves. We see such points clearly in the gospels, but do not so readily see that we feel the same resentment against others, the same satisfaction with ourselves. The interplay of attitudes to Jesus' call to "repent and believe", as pictured in the gospel record, lends enduring human interest to the public ministry upon which he entered after returning from the wilderness "in the power of the Spirit".

6. THE INNER CONSCIOUSNESS OF JESUS

The reader is seldom allowed to look directly into the mind of Jesus. The wilderness narrative is couched in impersonal terms, and "Son of man" is a term that has sometimes almost an air of impersonality about it;[32] it is as though Jesus were working behind a veil and shrank from showing his inner thoughts to any man, even those closest to him. For the most part, his work is represented as an outgoing one, dealing with the needs of others. Seldom does the record reveal his inner thoughts. The subject of his solitary prayers is not announced;[33] and he lived daily in a loneliness almost as complete as when he was finally deserted, for he had to work with people who could not share his deepest thoughts.[34] But in the wilderness, at Caesarea Philippi, at the Transfiguration, in Gethsemane, in occasional rhapsodic utterances, and in the words from the Cross[35] the reader is taken a step within the veil.

7. THE FIGURE OF SATAN

Satan (the devil is the Greek term) appears in the Temptation and elsewhere in the gospels, and gives rise to arguments as to whether people "believe in the devil". It is often said on the other hand that modern man believes in the devil, even though he does not believe in God.

What is meant by the figure of Satan is nowhere explained or defined in the Bible, and many of our popular conceptions are drawn from Milton or from medieval art. The devil provides for our minds the idea of a focus or personification of evil, and debate as to details of the idea is as inconclusive as it is sometimes acrimonious. It is evident that the Bible teaches the reality and persistence but not the eternity of evil. It presents evil as emanating from "the father of lies",[36] not as being a different, subtler form of truth. The "God of truth" and "Father of light"[37] is the only eternal Being, the only ultimate Lord.

We are dealing here with the difficult language not

only of metaphor but of personification. Personification is a necessity of thought and speech, for sophisticated and unsophisticated thinkers alike; but only the sophisticated stops to ask himself what he is doing, and whether the personification is adequate and consistent. The Bible is reticent about personification, although Paul speaks of "sin" and "death" almost in personified form, as *Proverbs* also speaks of "Wisdom".[38] That the "four horsemen of the Apocalypse"[39] are more than the passing symbols of vision is unlikely: but they do personify the dread forces of war, pestilence, death and hades. But Satan is not a momentary symbol. It is the continuing term for the personification of evil, though not a consistent one, as any study of the Old Testament will show. Satan always appears as a rational and attractive agent bent on perverting reason, but sometimes he is a cynical accuser among "the sons of God",[40] sometimes "the enemy",[41] sometimes "the power of darkness" or the "ruler" or "god" of "this world".[42] Except for references to the "old dragon",[43] he is always disguised, sometimes as an "angel of light".[44] Evil always strives to be taken as good, a compliment to goodness that should not be overlooked.

Devout Christians are puzzled as to what is meant by "Satan", although they see clearly enough what the Bible means by evil. In the main, what Augustine said on another topic is applicable to the personification of evil, "We speak thus, only in order not to be silent." There is no better word to use, and some of our other terms, such as anti-social attitudes, negative impulses, aggressive drives, are only convenient labels to enable us to sidestep the philosophical problems of the origin and nature of evil. How far Jesus used the term as a necessary one if his hearers were to understand anything, and how far the personification was clearly defined in his mind, cannot be determined. He was far from "blaming everything on the devil". He traces overt evil acts to previous small surrenders on the part of an individual,[45] not to some sudden onrush of a clutching Adversary.

At least the following considerations from the Bibl~ must be kept in mind:

(a) In the Bible, evil is always subordinate and destined to defeat. Although its origin is nowhere explained (the subtle serpent in Eden is already evil), there is no dualism (the idea that good and evil are co-eternal, usually with the material world as the product of the evil Power), and no "twilight of the gods" that anticipates the defeat of good by evil at last. That "all this authority" has been given to Satan is a satanic lie,[46] not a gospel truth.

(b) Moral evil is always traced to the perversion of the will, never to the existence of matter. The type of ill or evil that has its expression through matter, physical evil, such as storm, drought, disease and physical death, is one of the conditions of life in a physical universe; but such "evil" is not moral evil.[47] Most ancient religions traced even moral evil to the matter of the physical creation; but the Bible teaches that the created world is essentially "good", that the earth is the Lord's, that God loves the world, and that nothing is unclean of itself.[48] Physical and moral evil are intertwined, but the only real evil arises from an evil will.

(c) The evil will is, however, not man's alone. Evil is active not only in man but beyond him. Man cannot claim to be the only intelligent being in the universe in addition to God. But what these evil intelligences may be we are not told: evil principalities and powers, and spiritual wickedness in high places[49] are not defined or described.

(*d*) Man is not to fear evil, since he can be delivered from it: it is doomed, and helpless to harm the soul that is "stayed on God". The "Son of God" appeared in order to "destroy the works of the devil".[50]

Although no one can know exactly what is meant by "Satan", beyond the personification of moral evil, there is no other word that can be used that so well suggests the mixture of deception, self-deception, cynicism, rebellion, bondage to fear and ignorance that constitutes evil. Sometimes, we prefer to use an impersonal word, such as "evil" and "sin", as the New Testament writers also sometimes do;[51] but that is only to postpone, not to solve, the philosophical and theological problem. Evil is obviously a "Power" in the Bible, but the absence from ancient thought of our idea of "personality" (none too clear even to us) makes it impossible to say in what sense that power is a "person", except that it has the marks of personality, in intelligence and will, both perverted. For any further inquiry, recourse must be had to biblical dictionaries and wordbooks. One feature of the Temptation narrative is that "Satan" appears as a deceptive "angel of light", not as a foul fiend.

CHAPTER XI

THE COURSE OF JESUS' PUBLIC MINISTRY

He went on his way through towns and villages, teaching,
and journeying toward Jerusalem.—Luke 13:33

I. A GENERAL PATTERN

Although it is not possible to recover a step-by-step
account of Jesus' public ministry, because the gospels
were not compiled with this in view, a general pattern
is discernible in *Mark*,[1] which Luke and Matthew also
use. *John*, although based on a different plan, sheds light
at certain points. Granted that the chief interest of the
evangelists is theological and catechetical, some biographical reconstruction can be attempted. Among many possible analyses of Jesus' brief public career, the following
division into six stages has the advantages that tell-tale
phrases in the narrative, such as "After John was arrested,
Jesus came into Galilee", or "Behold, we go up to Jerusalem",[2] and illustrative incidents can readily be associated
with each stage, so that the reader can be conscious of the
main turning-points.

The six stages are: (*a*) an early ministry in Judea;
(*b*) a synagogue ministry in Galilee; (*c*) a countryside
ministry in Galilee; (*d*) a period of withdrawal for the
purpose of training disciples; (*e*) a last journey to Jerusalem; and (*f*) a week of challenge and rejection in Jerusalem. But any such division must be qualified by the
insistences that we do not know the duration of any
stage, whether weeks or months, and that these stages are

not sharply divided from each other. For example, that "his custom"[3] ceased to be that of Sabbath visits to synagogues does not mean that he never darkened a synagogue door again; and that he deliberately withdrew from the public gaze[4] to instruct his disciples does not mean that he spoke no public word during that time. It is a question of emphasis, not of exclusive emphasis, in each stage.

The record is not a "sweet story": it is a rather grim one. It indicates real stages, not successive acts in a dramatic script known before the action began: Jesus "learned obedience".[5] Changes in his method were evidently dictated by changing circumstances. Even the dominating theme of the suffering of the "Son of man" emerges from vague hints to clear anticipation,[6] and one may reverently suppose that it grew in clarity in the mind of Jesus. This discipline of learning obedience may well have been one of the themes of his solitary periods of prayer, of which occasional notice is given.[7] The things that he "suffered" included the stupidity of apostles,[8] the fickleness of multitudes,[9] the rooted prejudices of officials,[10] the ingratitude of those he healed,[11] and man's stubborn unwillingness to "repent and believe the gospel".[12] Yet, though it is not a sweet story, it is a comforting story, both in the old sense of comfort as strengthen,[13] and in our modern sense of giving ease to the spirit.

2. A FIRST MINISTRY IN JUDEA

Although Mark, followed in this by Luke and Matthew, begins his narrative only with Jesus' withdrawal into Galilee,[14] John indicates that Jesus' earliest public work was in Judea[15] and was contemporary with that of John the Baptist. Among its results was probably the gaining of trusted disciples resident in the Jerusalem area, who emerge in the story of the Passion. A peg for the memory is the arrest of John the Baptist, and the consequent change of scene to Galilee.[16]

3. A SYNAGOGUE MINISTRY

The record, both early and late, is dotted with synagogue references.[17] Jesus' first public teaching in Galilee was done chiefly in local synagogues, where he spoke as a distinguished Sabbath visitor. It may be assumed that he hoped the existing framework of religion could be adapted to his message, that the tree already planted would bear fruit;[18] but it became evident that the old wineskins could not hold the new wine, nor could the old garment be patched with such new cloth.[19]

Few details are preserved, probably because Jesus was still unaccompanied by permanent followers to record them. The impression is that of a relatively solitary figure, touring Galilee and preaching in synagogues. Something of what he said is presumably reflected in the substance of the Sermon on the Mount. The causes of offence were his implied assumption of authority as the "Son of man" and his claim that the ancient promises were being fulfilled and that "the kingdom" was "at hand".[20] For a time he met with courtesy from the rulers of synagogues; the day had not yet come when he was suspected of being either mad or blasphemous.[21]

It is plain that this "custom" gradually ceased owing to slow response or active hostility, and that he withdrew. This does not mean that entry to all synagogues was denied him; they were locally governed and he was found in them later.[22] It only means that the form or emphasis, and possibly the expectation, of his ministry changed. The most convenient peg for the memory is the Nazareth incident, with its violent conclusion;[23] but whether this

incident came early or late in this period is as obscure as
is the length of the time when the synagogues were his
chief platform.

4. A COUNTRYSIDE MINISTRY IN GALILEE

Jesus started no secret movement when he left the
synagogues: he began a different kind of public proclamation. It was not customary for rabbis (teachers) to
speak to the untutored,[24] but Jesus turned to them out of
compassion for their need,[25] teaching by the sea, in open
fields and in private houses. Because of his hearers'
ignorance, he could not emphasize "It is written" or
"Have ye not read?"[26] and therefore he taught them in
parables,[27] taking illustrations from their own background,
their daily work and customs, not from the Old Testament
and the tradition familiar to synagogue congregations.
This part of his ministry still appeals immediately, since
many modern readers also lack any background of
religious reference material apart from their daily round
of duty and leisure.

For a time the response to his words and his healing
was overwhelming: thousands crowded to hear. The
drain on his strength was so great that his friends, according to Mark's startling comment, at one point feared for
his sanity.[28] But the response faded. Sustained interest in
his spiritual demands regarding "the kingdom" proved to
be slight. The gospels do not encourage any naïve enthusiasm for "the common man", as being more lastingly
responsive than the cultivated. Seed could be as fruitless
on the wayside and in shallow soil as where the thorns of
power and riches grew.[29]

Anticipation of failure to retain the loyalty of the
crowds is possibly one reason for his selection of "the
twelve" to be with him as "apostles",[30] an action that may

have taken place a considerable time after his open-air ministry began. Earlier and looser ties[31] gave place to a daily attachment that marked this inner circle off not only from outsiders but from a substantial though undefined circle of "disciples" or learners. These twelve were sent out to preach and to heal, with marked success.[32] But they required careful instruction if they were to be responsible and effective leaders. Each must be made into a "householder",[33] with a reserve of knowledge and wisdom, now that scribes already trained were not to be available. Not every one who volunteered for intimate discipleship was acceptable.[34]

In this period, therefore, Jesus must have done much more than tell apparently simple parables to illiterate crowds. The Sermon on the Mount is addressed to groups, mainly disciples,[35] who had a serious interest and some knowledge of law and tradition. At least parts of it must belong to this period.[36]

The Galilean multitudes crowded to hear Jesus, but the day came when they deserted him. Because it stresses both this enthusiasm and this desertion, the Feeding of the Five Thousand[37] is a peg for the memory. There is and can be no satisfactory explanation of the wonderful work that occurred; but *John* makes it clear that the result was tragic: the back of popular support was broken because Jesus refused to become the Messianic king of popular and Zealot expectation. The common man wanted free bread, not disturbing and demanding truth, and "many of his disciples" shared that feeling. So Jesus' method and emphasis changed again.

5. A PERIOD OF WITHDRAWAL

Jesus withdrew[38] into less frequented places, possibly into parts inhabited chiefly by Gentiles, and once went

outside Palestine altogether into Phoenicia.[39]   It cannot
be said that he declined to speak to crowds, since a
private interview sometimes grew into a public occasion;[40]
but he is reported as speaking chiefly to "the disciples",
often to "the twelve" alone, and sometimes to Peter, James
and John only.[41]   He was evidently intent on the training
of the twelve.

Because private teaching is more conversational and
informal than public utterance it is less easy to report, and
less easy to use with catechumens.   Through the fragments preserved for us[42] everyone is familiar with the
child that came into their midst, the duty of forgiveness,
the ideal of marital fidelity, and the repartee of the Syro-
Phoenician woman.   Childlikeness is not childishness,
but a teachable and trusting spirit;[43] forgiveness is not to
be a matter of arithmetic but of genuine repentance and
a forgiving spirit;[44] lifelong, unbroken marriage is demanded but is an ideal that not all men can achieve;[45] and
Gentile faith is to be honoured, even though Jesus feels
he should limit himself to Jewish cases.[46]

This period of comparative privacy, again of undefined
length, apparently ended soon after what has been called
the watershed of Jesus' ministry, the Messianic confession
at Caesarea Philippi,[47] one of the most difficult passages
in the gospels.   That Jesus then acknowledged the correct-
ness of the apostles' conviction that he was the Messiah
does not mean that there are no previous hints that he
held this conviction himself.[48]   That he swiftly bound
them to silence can only mean that the time was not
ripe for any public announcement.[49]   That Peter expressed
their repugnance for the idea that the Messiah was to be
the Suffering Servant shows how slowly they could break
free from popular ideas; and even the later record of the

Transfiguration pictures them as puzzled rather than convinced.[50] But that the rather cryptic utterance at Caesarea Philippi was intended to give Peter and his official successors supreme authority cannot be clearly demonstrated from the reference to the "rock" and the "church",[51] nor does the rest of the New Testament confirm any such Petrine claim. Matthew's record of this incident has given rise to many serious disputes with widespread political ramifications.

6. THE LAST JOURNEY TO JERUSALEM

Shortly thereafter, Jesus turned south, as one driven out with "no place to lay his head",[52] and began his purposeful last journey to the capital.[53] This he did partly to avoid courting further danger where he was,[54] since that was not the danger he felt challenged to face in fulfilling the will of God.

The atmosphere of the gospels changes markedly at this point. There is a new air of foreboding, and the words of Jesus become sterner and more sombre.[55] That he taught that the Son of man must be rejected need not mean that nothing else could possibly happen, since all prophecy in Scripture is conditional,[56] but that this must happen if faith and repentance could be evoked by no other means. This period is given most attention by Luke, who devotes more than one-third of his gospel to it; the other two synoptists give it little space.[57]

There was evidently no public mention of his Messiahship;[58] but that something decisive was about to happen was announced by seventy disciples,[59] who received instructions anticipating an imminent advance by Jesus through Judea, authorizing a strictly limited proclamation, and stressing that time was running out. The presence of many half-convinced pilgrims in Jerusalem at the time of Jesus' arrival there suggests that "the mission of the seventy" resulted in widespread expectation, to the dismay of the officials.

Memorable among the material of *Luke* for this period are the incidents involving the rebuff of three enthusiasts,[60] the encouragement given to the repentant Zacchaeus,[61] and the great parables of the Good Samaritan, the Prodigal Son, the Pharisee and the Publican.[62]   The reference in *Mark* to this journey indicates that the followers of Jesus were uneasy and reluctant to go on;[63] but both *Matthew* and *Luke* record Jesus' feeling that he must go on because he was now hemmed into a narrow path and destined for a baptism ordained by God.[64]   But the journey was leisurely, despite its urgency; and, since from Caesarea Philippi to Jerusalem is not a great distance, there was an opportunity to spend time in Jericho and beyond the Jordan.[65]

7. CHALLENGE AND REJECTION IN THE HOLY CITY

The sixth period begins with Jesus' arrival at Jerusalem, and includes the events and utterances from the Triumphal Entry to the Resurrection.   His last journey had been deliberately timed to make his arrival coincide with the approach of the Passover.

A few days before this feast, Jesus approached the city in such a way as symbolically to claim authority.   The consequent debates and actions occupy a large part of each gospel.   The gospels leave the impression that, except to those with eyes to see, Jesus remained unknown to the end.   He was unknown by the men in whose midst he stood,[66] and he prayed at the last for men who did not know what they were doing.[67]

8. THE WORDS AND WORK OF JESUS

The gospels, studied as a record of the changing emphases of Jesus' ministry and of the way the repeated failure of men to respond caused him to alter his approach time and again, provide a framework into which must be fitted the consideration of his "words", his "works" and what is called his "work for our salvation". His work is something to which his words and works are contributory and which in Christian thought is the most important aspect of the gospel story. This work was nothing less than the revelation of the essential Nature of God. It is expressed in the Fourth Gospel thus, "I have . . . accomplished the work which thou gavest me to do . . . I made known to them thy name, and I will make it known, that the love with which thou hast loved me may be in them, and I in them."[68]

Such a declaration of "the Name of God" ("name" means nature or character) is not thought of in terms of enlightenment alone. God is Redeemer as well as Light. Hence Jesus is regarded in Christian thought not as a Revealer only, but a Saviour. Words, works and work are the themes of the following chapters.

CHAPTER XII

THE TEACHER SENT FROM GOD

This is a hard saying, who can listen to it?—John 6:60

I. IMPOSSIBLE DEMANDS, COMFORTING ASSURANCES

Everyone, except those who share Nietsche's contempt for what he called "slave morality", recognizes Jesus as the Great Teacher; and sometimes it is recommended that Christians confine themselves to the "simple gospel" of his teachings, leaving aside great theological claims. The trouble with this is at least twofold: in the gospels profound theological claims are plainly coupled with Jesus' moral counsels,[1] and without the assurances connected with such claims, his moral demands would only result in reducing any serious person to despair. The demands of the Sermon on the Mount are impossible to fulfil: every level of obedience only serves to bring into view a higher level.

The impossibility of full obedience is no argument against the rightness of Jesus' moral judgments, any more than the racial struggle in America is proof that the "self-evident truth" of the equality of men is false. Alfred North Whitehead has said, "So long as the Galilean images are but the dreams of an unrealized world, so long they must spread the infection of an uneasy spirit."[2] But Jesus did not come merely to spread the infection of an uneasy spirit: he came to call men not only to repentance but to faith. Along with impossible demands he offered most comforting assurances; the two together make the life of Christians a combination of a warfare that knows no ending and a peace of God that passes understanding.

No study of the words of Jesus can be fair to the gospel record or to Christian experience if attention is confined to his acute observations on the motives, morals and duties of men. Once this is pointed out, however, it is profitable to begin by examining his teaching for its artistic skill, its originality, its methods, and even its omissions. But no one must suppose that anything he said was simple, or that his first hearers were anything but shocked and repelled, or at least bewildered, by much that he said.[3]

2. THE VIGOUR AND ARTISTRY OF JESUS' SAYINGS

That his words were lively is obvious: the Fourth Gospel calls them "spirit and life".[4] No other teaching is so memorable, so easy to quote, so difficult to misquote. The apostolic words, "the love of money is the root of all evils",[5] are easily misquoted as "money is the root of all evil", but the words of Jesus are as difficult to twist out of shape as they are easy to recall. This is not, of course, to say that they cannot be misunderstood, at least at first: *Luke's* "blessed are you poor",[6] addressed to the disciples, has often been misquoted as "blessed are the poor", as though it referred to all the poor as such.

The secret of the vigour of his words lies partly in their artistic perfection,[7] involving a rigid economy of adjectives and preachment that gives an impression of effortlessness, partly in their bold use of hyperbole, or provocative overstatement which appears so frequently as to be almost normal.

Hyperbole is a form of wit (not quite the same thing as

humour).[8]   The subtle, paradoxical turn of a phrase arouses the mind to an initial incredulity, supplies a barb to make the truth stick into and irritate the mind, and makes literal obedience absurd or impossible. People with literal or humourless minds have special difficulties. Not even they can take the log and the speck in a man's eye literally, but some have argued that the needle's eye and the removal of mountains must be literal in reference.[9] People may differ about literal interpretation but argument at least serves to keep the words alive in their minds.

Jesus was deliberately provocative in what he said, apparently relying on the total effect of what he taught to restore a balance to minds inflamed or stunned by individual sayings, content to risk misunderstanding as the price of awaking thought. Sometimes he would explain patiently, but with some listeners he declined to do so.[10] He anticipated that some words would lie dormant in the memory, to be aroused from sleep in due time.[11]

It is remarkable that the evangelists resisted so successfully the temptation to dull his words by prolix comment.[12] The reader is left to discern for himself, for example, that when the predecessors of Jesus are called thieves and robbers,[13] the reference is to false claimants to Messianic dignity and not to such leaders as Moses and Elijah, who are praised elsewhere. The same reader must not take "Neither be ye called teachers"[14] as forbidding all learned or civil authority, but rather as commanding humility in its exercise: obedience to authority is elsewhere enjoined,[15] and graduated earthly authority is approved as the basis of several parables. That Jesus bade men "hate" their parents for his sake must be interpreted in the light of his alternative use of "love less", his denunciation of those who cheated their parents, and his loving concern at the last for his own mother,[16] whom he had not hesitated to rebuke or rebuff on earlier occasions.[17] That he forbade men to buttress their words with oaths must be interpreted in the light of his own acceptance of a legal oath at his trial.[18] That he insisted that his followers turn the other cheek to the smiter does not alter the fact that he did so not literally but only in spirit, when his own face was buffeted.[19] That he warned against relying on voices from the dead to teach men moral lessons already made plain[20] does not detract from the importance of his own Resurrection, which was not designed to teach any moral duty but to vindicate the character of God. That he commanded love toward all does not mean that he did not himself feel a special affection for certain individuals.[21] It is made plain by frequent hyperbole that the spirit of moral action must be elevated to a level unattainable by those who scrupulously observe the letter of moral requirements.[22]

In most of the above instances, the instructed reader feels that he sees the point and understands fairly clearly. But there are other cases in which he feels that like the apostles he is "without understanding" and is "afraid to ask".[23] Such hyperbolic counsels as those dealing with non-resistance, lending to all borrowers, and refraining from passing any judgment[24] are "hard sayings" that men can scarcely "receive". It helps, regarding the first of these, to point out that the forbidding of resistance or retribution refers to wrongs suffered by oneself, not to wrongs being inflicted by evildoers on others. Jesus endured injury himself, but was ablaze with anger against those who wrong little children;[25] and there is nothing to suggest that the parable of the Good Samaritan was intended to teach that, had the Samaritan arrived a bit earlier, while the robbers were bludgeoning the traveller, he ought to have refrained from stern action because of scruples of conscience.[26]   It helps, regarding the second, to point out that limitless borrowing and the repudiation of legal debts are forbidden in the New Testament,[27] even though the Christian may suffer from them.   Nonetheless, the hyperbolic form of the command about lending makes it awkward material for a missionary being tested by unconverted tribesmen.   It helps, regarding the third, to recognize that the blanket order, "judge not", is to be balanced against commands not to judge according to the flesh, and to note that Jesus encouraged the exercise of private judgment and conciliation when he urged that personal quarrels be settled privately, if possible.[28]   But the bold, uncompromising demands of Jesus go on and on, and we follow only afar off.

One difficult group of sayings concerns divorce,[29] an ugly feature of life that had the sanction of the ancient law.   The ideal of lifelong monogamous loyalty shines in its own light; but it casts long shadows.   Jesus is recorded to have admitted, in the face of apostolic protests, that it was not "given" to all men to "receive this saying".   He was as merciful as he was uncompromising.   But a man has to desire the uncompromising ideal before he has any right to entreat for that mercy that makes "the gospel" a gospel and not a manual of despair.

3. THE ORIGINALITY OF JESUS

That "never man spake like this man", and that people sensed that here was "a new teaching",[30] does not mean that Jesus was absolutely original in everything he said. He borrowed from and built on the Old Testament,[31] not only in what he said but in what he was able to take for granted in the minds of his hearers.   The very themes of Messiah and Son of man were Old Testament ideas that he inherited and changed. It is also evident that, outside of the Old Testament, many great moral teachers have said things that sound very like certain of the words of Jesus. This need surprise no one; absolute originality has no place among sane men. But Jesus was startlingly original in the way he pointed up neglected aspects of duties and services, giving truth a new look and a new life.[32]

This aspect of originality can be appreciated if one looks for the reason behind a saying, as well as at its form. Many serious moralists, biblical and non-biblical, for example, have said something quite like the Golden Rule.[33] Frequently it has been negatively expressed, "Do not to others what you would not have done to you", rather than positively as Jesus put it, "Do unto others what you would have them do to you." But the difference introduced by Jesus is not so much in the positive form as in the motive involved. It is like the difference between "Be good for heaven's sake", "Be good for goodness' sake", "Be good for your own sake", "Be good for society's sake", and "Be good for God's sake" or "for Christ's sake". Is the Rule the road to self-esteem, to that self-knowledge, self-reverence, self-control of which Tennyson rather loftily wrote? Is it the road to becoming a superior person by putting others in your debt? Is it to be followed because it pays off, on the dubious supposition that he profits most who serves the best? Is it to be confined to friends and lovable people? Is it the way to be at peace with oneself? Does it apply only at the highest level of selfhood, or does it hold for low desires also, thus encouraging a drunkard to treat everybody in the hope of numerous free rounds later? Or is this way to be followed simply because it is the will of God, because other men have needs and because one has ceased to think of oneself? The Rule can obviously be a different thing on different lips. On the lips of Jesus it is a vocation in obedience to the will of God, because God is like that.*

4. HIS FORMAL METHODS
OF PUBLIC TEACHING

Jesus' sayings are found in public utterances, private discourses with disciples, and conversations with individuals. That they were not presented and cannot be arranged as a system does not mean that they were not presented by definite methods. There are many legitimate and effective teaching methods that Jesus did not use, such as the Socratic dialogue, the drama, the formal lecture and the philosophical treatise. He used and brought to perfection two methods, still exceedingly effective, that were familiar through use by Jewish rabbis: the apophthegm and the parable. These make his teaching "occasional", that is, prompted by an occasion, rather than systematic.

(*a*) *Apophthegm*, sometimes called paradigm, means much the same thing as aphorism or epigram, a relatively short, self-contained utterance not part of a sustained argument, which sets forth a principle or comment. Examples of the apophthegm abound in the gospels,[34] particularly in the Sermon on the Mount, and most of them are hyperbolic in emphasis. Doubtless, Jesus repeated certain sayings on many occasions and in slightly varying forms. Doubtless also, he expanded and commented on the intellectual shorthand of these utterances, although little of such expansion has been reported. This gives his reported speech an oracular quality strange to

* For further illustrations of his originality, see Chapter XIII, Sections 2 and 3.

our ears because we are normally taught by other methods.

Sometimes Jesus adapted and improved existing sayings by adding a subtle change in a familiar saying to make it doubly effective. There are extant rabbinic sayings much like many parts of the Sermon on the Mount: it is the occasional difference that is important.

We know the force and the capacity for indefinite expansion inherent in apophthegmatic speech. Francis Bacon was memorably aphoristic;[35] Ernest Hemingway wrote a long novel to expand the words of John Donne (1573—1631), "never send to know for whom the Bell tolls; it tolls for Thee"; and Thornton Wilder wrote a book to expand the penetrating comment he had put into the mouth of one of his characters, "Of all the forms of genius, goodness has the longest awkward age." Paul did not habitually use this method, but sometimes he wrote apophthegmatically, as in "We can do nothing against the truth, but for the truth",[36] a saying that was to inspire Albert Schweitzer. Jewish rabbis have used this method often and skilfully.[37]

The pitfall in apophthegmatic speech is that it may be merely clever, or a superficial "wisecrack" or, worst of all, prosy. The words of Jesus do not impress us as clever; they make superficiality seem unclean; and they never stifle the mind with stodginess.

(b) Parables, or "like-sayings", are stories. They are really expanded metaphors and similes, and there are parabolic sayings of Jesus that hover on the edge of becoming stories.[38] Strictly speaking, "parable" can mean any type of story suitable for moral and religious instruction, including fable, legend, allegory and myth, but usually these other forms are called by their own names.

The fable, in which animals and other creatures speak, is found in the Old Testament,[39] but it is not used by Jesus, who avoided even the pathetic fallacy, as noted below. The legend, the type of imaginative and symbolic tales that become attached to historical persons, can be didactic and edifying, and is familiar to all through hagiography and Christmas lore. It is not unknown in biblical references,[40] but Jesus did not use legends, unless the colloquy of the dead Rich Man with Abraham could be so described.[41] An allegory, in turn, is a story in which every character and incident represent something, as in Bunyan's *Pilgrim's Progress*. It was a familiar Old Testament device,[42] and was often employed by rabbis, as is shown by Paul's occasional allegories,[43] but it was used surprisingly little by Jesus. The myth (a term to be used cautiously, both because of the erroneous popular supposition that any idea expressed in myth form must be false or heathenish, and also because of today's widespread theological interest in what are technically called the necessarily mythological elements in the Christian faith and creeds) is a special and fruitful study in itself. Traces of very ancient myths remain in certain Old Testament metaphors,[44] and in the scholarly sense of the word, the framework of the Parable of the Sheep and the Goats can be said to be mythological.[45] But Jesus' parables are not mythological; they are, instead, founded on everyday experience. The "kingdom of God" is "like" the things constantly before men's eyes.

Jesus based his parables on men's social life and work,[46] at least once on a historical incident,[47] and frequently on nature.[48] A feature of Jesus' use of nature is the absence of "the pathetic fallacy" or the attribution of human feelings to non-human things, as when we speak of the "hungry waves" of the sea or the "sad trees" of winter-time. Birds, when Jesus speaks of them, are birds, not busy housewives; and seed sown in a field does not "lie fast asleep".[49]

Parables appear in the Old Testament,[50] and probably some of Jesus' parables, like his sayings, are adaptations of existing current stories[51] into which a new element is introduced. His stories are masterful and memorable: they do not need and are not accompanied by heavy preachment. This is the more remarkable in that nothing is easier to make up than a prosy or precious edifying story, and nothing harder to create than a parable that endures and, like a jewel, shines with many lights as it is turned and examined.

Some of Jesus' parables were addressed to the untutored multitudes;[52] many were spoken exclusively to disciples;[53] some were for the enlightenment of curious or critical outsiders of wide learning;[54] in Holy Week some were veiled attacks on men in places of authority.[55] The original audience should be noted in every case.

As a general rule, a parable has one lesson to teach, however many subsidiary applications may develop. The Good Samaritan,[56] for example, is basically a lesson in the meaning of "neighbour", although the priest and Levite are also a warning to religious people not to substitute ceremonial niceties for plain moral duty. A parable should not be treated as an allegory unless there is clear scriptural evidence that this is permissible, as there is in the parable of the Four Soils.[57] Disregard of this rule will betray the reader into grave errors. It is absurd to suggest that "went down" in the Good Samaritan story means that some moral declension of the traveller led to his misfortune, since it may equally well be supposed that the robbers were on the way "up" and the Samaritan on the way "down", while the callous priest was almost certainly going up to Jerusalem. If we regard the parables as allegories, and insist that every circumstance, character, or event must have a particular meaning, we shall be bewildered to see how unedifying many of the characters whom Jesus praises really are. They are praised, in fact, only because they illustrate the point. The Wise Bridesmaids were wise, but no models of self-sacrifice.[58] The compulsion of guests is no illustration of Christian hospitality.[59] The uniform payment of labourers, whatever their hours of service,[60] is an example of God's grace but not of economic justice. And what shall be said of the story of the Unjust Steward, whose shrewdness is praised, but who is the hero of a tale in which owner, steward and tenants alike are rogues?[61] The Importunate Widow is a parable to encourage spiritual persistence only, and it is clear that the judge has no likeness whatever to God as Jesus portrayed Him.[62] The colloquy on Satan casting out Satan is sharpened by an analogy scarcely intended to encourage Christians to commit armed robbery.[63]

5. DEALING WITH INDIVIDUAL CASES

By no means all of Jesus' teaching is preserved in the form of public discourses. Much was said privately to his disciples, much to such individuals as the Canaanite woman, the Roman centurion, the adulteress, the woman with the issue of blood, and the covetous brothers.[64]

Private conversations, even though they were overheard by bystanders, must never be treated as though they contained general statements for universal application, since the meaning of words privately spoken may often have depended on the tone of voice or the glance of an eye. One cannot suppose, for example, that either Jesus or the Canaanite woman thought he was really speaking like a race-proud Pharisee when he quoted (even in diminutive form) the conventional epithet "dogs";[65] or that laziness is to be preferred above industry, because Jesus praised Mary's attentive quietness and rebuked Martha's fidgety and needless activity.[66]

The Rich Young Ruler[67] illustrates how individual cases do not set up universal rules. Does the incident suggest that wealth is essentially sinful, or is it that here there was need for spiritual surgery?[68]—surely the latter. Because of this, the story applies to us all, not just to wealthy people. The problem of wealth was certainly involved, and Jesus' sharp command shocked even the apostles who like pious Jews then and many Christians since regarded property as a special sign of God's favour. But that the command was not a blanket condemnation of property seems plain, for Jesus nowhere condemned success or praised failure as such. He had friends among the well-to-do[69] who made his work possible by gifts;[70] some of the apostles also were men of substance;[71] he never identified the poor in spirit with the materially poor;[72] he refused to cater to the selfish expectations of the have-nots;[73] and he commanded no other individual to sell all, not even the covetous brothers,[74] since they would still have been covetous even if they had been bankrupt. He did tell his disciples to sell and give,[75] but they evidently understood this as a hyperbolic command to put their trust in God, not to rely on riches, for there is no evidence that they sold everything and started afresh. Jesus constantly warned against trusting in riches,[76] but the problem of wealth is to be solved by stewardship, not by dissipation of resources.[77] The Young Ruler's possessions had become like a diseased eye, that in his case had to be cut out before he could see.

Help may be had, however, for the interpretation of many of Jesus' general public statements, by noting his private instruction and his example when specific situations arose. For example, it is clear that the hyperbolic command to go the second mile[78] is no excuse for impertinent effusiveness in obedience or for a supposed accumulation of merit, and that there can be no "second mile" when a clear principle is involved. Jesus refused to go the first mile under compulsion in the case of rigid sabbatarianism,[79] even though he never defied tradition merely for the sake of defiance.[80] Again, his affirmation that God is "kind to the unthankful and the evil"[81] is not an indication that God is morally indifferent, but is an immensely important declaration that Nature is so designed by God as to be morally neutral. That God demands moral niceness in the field of man's humanity to man is shown on the other hand by such sombre private words as those about the punishment of men who mistreat children, about those who create stumbling-blocks, and about unfaithful stewards.[82] His sweeping generalization about truth-telling does not mean that Jesus intended us to tell everybody everything on every occasion, as his reserve in speech and his shrewdness in debate make plain.[83] That all men are brethren does not mean that all are to be on the same level; the requirement that the leader be the servant, so that ambition may be sanctified by humility, is not designed to reduce the former to the ranks, but to make him more clearly the chief.[84] Jesus did not always agree with his adversaries quickly, however clearly he counselled a conciliatory attitude to the Romans and condemned gratuitous mulishness.[85] On many occasions, he resisted him that was evil; but his resistance was never for selfish reasons, nor was it by force; the apparently forcible cleansing of the Temple can be taken as the exception that proves the rule.[86]

It is apparent, from this swift survey, that the words of Jesus need not only to be memorized but to be cross-

referenced in the mind. The fact that they were "occasional" rather than systematic requires this; and the fact
that they were so often hyperbolic makes it necessary to
balance hyperbole against hyperbole. No saying is ever
exhausted by a single act or type of obedience. Like the
sword of the cherubim at the gate of Eden, these words
turn every way.[87]

6. THE GAPS OR OMISSIONS

Jesus did not say something on every conceivable topic.
His sayings have a wide range, bearing on honesty, justice, sexual faithfulness, formal religious practices, the
moral neutrality of the physical world, man's natural
powers of discernment, ingratitude, the snares of wealth,
covetousness, worry[88] and much else. But it sometimes
comes as a surprise and disappointment that little or
nothing is said in the gospels about many things that
interest us greatly, such as church work, education, the
use and abuse of music, industrial relations, scientific
method, complexes, fixations, courtship, total abstinence,
prison reform, forms of worship, rules for holiness, slavery,
the use of leisure, gambling, diet, dress, juvenile delin-
quency and child psychology. There were possibly many
things that Jesus did not need to say. At least, there is no
record of his having said them.[89] The ancients were not
completely ignorant on such matters as those listed; and
Paul's extraordinarily modern-sounding comments about
parent-child relationships (that one should not frustrate
or discourage the young, or live off one's children)[90]
show that earlier generations were not so muddle-headed
about practical matters as we sometimes like to think.

The gospels, then, while their material should be cross-
referenced in the mind, are not a moral card-index of
ready reference for all occasions like a book of spiritual

etiquette. But those who know the words of Jesus well are seldom bothered by the omissions in the gospel material. As Paul said, they have, in some measure at least, "the mind of Christ".[91]

CHAPTER XIII

KINGDOM, SON AND CHURCH

> To those who are called, both Jews and Greeks, Christ
> the power of God and the wisdom of God.
> > —I Corinthians 1:24

1. THE GREAT CLAIMS
THAT DOMINATE THE GOSPELS

To confine the study of the recorded words of Jesus to his moral rebukes and commands would be not only to leave out the parts hardest to understand, but to disregard the dominant emphasis of the New Testament. There are in the words of Jesus important references to the "kingdom of God", the "Son of man" and the "church" (or Messianic community). Every saying of Jesus is a hard saying, but these are hard in a special way. Yet they are the basic reason for the gospels' being written at all, and they make the gospels hopeful documents, with an air of energy and optimism not characteristic of manuals of morality. They supply what is properly called "the gospel", good news about God. Manuals of morality are often bad news about men, denouncing what men are and insisting that they act as they rarely can or intend to.

The rest of the New Testament seldom refers to or quotes the moral sayings and parables of Jesus. This surprising phenomenon, while traceable in part to the assumption that catechumens had already been taught to "remember the words of the Lord Jesus", is much more to be interpreted as evidence that it was a "church" that had been brought into existence by Jesus, not an ethical club. The Mosaic law can exist apart from the person of Moses,[1] Platonism apart from Plato, Confucianism apart from Confucius. These are ethical, speculative or legal systems. But the Christian faith does not exist apart from Christ, who is worshipped as well as obeyed. Because of this, it is necessary to look briefly at three terms that dominate the gospels—kingdom of God, Son of man and church—however strange they may sound. They join Christian morals with Christian theology.

Jesus reinforced the connection between religion and morality, a connection that had been insisted on by the Old Testament prophets. It is by no means inevitable. Many religions have had only a sketchy connection with morality, as Baal-worship and Moloch-worship in the Old Testament show; and much modern morality prides or comforts itself on living by its own strength, without benefit or handicap of religion. Jesus identified moral principles with the will of God, not with agreed social customs and sanctions, and he was angered when "traditions" fell short of the justice and mercy that he insisted were exhibited and demanded by God.[2] He did more. He claimed authority to change and refine moral and religious concepts, because he claimed to represent God among men. It was this that made early Christian preaching seem "foolishness", a rock of offence.[3]

Certain words of Jesus can be accepted without reference to "the faith" or to any kind of faith, since they do not immediately involve religious convictions. "Judge not", "take the log out of your own eye", and "what do you more than others?"[4] are more or less self-evident truths that would be true no matter who said them. Other words presuppose in his hearers some religious conviction, although not necessarily "the faith". Men are to be

judged by their professed convictions, for example, when
making an offering to God before being reconciled to an
outraged brother, or when praying and giving alms with
an eye to publicity, or when observing the Sabbath for-
getting that David himself broke the ceremonial law in
an emergency.[5]   But dotting the record are still other
words, that involve either a claim to unique authority on
the part of Jesus or an unwarranted ascription of such
authority to him by his reporters.   These include "my
words shall not pass away", "all things have been delivered to me by my Father", "many will say to me in that
day . . . and I will declare . . . ", "son, your sins are forgiven", "whosoever is ashamed of me and of my words,
. . . of him will the Son of man also be ashamed . . . ", "I
appoint you a kingdom",[6] and many others.

It was because of this attitude that Jesus was called a
blasphemer and his crucifixion manoeuvred.   He was not
put to death because he consorted with publicans, or
broke the Sabbath, or neglected ritual handwashing, or
because he said that the kingdom of God was like a
treasure hid in a field.[7]   That the type of far-reaching
claim referred to appears because his reporters totally mis-
represented him by reading back into the record what
they thought needed to be there, has often been suggested.
But it can hardly be the explanation, however much it is
admitted that certain gospel sayings reflect the faith and
needs of the early churches.   In the first place, the record
is too natural, too little organized and pointed for that;
in the second, the fact that the terms "kingdom of God"
and "Son of man" tended quickly to give place in the
New Testament to other terms[8] makes it unlikely that later
piety invented or deeply coloured the passages that involve
these words in the gospel record; in the third, anyone who
knows how second-rate early Christian literature usually

was, when men started to invent ideas, cannot credit any known group with the talent necessary to invent the impression the gospels give. The reader must always, of course, face the possibility that Jesus himself laboured under a noble but tragic delusion, a religious madness; but the atmosphere of the record, and the historical results that have arisen from what it sets forth make any such dismal assertion difficult to justify. The Christian believer feels it proper to assert that Jesus said this kind of thing because he had some unique authority to say it.

2. THE KINGDOM OF GOD
AND THE GOD OF THE KINGDOM

The "kingdom of God" or "the kingdom" was not a phrase originated by Jesus. It had appeared in *Daniel* and on the lips of John the Baptist,[9] and it was "in the air" because of its use in non-canonical Jewish writings. But Jesus put fresh meaning into both "God" and "kingdom". The frequency of the term in the gospels makes it impossible to mention all relevant passages. It is evident that Jesus believed that he was both ushering in and preparing men for "the kingdom". He never defined this kingdom or kingly rule, or discussed it systematically. He attempted only to convey an idea of what it is "like".[10] It is one of those terms for which analogy is better than definition.

What the kingdom is like depends on what God is like. Some definite impressions of both kingdom and God emerge from the many analogies Jesus used. If "the great King"[11] were legalistic or nationalistic, governing according to a set of literal rules known only to one people, His kingdom might well be thought of as reserved for a limited group of scrupulous and literal-minded subjects. And if such a group were to feel assured of so special a privilege, they could readily come to regard themselves as favourites, and might degenerate into time-servers. Jesus saw that just such degeneration had set in. Because he could entertain no such idea of God, he sternly rebuked those whose actions suggested that they hoped for such a kingdom.[12] But if the King is "Father", in a sense nobler even than man's highest conception of that word, then the kingdom will be a family of God, reflecting His character, and the citizens of the kingdom will be like happy children. They must, however, be "sons", in the sense of persons who share the purposes of the Father, not children, in the sense of those whose claim is based on ancestral descent.[13] The New Testament insists that God's character is of this second type, and that He is revealed in Christ. The point is not so much that Jesus was like God as that God is like Jesus, who reveals the true "Name of God".

That Jesus shifted the emphasis and enlarged the scope of man's conception of God can be gathered not only from the general impression left by the gospels on the reader but also from one outstanding illustration. It is widely agreed, even by non-Christian scholars, that, although Jesus was not the first to call God "Father",[14] he was the first to teach clearly what is called "the Divine Initiative". He taught that God is One who seeks out lost and wayward men, coming to call them,[15] not waiting for them to come to their senses and seek Him out.[16] It is always more accurate for Christians to confess that God has found them than to claim that they have found God or "found Christ".

The Pharisees were quick to sense how radically Jesus was departing from the orthodoxy of characteristic Old Testament positions.[17] They resented, as logically they well might, the teaching that God was seeking out the unworthy sinner: it was a bad precedent to set, an affront to God and a failure to recognize the deserts of righteous men. But the New Testament teaches this idea without reserve, and is filled with the atmosphere of the kingdom that must belong to such a God. It is a radical idea. It cuts the nerve of pride and self-confidence by reducing all men to the status of the undeserving; it attributes man's acceptance by God to His grace alone.[18] This largely explains Paul's initial bitterness toward Christians before his conversion, and his low opinion of the "law of Moses" afterwards. His autobiographical record of despair in Romans 7 recounts how his passionate zeal to fulfil meritoriously the requirements of obedience led only to frustration and despair, until his pride broke[19]—it never completely disappeared from this proud and difficult man— and he learned to receive a gift rather than deserve a reward.[20]

Concerning the "kingdom" of such a God, Jesus taught that men of childlike spirit alone can enter it (in another passage he says that birth "from above", or a second birth, is necessary for entering or seeing it),[21] that God "gives" it,[22] that no one can demand a place in it,[23] and that many who count on being in it will find themselves outside, while others will unexpectedly find themselves inheriting it.[24] The kingdom, like seeds or yeast,[25] has a hidden energy beyond man's control. It is a new dimension within a man.[26] It is a healing force to restore men to true self-possession.[27] But it has a dark side as well. It is "like" the grim reckoning with a slothful servant, the shutting of a door against unprepared bridesmaids or villainous visitors, or the action of an outraged king not only in substituting a new guest-list for the original one but in requiring that the new guests come decently garbed for the wedding of his son.[28] These are but a few of the analogies that teach that men cannot force or buy their way into the kingdom, but that they can bar themselves out of the kingdom by pretence, by betrayal of trust or by being rude when invited.

A puzzling question is whether Jesus taught that this kingdom exists here and now, or whether it is only to be looked for in the future, or both. He evidently taught that because he had come the kingdom was actually in operation. It had come.[29] He called it "my" kingdom, and appointed men to it.[30] But just as clearly, he taught that it is yet to come. Men are to pray for its coming; they will inherit it at the final judgment; and it can never be identified with or by any outward evidence.[31] The kingdom has come, yet is still to come.

This duality of reference, while it has given rise to great differences of opinion, is not unintelligible. Those who seek the kingdom[32] know, from experience of what is in themselves and in the world around them, that tension and incompleteness will never be absent, that full fruition will never come. And they also realize that there will be times when the tension becomes too great, when the kingdom comes "with power", as it was to do typically at the Fall of Jerusalem.[33]

This expectation of "power" has been a trouble and a comfort for Christian people. It was a troublesome idea in the first generation, for it is evident that in spite of the recorded warning of Jesus[34] the earliest apostolic preaching reflected the expectation of an almost immediate "establishing", the approach of "the end".[35] It appears that Paul, in his earlier writings, had this foreshortened view, but that he shifted his emphasis in his maturer and later epistles. The Fourth Gospel, in turn, interprets the "coming" more in terms of the constant "Presence" of Christ with his people through the Spirit.[36] Thus variously did men equally devoted to "the faith" understand the difficult language of what we call "eschatology", or "the Last Things". The same variety exists to this day, giving rise to deep cleavages among Christians of different temperaments.

A generation ago a new type of interest was aroused by those, including Albert Schweitzer, who held that Jesus himself literally expected "the end" to come quickly, and was to that extent in error. In answer to this, the idea of "realized eschatology" has been expounded, the conviction that the judgment of the world is continuous, that "the end" is involved in every moment of history, so that "now is the judgment of this world" is a truth that does not wait for the winding up of history and the end of time. The historical and eschatalogical are, as it were, parallel and not successive; and the end is never absent from the process. Jesus is believed to have spoken in this sense rather than in erroneous expectation.

The doctrine of "realized eschatology" seems to be justified by John's contention that "eternal life" is something that already exists,[37] not something that begins after death.

3. THE SON OF MAN

Like "kingdom of God", "Son of man" was a phrase taken by Jesus from *Daniel*[38] and from non-canonical Jewish literature. It could, men had felt, refer to an ideal Israel, or it could refer to the leader of that ideal community, who might be the Christ. Like "kingdom", "Son of man" has a dual reference in the gospels, to the Son as present and as still to come. Apparently, the name "Son of man" fell swiftly out of use in the early churches; it appears but once in the New Testament outside the gospels. Its place is taken by "Christ" or by "Son of

God", which latter term appears in the gospels less frequently on the lips of Jesus himself than does Son of man.[39] "Son of God" may have practically the same connotation. Scholarly investigation of this perplexing name, "Son of man", is still far from completed, and only the simplest introduction to its meaning can be attempted here.

As with "kingdom", so with the term "Son of man" Jesus introduced much that was new and different. He identified himself as the Son of man, a term evidently close in meaning to "the Christ".[40] But he stripped from the title any suggestion of immediate power or glory, making the Son of man a humble figure, come "to seek and to save the lost", to act as a "servant", to reveal the Father, not to judge the world.[41] The form of words preserved in the passage preceding, "Come unto me", appears to suggest that the Father is thus truly revealed but that the Son can never be clearly understood even by those to whom God is revealed through the Son's mysterious presence among men.[42]

These difficult Son-of-man and Son-of-God references can be approached through remembering that "son of" is a Hebrew grammatical form indicative not so much of physical paternity as of spiritual affinity, a likeness or a sharing of character and purpose. Since man was made in "the image of God", the Bible teaches that there is for every man the possibility of true communion or sonship. Men can become "partakers of the divine nature". But this can come to pass only if God provides for man a way out of the estrangement or "death" resulting from sin.[43] So there is need for a "mediator" or "umpire"[44] between God and men, someone who can represent and interpret both. The "Son of man" is therefore "son of" man, the ideal man truly in the image of God, man's ideal representative before God; and the "Son of God" is "son of" God, the "image of the invisible God",[45] His appointed and anointed (Christ means Anointed One) representative to man. The hunger for such a meeting of God and man is satisfied, according to the New Testament, in the Person and work of Christ.

According to the gospels, the Son of man, like the kingdom of God, is present now. Even more clearly than it asserts the actual presence of the kingdom, the gospel story asserts the presence of the Son of man in Jesus. Jesus makes the identification often, "Son of man" being unmistakably equivalent to "I". The "Son of man" has nowhere to lay his head, he came eating and drinking, he is lord of the Sabbath, he sows good seed, he is betrayed with a kiss, he has power on earth to forgive sins; and his presence makes stern demands, so that men must not be ashamed of "me", but are to acknowledge "me", if the "Son of man" is to acknowledge them.[46]

But, as in the case of the kingdom, the Son of man is still to come in power and glory, and his coming "in power" has in it the awful element of judgment, or the breaking of unbearable tension, whether typically in the Fall of Jerusalem or through any other baring of his arm. This future "appearing" of the Son of man can be described only in analogy and symbol, the terms used being by no means original in the New Testament. It is couched in highly figurative language, involving clouds, angels, "the glory of his Father", and a delay that will try men's faith. It will be an unheralded irruption of power, glory and judgment, unmistakable for those who have eyes to see. The nations are to be gathered before his glorious throne, and he is to send forth his "angels" for the harvest.[47] Paul carries this figurative anticipation even farther, picturing the triumphant Son delivering up the kingdom to God at the last.[48]   Language can go no farther, and many may feel that they cannot follow it so far.   It is the language of vision and interpretation, not of a map or photograph.   There is no good reason to doubt that such metaphors in the New Testament had their source in words of Jesus.

This duality of reference is not altogether unintelligible.   Men of understanding know that the work of Christ is already complete, and yet is never completed.   That work was sufficiently accomplished in Palestine long ago, so that the Son of man is already like a vine of which his members are branches.   But in another sense it was not completed; it must go on and on until the unimaginable end.

4. THE CHURCH

It is surprising, considering how often "the church" is mentioned in the rest of the New Testament, that it is mentioned by that name only twice in the gospels (both times in *Matthew*).   Once it appears to mean the visible congregation of the faithful, met for discipline and worship, and once it seems to indicate the broad and indefeasible community of souls united to Christ and to one another by their faith in Jesus as "the Christ".[49]   Like "kingdom" and "Son of man", "the church" has never yet been given a satisfactory definition, yet is understood sufficiently.   By one analogy, it is the Body of Christ, who is its Head.

But, although "church" is seldom mentioned by that name, the idea of a community of faith is frequently met with in the gospels.   The Messiah is not the leader of separated island-like individuals, but of a Messianic community, analogous to the "Israel" of the Old Testament.   Twelve apostles are appointed over "twelve tribes"; men are to meet together in Christ's "name", even if only by twos and threes; natural ties of blood must give place to a relationship of grace, families being divided because their members are loyal to different spiritual communities; there are to be leaders, who must be true "benefactors"; and the disciples are to eat together in the presence, and ideally in the spirit, of their Master.[50]

Jesus is not recorded as having laid down any set pattern of organization; but that he anticipated a beloved community seems plain. This community, this "church", is of necessity a new organization. Followers of Jesus are warned that the synagogues will cast them out, that governors will oppose them, that as Christ's "sheep" they must live amid "wolves"; but they are assured that they will be a new "nation" that will truly inherit the ancient promises.[51] They must watch lest in their turn they grow proud and exclusive, rigidly insisting on a visible uniformity of spirit. For this reason, the Prodigal and the Elder Brother must learn to live together in the Father's house, in which they have equal status; all must realize that the Good Shepherd has a "flock" that exists in many "folds", possibly unknown to one another; and disciples must be tolerant, knowing that, as truly as he that is not with Christ is against him, those who are not against him are on his side.[52] For his "sheep" and for his "friends" he was to lay down his life, in dying as he had in living.[53] This use of the plural is consistent in the New Testament, and suggests the community rather than the solitary individual. The word "saint" never appears in the singular in the New Testament, but always as "the saints", who are by no means always what we think of as saintly.

If it seems plain that this church was not to be an exclusive club of like-minded and respectable people but a fellowship of repentant sinners and still imperfect saints, it seems equally plain that it was not to be a community hived off from the world, as Essene communities were. Families might be spiritually divided, but they were not necessarily to be socially and physically separated.[54] Jesus declined to pray that his disciples be taken out of the world.[55] Not much is said in the gospels about undertaking formal responsibilities in and for the world; but the example of Jesus and the total absence of any command to separate themselves from human society led the early Christians gradually to take responsibility for the poor, to do good to all men, to learn to obey the magistrate, to pay taxes as common citizens, to seek a good reputation among outsiders.[56] As William Temple put it, the Christian faith is the most worldly of all the world's great religions. Whether the kingdom and the church are in any or in every sense equivalent terms is a problem of interpretation on which widely different opinions are held.

CHAPTER XIV

THE MIGHTY WORKS AND SIGNS

No one can do these signs that you do, unless God is
with him.—John 3:2
Truly, I say to you, no sign shall be given to this generation.—Mark 8:12

I. THE DISTURBING STRANGENESS

The student of the gospels often feels uncomfortable
when he reads those parts of the story that record "wonders" and "signs". It is a different kind of discomfort
than he feels over the commands of Jesus. With regard
to the commands he feels that they are right and he is
wrong, whereas concerning the mighty works he feels
that there may be something wrong with the record. At
least it is strange, and sometimes meaningless. This is,
he recognizes, almost a reversal of what he felt as a child.
A child may feel relatively little concern over the commands of Jesus, which he is not old enough to analyze;
but he is moved to a grateful wonder as he gets his first
assurance about "the goodness and loving kindness of
God our Saviour"[1] from the stories of the active goodness
and kindness of Jesus, who "went about doing good".[2]
On the contrary, the adult often shrinks from this part
of the record, not only because, firstly, he wonders whether
it is true; but because, secondly, he feels little or no need
for this kind of help; and because, thirdly, if he reads carefully, he discovers that the permanent results for good
were apparently small. In addition, he feels uncomfortable
about such words as "miracle" and "supernatural".

But balancing considerations soon suggest themselves. The reader discovers that many of the people Jesus helped did not consciously feel their need, either. They were usually brought to him,[3] scarcely knowing what was the matter. Our world is full of problem cases of this kind, people to whom it is not helpful to recite the Sermon on the Mount, because their illness or their retreat from life has been caused by unrecognized fears, worries, suppressed guilt-feelings, or tensions in personal relationships. Such people have to be brought back to the threshold of sanity or self-mastery before they can begin to obey moral precepts. When the reader sees that, in this side of his ministry, Jesus was met with ingratitude as well as gaping wonder, and was seldom able to rely on those he helped, he recalls being told that physicians today have few "grateful patients". If he does not understand such a word as miracle, he can comfort himself with the knowledge that no one ever has understood it. If he dislikes the idea of the breaking of laws of nature, he can readily learn that informed Christians do not like such an idea either, and that this "modern" attitude is much older than he thinks. It arose quite early in Christian history, although it was not one that would have occurred to Jesus' contemporaries, who did not talk of laws of nature but thought of everything as a direct act of God.

The term "miracle" is used less often in the Authorized Version than people suppose; and it appears rarely in the Revised Standard Version, the better translation being "mighty work" or "power". This is frequently coupled with "sign". Sometimes it is "mighty works and wonders and signs" all together.[4] These words are descriptions, not attempts at explanation. They are acknowledgements of ignorance rather than definitions of knowledge. "Miracle" means simply something to be marvelled at, and we use it constantly to describe our reaction to microscopic life, atomic power, flowers, sunsets and falling in love. As for "sign", it means simply an occurrence that points to something. But of what is a mighty work a sign? To Jesus it was a sign of "the power of God" being "present to heal"; his opponents professed to see in it a sign of league with the prince of demons.[5] A sign can always be explained away, and probably for this reason Jesus refused to approach his generation with the aid of "signs". He himself was a sign, but for many he was a "sign spoken against".[6]

Some Bible readers may believe that reverence compels them to see in miracles a sign that the laws of nature have been suspended or broken; but most instructed Christians hold rather that reverence compels them to see here a sign that there are laws, and the harnessing of laws that we know nothing about, at least as yet. "Supernatural" is not a biblical word. It is an unfortunate term, because it so easily suggests the unnatural or the irrational or the magical. It, too, is a cover for our ignorance and not a clear statement of our knowledge.

2. OTHER MEN HAVE WONDERED

Ours is not the first generation to make puzzled inquiries. Early Christian theologians made some quite modern-sounding statements on the subject. Augustine wrote, in the fifth century, "A miracle, therefore, is not contrary to nature but contrary to nature as it is known to us," and, "God, the Creator and Founder of all natures, does nothing contrary to nature: for that will be natural to each thing which is done by Him from whom every kind of number and order of nature comes." Thomas Aquinas wrote, in the thirteenth century, "Those events are properly to be styled miracles, which happen by divine

power beyond the order commonly observed in nature."
But thinking has not always been as clear as this. For
example, that Jesus' miracles were either advertisement
or proof has been suggested; and people tend to recall
these wrong ideas rather than the clearer views of Augustine and Aquinas.

Although there is no suggestion of it in the gospels, the
idea that a miracle in Jesus' ministry was "the bell before
the sermon", to attract crowds to the teaching, had some
currency in medieval times. But it was left to the beginning of the modern age to suggest something equally
unsuitable, something Jesus did not claim, that the truth
of the gospel and even of the gospel ethics is "proved" by
the miracles.[7] This embarrassing argument is scarcely
ever heard today, except in uninformed circles. It should
never have arisen, in view of Jesus' refusal to work wonders as proof, his warning that false teachers could and
would work wonders,[8] and the evidence that few people in
the gospel were as greatly impressed by wonders as we
sometimes feel that they were bound to be.[9]

There are those who wish that this material was not
in the gospels at all, and that Jesus had been like John
the Baptist, who "did no miracle".[10] But the record is
what it is and, whatever reservations one may feel about
details here and there,[11] this part of the story cannot be
cut out, or explained away as pious fiction or hagiography.
There is no doubt that the work of Jesus was accompanied
by extraordinary incidents which he ascribed to "the
finger of God", the Father who was with him doing the
works.[12]

3. HOW COMPLETELY MODERN IS MODERN?

Before examining the record, it must be recalled that
there is a distinction between physical evil and moral

evil. These are logically distinct, but they are seldom separable in experience. They overlap in the areas of both cause and effect. Physical evil appears in such things as earthquakes, the breaking of an arm, the contracting of a germ-borne disease. These do not happen to people because they are morally bad, any more than sunshine falls on people because they are morally good. Jesus forbade any such conclusions.[13] But physical evil can result in moral evil. Earthquakes can produce paralyzing and irrational terror; a child who breaks an arm is often tragically spoiled by the special attention he receives; a child whose arm is broken by a vicious adult is more seriously scarred inwardly than outwardly; and there is good evidence that germs most easily infect people who are under stress of anxiety or fear. Moral evil in its turn may be the cause of physical evil, as when paralysis is produced not by physical lesion but by a hidden fear or wish. Jesus often worked in the twilight zone where moral and physical evil overlap.

Even the most reverent reader is aware that his mind is largely governed by certain "modern" considerations. But he may not notice how much in line with these the gospel evidence is in some respects. The following comparison of nine "modern" and gospel ideas has some value.

(a) We feel that God's power and kindness are more evident and convincing in the orderly workings of Nature than in anything extraordinary. But Jesus also put his greatest emphasis on God's orderly provision, and illustrated his sayings from common experience.[14]

(b) Mind, body and spirit are so interdependent that modern medical thinking traces over half of man's sickness to "spiritual" (which is not the same as to say religious, moral or theological) causes. Emotions account for as much illness as all other causes combined; and they are real illnesses, not just something "in your mind". But it is evident that many, though by no means all, illnesses in the gospels were likewise of a functional rather than organic type, as in the cases of the subconsciously guilt-ridden paralytic and the woman who was afflicted with constant bleeding.[15] As for "faith" it is not suggested in the gospels that these two people exercised what could be called specifically "Christian" faith. Many gospel cases of mental disorder closely resemble what we know today, and unwavering kindness such as Jesus showed is still vital to successful cure.

(c) "Faith-healing", as we hear of it, does not always come through or to people of sound moral character, nor does it always result in improvement of character. Such healing seems to have no exclusive tie with Christian faith or doctrine, since it occurs at primitive levels and in primitive religions and is often tinged with superstition. Moreover, we are aware that people can be killed as well as cured by faith, as through African death-curses. We also observe that faith-healing seems to work less effectively the higher one goes in the spiritual scale. Men with a healthy religious faith are subject to fewer of the illnesses that faith-healing can touch, yet may suffer from maladies that are chronic or permanent.

All this has its parallels in the New Testament. Jesus admitted that his own disciples would have no monopoly in the field, that Jewish exorcists, and even charlatans, could be effective.[16] He was faced with the discouragement that many who were "saved"—healed or made whole—from disease showed no real desire to be "saved" in any more profound sense.[17] To be made well was enough: to be made good was something else again. Jesus did not equate "faith to be healed" with "saving faith", and did not want the two to be confused, as is shown by his repeated and generally useless commands to those who were healed to keep quiet about it.[18]   He condescended to men of primitive and superstitious outlook, as when he cured the obviously ignorant blind man by using spittle,[19] which is still regarded by primitive peoples as a specific medicine, particularly if it comes from a great person. The New Testament shows that men of primitive faith and cunning could die by the exercise of faith, as Ananias did (for religious terror is a form of faith),[20] as surely as others, such as the lame man who was laid daily at the Temple gate (a sign of persistent expectant faith), could be cured by faith.[21]   As for the permanence of handicaps endured by men of great religious faith, Paul stands as a lasting and comforting example of a man of deep faith, not unacquainted with ecstasy, who was bluntly told to stop praying for the removal of his "thorn", since God's grace was all he needed and all he was going to have.[22] The greatest spiritual triumphs are those of people who have faith in spite of crippling handicaps, not those who get rid of certain handicaps through a certain type of faith. A Paul unhealed is of more value than many healed Gadarene maniacs.

(d) Most of us profess to be helped by the "wisdom" of Jesus more than by his "mighty works", which do not seem to touch our need or our capacity at ordinary times. Our Christian faith did not arise and does not persist because of miracles. We may believe in the miracles because of Christ; but we do not believe in Christ because of the miracles. This, too, has a familiar gospel ring to it. The faith of the apostles was not drawn from "signs". They might occasionally be wonder-struck, but their faith had a deeper source.[23]   Neither they nor the Pharisees and scribes ever exercised "faith to be healed", although they helped other people to exercise it.[24] Jesus did not appeal to his own wonders as a basis for faith, except as a second-best.[25] The early church scarcely ever argued for the truth of "the faith" on the basis of miracles: there were too many instances of such things in the heathen world for that.

(e) People cured by faith seldom become capable of responsibility or leadership. That, too, is gospel truth. No healed person is recorded as having been given respon- sibility, though Mary Magdalene became a faithful servant of Christ.[26] The Gadarene demoniac was forbidden either to join the company of Jesus or to make public announce- ment of his cure, which latter command he excitedly disobeyed.[27] Emotional maturity is not gained at a bound, especially by those who have been immature. Jesus could not lean heavily on bruised reeds.

(f) Faith-healing can be followed by serious relapse, in the same way that many converts at high-pressure revival meetings backslide after the first emotional up- surge has spent itself. This, too, is reflected in the gospels. Jesus did not promise that his cures would be permanent, nor were they all instantaneously successful. He warned that relapse would follow failure to achieve spiritual sta- bility.[28] Goodness and wisdom were not automatic re- sults of being healed, but goodness and wisdom were impossible for these people until they were healed. One cannot talk to the stone-deaf, or teach subtle truths to the distraught. Moral obedience is possible only when the threshold of moral responsibility has been reached. Some- times that threshold is immensely difficult to reach. Jesus could on occasion effect cures only slowly,[29] sometimes not at all.[30] The apostles were puzzled by their own power- lessness at times.[31]

(g) "Demon-possession" is, to our minds, an unwelcome explanation for disease and human torment. Here we feel special difficulty about the record. It must at least be noted that by no means all diseases were traced to this cause, and that leprosy in particular was not traced to demons and was never used as an analogy for moral uncleanness.[32] We should appreciate also that demon-possession was in principle a kindly type of diagnosis, much preferable to the later attitude of blaming and punishing the distraught, which dominated men's actions until recent times. The ancient diagnosis was morally and therapeutically superior, even though it may have been scientifically inexact, since according to it no one was considered to be guilty of some awful sin if he was mentally unbalanced.

No one can prove how far, if at all, Jesus himself shared the popular belief that demons were swarming around men, but we can appreciate that there was no use in his talking to afflicted people in any other terms, any more than a modern doctor can help a distraught patient by a learned discourse on mental lesions. Moreover, considering the revival in recent learned European theological thought of the idea of "demonic" powers that drive men and nations to bestiality and moral suicide, and the puzzling evidence of "possession" that comes from both missionary and anthropological annals, as well as the Freudian insistence on "unfriendly powers", we cannot speak with quite the same confident scorn as our forefathers on this topic of demonism.

(h) Numerous occurrences on the lunatic or primitive fringe of religion repel us, including people walking on live coals, handling snakes and falling into raving ecstasy. We admit that these phenomena occur, but they do not appear to have any value in the area of deep religious conviction. The New Testament is with us there, too. Abnormal manifestations were regarded as belonging to the fringes, not the centre, of serious religion. Jesus refused to permit or build on the penetrating, fear-dominated, ejaculatory praise of the mentally deranged,[33] although they were more sensitive to the atmosphere of power around him than were many of the sane. Paul showed a similar distaste at Philippi,[34] and at Corinth gave a low evaluation to "tongues" as compared with a "sound mind".[35]

(*i*) It is admitted by us that strange gifts appear among men (including George Fox, the early Quaker, and Paul Kruger,[36] the Boer leader), and that there are known cases of healing at a distance and of seeing beyond the range of vision. This can lead us to take seriously Jesus' prevision of Nathanael,[37] and the records of effects wrought by him at a distance.[38] We ought not, however, to talk of charismatic vision in such cases as the probably pre-arranged borrowing of the Ass from a disciple or the carrying out of a prearranged plan for the secret holding of the Last Supper.[39]

Such comparisons between our modern approach and the evidence of the gospels may not finish the inquiry, but they certainly help to open it up. We cannot hope to fill in the record that gives us so little detail at many points.[40] The approach must be one of humility and reserve, and if this part of the record holds no immediate interest for a particular reader, he can turn to other parts. In examining the wonderful works in the gospels, there is no profit in either of two extremes: a nervous and belligerent reverence that refuses to inquire, lest a professedly simple faith be challenged by unwelcome considerations; and an arrogant scepticism that dismisses the whole thing as pious fiction, or rationalizes it as not very remarkable after all, or takes refuge in the silly suggestion that diseases that cannot be successfully treated by drugs and surgery are not really diseases but are "all in the mind". Certainly, medical opinion would not support this last suggestion.

It is inevitable that the first step in an approach to the mighty works should be taken by way of the works of healing, because although we only "see in a mirror dimly",[41] we do see something. But it must not be supposed that Jesus can be adequately described as some cheerful advocate of mental health. Nor dare we think that by drawing an analogy between the Great Physician and a skilled psychotherapist we have explained either the Physician or anything else. Description is never explanation, and "how" never reaches the level of "why", no matter how far one goes in tracing processes. When we talk about plumbing the depths of man's subconscious mind, what are we really saying? When we have admitted that iodine (let alone a placebo) can produce cures like those produced by faith, what have we explained? We have only said that, after years of patient investigation, we have managed to find a key to unlock natural powers that have, on occasion, been unlocked even more effectively by a word or touch. We can rejoice that God has "given" great "authority to men",[42] but we do not know why it works, or why the universe and the delicate mechanism of man respond.

4. MYSTERIES WITHOUT A KEY

Any further step in the study is more difficult. There are wonder stories in the gospels of a type that baffle us, because the record is fragmentary and our present knowledge does not help us understand. But in certain cases our bewilderment has another cause. We are frankly more bewildered as to what moral or spiritual purpose was served by these incidents than we are by the question of their possibility as occurrences. We can see that healing had a purpose. It was evidently an act of compassion, as well as a sign of God's presence. It aimed at bringing men up to the threshold of moral responsibility through saving or healing them bodily; and thus it gave them a new chance at life. But what can be said about any purpose served by the "nature miracles", the stilling of storms and the feeding of multitudes? Stray gleams of light are shed on these incidents that involve physical Nature, when we appreciate the occurrence of swiftly passing Galilean storms, and when we recognize that to feed a Palestinian group involved much less food than we would demand. Light on what may have happened is shed, or the absence of light explained, if we recognize that, in the telling, limited aspects of incidents can become the whole story, the rest being unrecorded. We spiritualize, and we were intended to, the sinking feet of Peter or the laboured rowing of the disciples against the wind;[43] we see in the Feeding of the Five Thousand, as we were intended to, a miracle of compassionate sharing, such as belongs to God's kingdom. But when such edifying spiritual meanings have been extracted, we are left with nothing to suggest any satisfying reason for the original occurrences as they are recorded; and are puzzled that the immediate results of the incidents were so insignificant or, as in the case of the Feeding, so negative.[44] We must be content to wonder rather than worry. No one has yet said the last word here.

5. THE RESERVE OF JESUS

Few things are more noticeable than the reserve of Jesus in the use of "power", coupled with his reverent discernment in it of the presence of "the kingdom". He refused to invite or force consent through mighty works, and fled from places where local excitement over them obscured the real purpose of his mission,[45] because he saw clearly that there was no necessary connection between being wonder-struck, or "astonished", and being inwardly converted. Whatever our interpretation of the hyperbole or symbolism of the language used, his refusal to ask for God's physical aid in his own crisis, after the painful decision in Gethsemane, was evidently deliberate.[46] The record also shows his reserve in that he left men to do whatever men were able to do for themselves, whether feeding Jairus's daughter or unwinding Lazarus' grave-clothes.[47]

Yet, though he worked with such deliberate reserve, there is no doubt that he saw, in such mighty works as he took time to accomplish, the presence and power of the kingdom of God, not his own power exclusively; he saw in them also the defeat of Satan, the binding and plundering of the "strong man".[48] This constant awareness of the presence and power of God resembles the reverent and awe-filled feeling of physicians, who know that they are not doing anything by their own power but are only clearing the way for something to be done by a power beyond themselves. It is in line with the attitude of reverent scientists, who pause to consider that everything they are discovering or manipulating has been there all along.

6. THE INTERPRETATION OF SOME PUZZLING INCIDENTS

Occasionally, incidents are so recorded as to raise another kind of difficulty, the suggestion that Jesus sometimes acted at variance with what we believe to have been his settled character. Either a misguided reverence or a captious unbelief can seriously misconstrue these passages.

There are at least three such instances, and these cases are for this reason examined in greater detail here. No other reason exists for singling them out, because, apart from the interest they arouse, they are of practically no importance to Christian thought. The case of the Gadarene demoniac is one of cure by suggestion, the only way in which the mind of a maniac could be reached. The coin in the fish's mouth may be a figurative way of expressing a command, or it may refer to a marvellous catch; but the real point at issue was a coin in a tax collector's hand. The case of the withered tree is an example of symbolic action or acted parable, and it necessitates some exercise of critical judgment about the text of the record, since the two gospels that record it differ significantly as to the time factor involved. We instinctively follow *Mark*, as we do also in normally thinking of one Gadarene maniac rather than of *Matthew's* two.

(*a*) *The Gadarene Demoniac* (Mark 5:1-20; Matthew 8:28-9:1; Luke 8:27-40)

This story shows how the only public tour attempted by Jesus in the Decapolis was stopped almost before it had begun, since his act of compassion to a demented man angered the populace because of the coincidental destruction of their swine. In the face of their anger he withdrew, and never thereafter visited the district except in a hurried and secret journey.[49]

An explanation must be sought that does not multiply marvels only to raise moral and other questions. It must be recognized to start with that, in this predominantly Gentile area, pigs were not forbidden, but were a legitimate means of livelihood;[50] and that the memorable conversation was between Jesus and a maniac, and is not to be

judged as though it were between him and the Rich
Young Ruler or the inquiring lawyer.[51]

There is no doubt that the maniac and the populace
thought that Jesus deliberately destroyed 2000 pigs belonging to them, and did so without apology or sign
that he felt responsible. But Jesus nowhere commanded
such destruction, or appeared to desire it. His giving
leave to the demons[52] can be taken as a response to the
maniac's request that the herd, already in a panic from
his ravings, might carry his "legion" away with them.
The animals' panic was a means of cure by suggestion.
There is evidence that this cure was a difficult one, since
the tense of the Greek verb in "he had said, Come out of
him", suggests either an unsuccessful first command, or
a command repeated at intervals in the man's ravings,
until Jesus had gradually subdued the man who had
become the terror of the neighbourhood.

To interpret the story otherwise is to raise a host of
unnecessary problems, such as: (*i*) to regard a conversation
with a maniac as though it were a normal exchange of
ideas; (*ii*) to suppose that a man can be possessed by up
to 2000 demons; (*iii*) to assert that the man's real name
was "Legion", whereas either he had forgotten it or his
mad cunning made him refuse to give his name, for fear
of putting himself in the power of this stranger; (*iv*) to
suggest that demons can be transferred to animals; (*v*) to
admit that demons can drown; and (*vi*) to suggest that
Jesus deliberately destroyed other men's property. None
of this is either tolerable or necessary.

The result was that the man was cured, but that the
mission tour was stopped. Jesus' refusal of the man's
request to join his company has already been referred to.
The man's enthusiastic disobedience to the only command
Jesus gave him, by spreading a probably garbled account

far and wide, throws light on Jesus' repeated command
that cured persons keep silent. It also emphasizes the
contrast between their irresponsibility and the obedience
of the disciples when they were bound to silence.[53] Such
irresponsibility could and did handicap Jesus.[54]

Few healing incidents are recorded in such detail, and
it is fair to assume that the high drama of this one fastened
attention on the exciting accompaniments more than on
the result accomplished or the disease involved. It is not
clear whether Jesus was accompanied by disciples on this
occasion, or was alone among strangers.

(b) *The Coin in the Fish's Mouth* (Matthew 17:24-27)

This is probably a case of a miracle of coincidence,
which is just as marvellous as any other kind. It may
possibly, however, be an example of hyperbole in speech
and report. The problem is that the atmosphere of the
story differs from the basic impression of Jesus that the
reader gets from the rest of the gospel record. The point
of the incident lies in the possibly embarrassing consequences of a coin promised to a tax-collector without
Jesus' consent. This story is found only in *Matthew*, the
gospel interested in Jewish law and custom as these might
affect Christians, and deals with a point without interest
for readers of *Mark* and *Luke*. It has to do with Jesus'
attitude to one custom, and with Peter's characteristic and
embarrassing impetuosity.[55]

About the time Jesus was preparing to go to Jerusalem
to claim the highest authority, Peter was asked whether
Jesus paid the half-shekel tax given by pious Jews for the
support of the Temple. Without reflection, he answered
"Yes". Jesus asked him whether members of a royal
house paid taxes, to which Peter replied "No". The point
he had overlooked was that by promising the tax he had
wrongly included his Master among the subjects of the

Temple hierarchy. Jesus did not press the point, since the time had not come to give "offence" to the authorities, as he was deliberately to do later. He therefore commanded Peter to pay the tax, but not out of the common purse. It was to be Peter's own payment, secured by working at his trade of fishing.

At this point the fish's mouth is mentioned, but what was involved is neither clear nor important. There are fish in the Sea of Galilee that carry their young in their mouths and sometimes pick up bright objects. It is quite possible that the first fish Peter caught had a coin in it. But Matthew does not trouble to say whether such a fish actually was caught, and therefore some interpreters feel that Jesus was, with characteristic hyperbole, commanding Peter to work out the tax and pay for his own impetuosity.

The problem was that of a coin in a tax-collector's hand, and what it might appear to acknowledge. The incident apparently had no embarrassing sequel. The offered payment of this tax did not become a subject of controversy in Holy Week, although the payment of taxes to Caesar was a burning question.[56]

(c) *The Cursing of the Fig-Tree* (Mark 11:12-14, 20-23; Matthew 21:18-22)

Here is an incident, recorded with a striking difference in two gospels, that might be taken to suggest that Jesus blasted a tree simply because he was hungry, an action all the less in character because "it was not the time of figs". The circumstances, however, make it plain that the point of the incident lies elsewhere. The fruitless but richly leafy tree was almost certainly diseased, and was a symbol to Jesus of a diseased and rotten socio-religious system that was about to "wither from the roots". This system, based on Sadducism and the Temple connected with it, was already, in his mind, far gone in corruption and doomed to be destroyed. It was destroyed after an interval, when Jerusalem fell. But Jesus had not caused the corruption of that system, nor did he purposely destroy it. It had outward show, but had doomed itself to die because of its unacknowledged inner decay.[57] In the same way, the tree, with the precocious leafage of a diseased plant but with no promise of fruit, would bear nothing and was near to death. Jesus did not cause its doom: he only recognized and pronounced it. As in his parables, he drew an analogy from what was plain to be seen, if men would turn aside to look. Some interpreters have held that this incident is a parable that has somehow been recorded as an action. This is hardly necessary, if one grants that the tree was already at the point of death, and that only an observant eye could see its condition.[58]

Whether this be the proper explanation or not, the reader must use some imagination in interpreting the story, since *Mark*, the earliest account, tells of the withering after an interval, while *Matthew* heightens the effect by having the tree wilt at once. One is almost bound to follow *Mark* here. In any case, it is unnecessary to think that Jesus punished a tree, or caused its blight.

7. THE REAL PRESENCE OF GOD
IN HIS WORLD

In this discussion of "wonder" and "sign", the important point is that the Christian believes in the "real presence" of God in the world, not His "real absence". Deism, the belief in a *deus absconditus*, has no place in Christian faith. But Christian theism does not suggest that God is given to suspending arbitrarily the laws by which He manages creation. It insists only that these laws are God's servants, not His masters, and that man's knowledge of them is limited. There is no hint of the suspension of the natural law in the words of Jesus, and certainly Augustine and Aquinas, already quoted, could permit no such anarchy of thought about a "faithful creator".[59] Prayer and other spiritual efforts can operate only in a stable universe, within the firm framework of which the earthly discipline of the soul is set. To the Christian, that framework is more of an open framework than it is in the minds of those who hold it to be a closed system, from which any deliberate action of God is excluded. But for both it is a firm framework.

CHAPTER XV

THE DEVELOPING CRISIS

Behold, the days are coming, says the Lord, when I will
make a new covenant with the house of Israel and the
house of Judah, not like the covenant which I made with
their fathers, when I took them . . . out of the land of
Egypt.—Jeremiah 31:31-32.

I. AN EVENT WITHOUT HEATHEN PARALLEL

The gospel-writers devoted one-third of their limited
space to a single week of the life of Jesus, not so much
because this was a week of memorable drama as because
it was crucial for "the faith".[1]

Early Christian writers drew attention to the fact that
there were heathen parallels for most parts of the gospel
story—possibly demonic imitations of the truth, possibly
foregleams of the light—but not for the Cross. Such
things as the virgin birth, the miracles, the homeless wandering, many of the moral sayings, the opposition and rejection, were by no means unknown outside the gospels.
But the Cross, they emphasized, had no parallel, no imi-
tation: it was a unique "mystery", that is, a secret now for
the first time made an open secret. In other cults or myths,
it was unthinkable that a godlike figure should die at the
hands of men. When threatened, Apollonius and others
had either escaped or been at the last moment delivered.
But in the gospels this had not happened, and because it
had not, it was either most troublesome or most comforting.

For the first time, the gospels become almost biographical in form as Holy Week arrives, following Jesus almost on a day-to-day basis. It is possible that the oral traditions on which the gospels mainly depended were of two kinds, a teaching tradition and a narrative tradition. The narrative tradition is elsewhere usually subordinated to the teaching, and used as a sort of cement to hold teaching sections together; but here the narrative becomes dominant and almost continuous. Catechumens evidently had to know the outline of the story and the immediate causes of the Passion, as a background for the preaching about its purpose and its ultimate source in the love of God.

2. THE CRUCIFIXION
AND THE FAITH OF CHRIST CRUCIFIED

To talk, however sentimentally or dramatically, about the Crucifixion is not necessarily to talk about "the faith of Christ crucified". Logically, the two can be separated, the one a moving drama and the other a religious conviction. In Christian minds, the event is important not as a dramatic tale but as a "sign" (or wonder or mighty work), outward and visible, of invisible and eternal truth. It is even what is called an "effectual sign", that accomplishes in the receptive individual what it sets forth. It is a matter of record that the mere telling of the Passion narrative has a remarkable effect on the mind, whether it be untutored or tutored.

The first spontaneous reaction of a child is indignation against those who treated Jesus thus, coupled with admiration for the heroism displayed by this lonely figure with the world against him and his friends in panic.[2] Maturer reflection suggests that quite other reactions to the death of Jesus can exist. This may lead the individual to a rebellious decision not to get personally involved, particularly not to be brought into judgment or feel any personal obligation because of a tragedy in which he had no direct part.[3] Or there may arise the stubborn suspicion that God, because He permitted or intended this to happen, is either less good than Jesus encouraged men to believe, or is helpless in the face of evil[4]—the old problem of the balance between love and omnipotence in God. But reflection may have the effect it was intended to have, and result in penitence[5] (indignation at and despair concerning oneself), and faith[6] (trust in the pardoning love of God in Christ). All these reactions can be seen in the New Testament, including the "don't blame me" outlook of the high priest in Acts 5:27-28.

A striking feature of the New Testament is the way the earliest preaching, which was at first based on indignation over the actions of others, the "cruel men" from whom hearers were exhorted to dissociate themselves, developed next into a merciful admission that the cruel men may have acted in ignorance, and at last into the conviction that all men were guiltily involved, including "me".[7] It ceased to be a matter of "their sin" and became "our sins". The Crucifixion ceased to be an act by limited groups of Jews and Romans and became a human act, "my act", as though each believer had been "there when they crucified the Lord". The new covenant thus resulted in each man's being led, in a new kind of exodus, out of bondage into freedom, out of himself and then back into himself, "crucified with Christ" in some inexplicable way. A man was "reconciled to God", not as he might become reconciled to rheumatism, but by finding inner peace restored.[8] By a curious double use of the same words, the New Testament speaks of God having been "in Christ" and of the believer being "in Christ".

The paragraphs that follow deal with the fact that

in the narrative there is evidence (*a*) of the sense of "doom" felt by Jesus as he worked, (*b*) of the conviction that Old Testament expectations were being brought to realization, and (*c*) of the fact that men of all kinds were aware of an impending crisis.

3. THE "DOOM" OF "THE SERVANT"

Very striking is the sense of doom (a word that means judgment as well as destiny) that was felt by Jesus. The idea of "the Servant" as found in the New Testament was probably somewhat elaborated by the early church, but there is strong, critical scholarly opinion that Isaiah 53 was prominent in Jesus' thinking and that Jesus' conviction about "the new covenant" belongs to "the bedrock of the tradition".[9] In his Passion, something was occurring that had been "prepared from the foundation of the world"; this was his "hour"; this was Jerusalem's "time of visitation"; this was the very battleground between good and evil, and beyond the earthly struggle of the moment could be discerned the shadowy "power of darkness", apparently victorious but actually in the throes of defeat.[10]

Jesus strides through his last days in the grip of a compulsion that had long "straitened" him. That even he did not fully comprehend it can be reverently suggested, if only because of the mysterious agony in Gethsemane. In any case, the record indicates that, although he was utterly sure that he must die at the hands of "sinful men",[11] he nowhere explained why. We have been wondering why ever since. Only twice does he approach this theme, and then to speak of results rather than reasons. The result would be the ransoming of the enslaved and the true sacrifice leading to the forgiveness of sins.[12] No reason is suggested, except that this was the way of God's will, and that it "was necessary that the Christ should suffer these things."[13] This is not altogether foreign to our own experience. Many who have lived through crises not of their own making or choosing have felt, in a smaller way, that they were part of something greater than themselves, that they had somehow been prepared for this hour, that they were instruments as well as actors in what was done.

It may be that no reasons are given because reasons cannot be given or understood in any act of love. Love does not give reasons: it gives itself. It goes not by logic but by sacrifice to its high ends. Whatever the explanation, it is one of the least noticed and most important facts in the gospels that Jesus said so little about why the will of God had to be as he discerned it to be. New Testament writers were, later and inevitably, to search for reasons. But men are still more often convinced by the act of love than by any reasoning about it.

So overwhelming is the sense of inevitability in all that happened that some may think of the Passion as something foreseen in detail by Jesus and unfolded like the prepared script of a play. But it was at every step a venture of faith, however clear its end might be.[14] Jesus being what he was, his conviction being what it was, Caiaphas and the rest being what they were, the Crucifixion was inevitable unless someone had a change of heart. But no one changed, and the Son of man went "as it was written of him".[15] The New Testament makes much of the obstinacy and evil of men as providing, without their intention, the means or occasion for the fulfilling of God's eternal purpose of grace.[16] No other type of inevitability can be considered. To do so would reduce the story to a set of morally meaningless movements by characters without self-direction, degrade the agony of Jesus into pretence, and make Judas a guiltless

and even praiseworthy instrument of God's purpose.
As Jesus had said, the world being what it is, occasions
of sin, including this one, would inevitably come, but the
voluntary shaper of the stumbling-block would be none
the less guilty.[17]

4. "THE HOPES AND FEARS OF ALL THE YEARS"

The story, with gathering momentum, involves situations, some apparently deliberately designed by Jesus,
some encountered in suggestive coincidence, that were in
harmony with haunting suggestions of the Old Testament. Jesus was conscious of this at times, and acted deliberately so as to focus attention on Old Testament expectations. There seems to be no other reason, for example,
why an ass was carefully borrowed for the Triumphal
Entry; and the choice of the Passover season for the crisis
was deliberate, associating the first exodus with the
second. The evangelists, as they looked back, became
conscious of many Old Testament details[18] that threw
added light on their conviction that here "the definite
plan and foreknowledge of God"[19] was overruling for
good man's obstinate wickedness.

It is not that the Old Testament is to be treated as a sort
of cryptogram or almanac, but that Old Testament hopes
and plans were often expressed in words startlingly suggestive of certain details of the Passion. An exact and
literal correspondence is not claimed; it is the fulfilment
of the spirit of expectation that counts. An example of
this is the striking parallel between the contemptuous treatment of "the Servant" and the mockery endured by Jesus.
It is not a case of literal exactness. Isaiah does not mention
blindfolding, nor do the gospels speak of any plucking
out of the beard. But so suggestive is the parallel that the

Christian who feels it is seldom aware that the gospel writers do not themselves draw attention to this parallel with Isaiah.[20]

The following list illustrates how the Old Testament served to anticipate, illustrate and, in some cases, deliberately affect the Passion narrative.

(*a*) A primary list would include:

(*i*) The meek (in the Bible sense of meek, as strong but not self-seeking) king comes to Zion: Zechariah 9:9; Isaiah 62:11, cf. Matthew 21:4-5; John 12:15 (not quoted in *Mark* and *Luke*).

(*ii*) The expected Lord suddenly comes to his Temple: Malachi 3:1-3; Psalm 69:9; Isaiah 56:7; Jeremiah 7:11, cf. Mark 11:17; Matthew 21:13; Luke 19:45; John 2:17.

(*iii*) The "ruler" who would be "Lord", and not a nationally-minded warrior: Micah 5:2; Psalm 110:1, cf. Matthew 2:6; Mark 12:35-37; 11:3.

(*iv*) The "new covenant" superseding the old: Jeremiah 31:31-34; Isaiah 55:3-4, cf. Mark 14:24; Matthew 26:28; Mark 22:30 (Luke 1:72; Hebrews 8:8; 12:24).

(*v*) The ransoming of the repentant from the power of the grave: Isaiah 53:10; Hosea 13:14, cf. Mark 10:45; Matthew 20:28 (I Timothy 2:6; Revelation 5:9).

(*vi*) The shepherd smitten and the sheep scattered: Zechariah 13:7, cf. Mark 14:27; Matthew 26:31.

(*vii*) The apparently forsaken yet unforgotten innocent sufferer: Psalm 22:1 (and possibly the whole psalm, since it depicts him as winning through to an unwavering trust), cf. Mark 15:34; Matthew 27:42-43.

(*b*) A secondary list can be compiled from the new meanings that came to ancient passages, as the interpreters of Jesus looked back, including:

(*i*) Men looking on their pierced victim: Zechariah 12:10, cf. John 19:37.

(*ii*) The zeal of God's house: Psalm 69:9; cf. John 2:17.

(*iii*) The Servant silent before his accusers: Isaiah 53:7, cf. Mark 14:60-61; 15:1-5.

(*iv*) His unbroken bones: Psalm 34:20, cf. John 19:36.

(*v*) The parted garments: Psalm 22:18, cf. Matthew 27:35; Luke 23:34.

(*vi*) Thirty pieces of silver: Zechariah 11:12-13, cf. Matthew 26:15; 27:9 (where a slip traces the reference to *Jeremiah*, through confusion with Jeremiah 32:6-15).

Another example of how the phrasing of an utterance could be suggestively seized upon to confirm a conviction, even though in this case the original utterance meant something else, can be seen in the quoting of the cynical comment of Caiaphas that "one man should die for the people": John 11:50, cf. John 18:14.

5. THE SENSE OF APPROACHING CRISIS

As noted earlier, John is the only evangelist who tells that Jesus' last visit to Jerusalem was not his first. It is evident that this approach was quite different from the others, when his "time" was "not yet".[21] It was deliberately timed to coincide with the high point of the religious year, when Israel's deliverance from Egypt with the help of God was celebrated. There was tension in the air, of which pilgrims and priests were conscious,[22] as were the disciples. The atmosphere of Jesus' ministry had changed.

(*a*) This popular expectation may be largely traceable to the recent preaching of "the seventy".[23] The pilgrims were not indifferent, however fickle they may have been, however wrong their hope of deliverance. Pilgrims shouted to see the Triumphal Entry, to the inevitable accompaniment of childish din,[24] and Jesus refused to silence them, in view of the significance of the occasion.[25] This popular mood may have given colour at last to the charge of seditious plans, and may help to explain the disturbed feelings of Caiaphas[26] and the expedient surrender of Pilate. The ends of government, religious and civil, seemed to require the forcible stopping of any excitement, and it mattered little to the authorities whether the victim was justifiably executed or not.[27] Doubtless, the lunatic fringe of the Zealots was prepared to capitalize on any rumours, as the popularity of Barabbas shows.[28] Some superficial excuse may be offered for Caiaphas and Pilate as nervous officials, but their essential callousness and self-interest cannot be disguised. It is not necessary to think of the bloodthirsty mob on Good Friday as involving the same individuals as shouted on Palm Sunday. In the East, a mob can be whipped up for any purpose at a moment's notice, and there were plenty of suggestible people around.

(b) The apostles also felt a change in the atmosphere, and their deep feeling of unrest is suggested by their combination of panic and jealousy, and by the way their stubborn worldly hopes, long since rebuked by Jesus, found fresh voice in quarrels and ambitious requests.[29] They seem to have had a lingering hope that Jesus would give up his queer, impractical notions, and become the Messiah of popular hopes. This may help to account for the defection of Judas when the facts became clear. Their evident lack of any clear sense of the nature of the crisis as late as the Last Supper, and their sleep (doubtless traceable in part to fatigue induced by unacknowledged strain) and panic in Gethsemane,[30] seem inexplicable on any other supposition than that they did not fully grasp the issue or were subconsciously running away from it. With the exception of Judas (and one wonders whether he was at the last really an exception)[31] they were in the end to find in their love something greater than their disappointed hopes; and the Resurrection was to bring them out of their despair.

(c) There is a distinct change in the tone, emphasis and circumstances of Jesus' words and acts, as shown in the following ways:

(i) He had formerly almost exclusively emphasized religion as inner, individual and relatively unorganized— all of which remains true—but now he was concerned with it as also something public, visible and organized under some authority. Individuals were less and issues more emphasized. Certain people appear only as illustrations, not as individuals to be interviewed, as do the generous widow and the inquiring Greeks.[32] "Moses' seat",[33] however unworthily occupied, stood for something indispensable, needing to be redeemed, not abolished.

(ii) Jesus' references to the kingdom of God take on a note of imminence and doom.[34] Judgment could not be evaded. This does not invalidate his earlier cheerful references to lilies and sparrows as evidence of God's loving care. Men are still to observe birds and flowers, and to be assured that their own value exceeds that of all other created things. The problem is that men do not grow as lilies do, and are a greater problem than all sparrows put together.[35]

(iii) Sadducees, who on only one previous occasion are reported to have taken notice of Jesus,[36] now become prominent as he comes to grips with "chief priests and elders".[37]

(*iv*) The Romans, who had apparently ignored him, except for a moment of superstitious anger on the part of Herod Antipas,[38] now enter the story and are to become his executioners.

(*v*) Certain parables and sayings have a local and immediate application. The Prodigal Son had been a timeless and universal figure, but the Wicked Vinedressers were understood to be actually present when Jesus spoke about them.[39]

(*vi*) The theme of the impending destruction of impenitent Jerusalem now becomes prominent.[40]

(*vii*) The theme of "the Servant" becomes more dominant, and may account for what sometimes appears to be a curious impersonality in Jesus' words and acts, as though he had identified himself with a destiny not of his own designing,[41] although he had voluntarily accepted it and was faithfully to fulfil it.

6. THE BROADLY HUMAN BACKGROUND OF THE EVENT

The scene was Jewish and Roman, because it emerged from the rich heritage and hopes of Judaism, and because Pilate was the Roman governor. But it was essentially a human scene. The catechumens for whom the gospels were written were expected to see themselves as guilty actors in the drama, not to think of the rejection of the Son of man as a peculiarly Jewish and Roman sin. There is no such thing as the guilt of a whole people, only of individuals, although consequent disaster can visit entire nations. Only a small minority of Jews, chiefly Sadducees, and essentially only one Roman, Pilate, were directly responsible for the tragedy. But the catechumens had to perceive, as we must, that every man had been involved because exactly the same rejection takes place in his own heart.

This feeling of personal involvement comes partly because the scene is peopled by ordinary men, with ordinary motives. Had Pilate been a monster like Hitler, instead of an undistinguished soldier, or Caiaphas a sadistic pervert, instead of an unremarkable ecclesiastical schemer, or the Trial of Jesus an exercise in brain-washing, instead of an exhibition of the kind of hate and fear that any man can feel in the presence of One whose greatness he cannot tolerate, the catechumens and ourselves might feel little or no involvement. One can think of Belsen and Dachau without feeling personally guilty, except as one sees in them a frighteningly possible but quite unlikely extension of the brutality that sleeps in every breast. But one cannot think about Calvary without feeling personally involved, at least on second thought, if only because Peter's cowardice, Judas's defection, Pilate's expedient desire for peace at any price, and the suggestibility of the mob are exactly the things we know in ourselves daily. They are not frighteningly possible so much as shamefully commonplace.

7. "PEACE THROUGH THE BLOOD
   OF HIS CROSS"

The frequency with which the blood of the Cross is associated with the forgiveness of sins is a striking feature of the New Testament;[42] and the assurance of the forgiveness of past sins became one of the chief reasons for the conversion of Mediterranean people to the faith.[43] But the reference can be distasteful to modern ears, because we lack both the background of blood-sacrifice and much of the anxiety about sin that men had in those days. The blood of Christ had the effect, firstly, of abolishing blood-sacrifice as being no longer needed or tolerable; and secondly, of bringing comfort in the face of anxiety. One New Testament passage says that the coming of Jesus had, in a sense, made sin worse rather than better.[44] This hyperbole serves to underline the connection between his work and man's need of penitence and pardon.

It may be that modern man is not troubled about his sins, feeling futile rather than guilty. But at least he talks about faults, particularly those of other people—delinquent parents, children, statesmen, employers, workmen, teachers and clergy. He shrinks from the word "sin", because it means that offences are ultimately (and also immediately) against God; and it does not seem to him necessary to admit anything more than offences against good taste or good sense or human rights. He is inclined to take God's forgiveness, if it is needed at all, for granted, as Heine did, saying, *"C'est son métier."* But he does not take human forgiveness for granted, and sometimes doubts whether it is possible or proper.

Whatever one's attitude to God's forgiveness, there are certain conditions surrounding forgiveness at the man-to-man level that the New Testament teaches hold also at the God-to-man level. The parables of Jesus on the subject[45] make it clear that: (*a*) there must be willingness on the part of the offended party to forgive; (*b*) there must be on the part of the offender a recognition that he has culpably trespassed against the rights of others, a willingness to be forgiven, and a sense of gratitude for the favour of pardon graciously granted; (*c*) a "price of sin" is absorbed by the forgiving party in the transaction, since forgiveness has to be freely given or it is not forgiveness.[46] Of these, (*b*) is the most difficult to bring about, since men find it even more difficult to be penitent and to accept forgiveness than to extend it. But (c) is the most difficult to justify theologically, since it involves the problem of justice and the honouring of the moral order.[47] We seldom see this as clearly as theologians want us to. Forgiveness requires two parties. One party cannot accomplish it alone, not even God. There is also a distinction between the guilt of sin, which can be forgiven, and the consequences of sin, which even forgiveness cannot fully prevent.

All three of these elements in forgiveness appear in the New Testament preaching of "peace through the blood of his cross"; and all three have been the subject of theological speculation. Sometimes the main emphasis has been on (c) above, and sometimes on (b); but the most basic consideration is actually (a). The love of God has first to be seen as certain, after which repentance can be invited and faith encouraged.

Anyone who inquires into the course of Christian thinking on "the Atonement" enters a field of fascinating complexity, disfigured by some well-meant nonsense but dignified by some of man's greatest and clearest thought. The typical lines of inquiry are: Is forgiveness necessary? Is it possible? Who has the right to forgive and be forgiven? Is forgiveness justified, or does it compromise justice? How is pardon made actual? Is forgiveness sure? Forgiveness by God's free "grace" is practically unknown outside of Christianity. Most modern literature suggests that evil has to work itself out to the bitter end, without hope. Many religions have taught that the results of evil must be worked out through existence after existence, until the scales are balanced by accumulated merit. Others have relied on magic to avert the effects of sin.

New Testament preaching is based on the Passion and

Resurrection, and the early catechumen was supposed to know the circumstances and stages of the story. It is certainly not a "sweet story" and, if it served only to reveal to man his sin, it could only result in deepening his self-hatred, which psychologists nowadays assure us is more deep-seated than we ever imagined. But the story is intended to bring release, not deepen despair. Self-hatred is no more the goal of religion than is self-laudation. It is only a half-way house between self-love and self-forgetting through the love of God.

CHAPTER XVI

THE SMITING OF THE SHEPHERD

Now is the judgment of this world.—John 12:31

I. A NARRATIVE BARE OF COMMENT

If, in this chapter, the Passion narrative seems to be presented in a rather matter-of-fact way, there are two reasons. Firstly, this is the way the gospels present it, with practically no preachment or apostrophe. No evangelist interrupts to say, "Oh, the pity of it!" or "Do let's be good." Secondly, this is the way it should be known if it is to be appreciated as a whole. Many tend to skip from the Temple Cleansing to the Upper Room, ignorant of what the record says about intervening events. Most people are aware of only the most general considerations concerning the Trial.

In the conflict of Holy Week, things said and done in public alternate with things said and done in private. The Triumphal Entry, the Temple Cleansing, the "Debate", the Trial and Crucifixion were public. The cursing of the fig tree, the "little apocalypse" and its attendant parables, the Last Supper, the final teaching as reported in John 14-17, the Agony, and the Resurrection were for the inner circle. Like the catechumens of the early generations, we are permitted to hear of both. To use another analogy, there is here something that resembles the weaving of a tapestry. The fixed warp was the dread vocation of "the Servant", who dominated his own defeat, made it coincide with the Passover, and died for every reason except that he deserved it. The moving and swiftly changing weft was the actions of other people, who strove to the end to evade the issue he raised.

The events can with some assurance be assigned to certain days. It is usual, in doing this, to follow *Mark's* order, rather than the undated narrative of *Matthew* and *Luke*.[1] For this reason, the Entry and the Cleansing are here put on Sunday and Monday, and the so-called Debate is assigned to Tuesday.

2. A CHALLENGE IN TWO SYMBOLIC ACTS

The two symbolic acts are recorded as occurring on successive days. Neither appears to have been planned as a public spectacle, since Jesus maintained secrecy about borrowing the ass and appeared in the Temple without preliminary fanfare. The shouting crowd at the Entry was not a planned gathering, and the disciples appear to have reacted on impulse, not on instructions. But Jesus could not be hid, and both acts were bound to excite comment and raise questions. Neither had any immediate tangible result, and neither was accompanied by oral explanation from Jesus. The Triumphal Entry of "Palm Sunday"[2] petered out after the city gate was passed; and the immediate sequel of the Cleansing[3] was probably that the offenders gathered up their scattered wares and went back into business.

But there were intangible results. Had not Jesus ridden into the city in such a way as silently and symbolically to claim kingly authority?[4] Men riding asses were common enough, but religious leaders walked. In ridding the Temple of irreverent and profiteering men, had he not asserted authority as Lord of the Temple, before whose sudden appearing none could stand?[5] Such acts by a widely-known figure demanded attention. The authori-

ties must do something, if they were not to stand dis-
credited. They must at least challenge him, in the hope
that by trapping him in his speech they might make him
appear to be absurd or a public menace.

3. THE "DEBATE":
THE QUESTION OF AUTHORITY

The next part of the record is therefore what can be
called a "debate", which Jesus invited by his presence in
the Temple on the following day (Tuesday).[6] Because
this debate is complicated and its references obscure, many
skip through it, scarcely seeing its importance as the last
appeal of Jesus to the public, and as leading to the final
plot to destroy him,[7] with Judas defecting as an informer.
During the colloquy the common people were present as
bystanders, but the participants were experts, armed with
subtle debating skill. It is not easy for modern readers
to follow the discussion, both because the points have to
be overheard rather than heard, and because Jesus'
opponents soon showed anxiety to avoid the very question they had raised. But Jesus kept the thread of the
debate in his own hands, and as at the Entry and the
Cleansing, retained the initiative.

The debate, which swayed back and forth as various
groups were involved, is reconstructed at length in *Matthew*,[8] as is natural in a gospel circulating among Christians with an ancestral interest in Judaism. It occupies
less space in *Mark* and *Luke*. The questions have an
immediate reference to Jewish leaders and hopes, but they
are continuing and universal questions, touching such
recurrent problems as legal versus personal authority,
church and state, principle and detail.

The course of the discussion is reported as follows:

(a) *The opening challenge*[9] from "the chief priests and

elders of the people" was as to his "authority" to act as he had done. It turns on the principle that there are two types of authority: constituted or delegated authority, dependent on public office, antecedents and customs; and personal or direct authority, not established by documentary or legal certification. No one really expected Messiah to come with written credentials; and Jesus' opponents found themselves, to their intense discomfort, quickly faced with the possibility that here was God-given authority, that could not be outwardly proved but that called for direct personal decision. Jesus demanded from them evidence of their competence and willingness to decide in such a case, by asking what they had concluded about John the Baptist. They professed to be unable to say, thereby confessing that they lacked either competence or courage, and were guided by expedience. They had acted as though they had formed a judgment on John, but feared to say so openly.

(b) *Three parables*[10] (the Two Sons, the Wicked Vine-dressers and the Marriage Feast) were then spoken by Jesus, each stressing the point that those who presume on privilege have forfeited it and will be replaced by others. These parables involve what was to be elaborated elsewhere in the New Testament, that the new Church was to become the true "Israel", a new "nation", heirs of the ancient promises.[11]

(c) *Three questions* are then recorded, introduced to distract attention from the embarrassing question of authority.

(i) Attempting to discredit him with the populace or with the Roman governor, Pharisees and Herodians, politically at opposite poles, raised the problem of Caesar's taxes,[12] only to be told that they had tacitly admitted

Caesar's rights by using his coins, and that the real issue was the rights of God, not necessarily tied to any political framework. Jesus' answer is deliberately obscure, which may seem to us unfortunate because the question of church and state is such a thorny one; but its immediate purpose and effect were to drive the questioners back to the real problem under review. It did rule out, however, any expectation that Messiah would be a political leader: his was to be solely a mission to arouse man's inner response to God.

(*ii*) The Sadducees, who probably rejoiced to see their own rivals worsted, then endeavoured to discredit him with an academic question, such as they had doubtless used to reduce Pharisees to angry silence. Whereas extreme Pharisees held that the reanimation of the flesh would be a condition of "the resurrection of the just", Sadducees observed the silence of the Books of Moses and affirmed little about immortality. The case of the woman with seven successive and childless husbands[13] presented, on Pharisee premises, a baffling problem. But Jesus demolished the question as meaningless, because, as Paul was also later to affirm,[14] the life to come will not renew fleshly conditions. That he dismissed it so abruptly is understandable, since it was designed to divert attention from the question of authority. He answered the Sadducees by citing a passage from the Books of Moses[15] (to which books they ascribed the highest authority) that pointed to survival after death but did not suggest the reanimation of flesh.

(*iii*) A liberal Pharisee, doubtless delighted along with his fellows that the Sadducees had in their turn been out-manœuvred, then asked Jesus concerning the great commandment of the law.[16] There was a courteous exchange between them, but Jesus did not elaborate on something on which he and his questioner agreed. It, too, was a question-begging inquiry. The debate then languished.

(d) Jesus is recorded as having broken the silence by returning to the real issue, in a form as clear to his opponents as it is obscure to us. It involves an unanswerable *argumentum ad hominem*,[17] as his earlier answers to their own questions had. Starting with the assumption, which at least no Pharisee would deny, that Psalm 110 was not only of Davidic origin but of Messianic reference, Jesus asked why, if David had anticipated a Messiah who would be only a greater Davidic warrior, he had called him "Lord", a term unsuitable for addressing one's own physical and legal descendant because it is applicable only to someone with God-like authority. The psalm pictured a warfare that would be in God's hands alone, with the "Lord" seated at God's "right hand", the place of authority. There is in the psalm no suggestion of documented or institutionalized authority. To such an awkward question about the Messiah no one ventured to reply; but it raised again the original problem, "By what authority ... and who gave you this authority?"

(e) The debate had been over the bystanders' heads, but they heard Jesus "gladly",[18] after the manner of the inexpert, who rejoice to see experts cut down to size and who often fancy that life would be better if authority were abolished. Jesus turned to them to state, in effect, that they must not think that he had come to introduce religious anarchy. They must respect lower authority before they could obey the higher authority he was introducing. But they must not think that they would be truly obeying authority if they were content to copy the unworthy example of those in authority.[19] Whether this sobering and vital warning was on this occasion brief as in *Mark* and *Luke,* or elaborately long as in Matthew's compilation of warnings against hypocrisy and literal scrupulosity, is a question to be decided in the light of the repeated device of gathering related material into a solid block of teaching in *Matthew.*

This is Jesus' last recorded utterance addressed to the public. The issue had been made clear. There was no more to be said. The "Servant" would no more "lift up his voice".[20] That night the chief priests—only *John* suggests that the Pharisees were more than fellow-travellers in the enterprise[21]—prepared a plot in which Judas joined them.

4. DOOM FOR THE SOCIETY
THAT IGNORES ITS DAY OF VISITATION

Much more is recorded as belonging to that day, but it was spoken only to the inner circle. The generous widow is pointed out as an example only to the disciples. The inquiring Greeks[22] belong to no identifiable day, and they too were an object-lesson only to the disciples. The main theme of intimate discourse was the impending Fall of Jerusalem, about which Jesus did not speak extensively in public. He sat on the Mount of Olives and spoke to his disciples about this topic, suggested by their rather fatuous admiring comments on the Temple,[23] the kind of small talk men cling to when they are out of their depth. Jesus is recorded as having broken into sombre speech, in part preserved in "the little apocalypse", in part in memorable parables.

What is referred to among scholars as "the little apocalypse"[24] is one of the most controversial of New Testament passages. Reduced to its simplest terms, it can be said to have twin themes which it is impossible and unnecessary to separate clearly, since apocalypses speak in such veiled language. These are, first, the Fall of Jerusalem, and second, the disasters like it that will occur and recur to the end of time, whenever and wherever "the Son of man is rejected". The two themes are parts of the same thesis: the certainty of judgment on societies that have rotted inwardly, a judgment that will fall on the whole society. No doubt, many early Christians thought that both themes were sufficiently exhausted by the city's fall, since they believed that "the end of the age" was near and the Fall of Jerusalem in 70 A.D. was fresh in their memories.

If the apocalyptic phrasing of this foreboding passage is hopelessly obscure to some readers now—and some of it is obscure to everyone—it may be partially clarified by examining the three privately spoken parables of doom that follow[25] and that illustrate this same theme of the judgment to fall on those who have forfeited privileges by failing to prepare for or recognize their "day of visitation". These terrible stories of the Ten Bridesmaids, the Talents, and the Great Assize (or the Sheep and the Goats) leave no room for easy sentimentalism about the creeping evil that poisons social organization and community life. That Matthew alone records them suggests again that his first readers would feel a keener interest in the fate of Jerusalem than would the first readers of *Mark* and *Luke*.[26]

So ends the record of that Tuesday, a day to which Matthew gives more space than to Good Friday itself. No one can skip over this complicated report if he is to appraise the issues and evasions of the Trial of Jesus three days later. "Who gave you this authority?" is the question raised for every reader of the gospels still, and he should know something of the circumstances in which it first appeared.

5. TWO DAYS OF SILENCE

For the two following days there is scarcely any record. The anointing of Jesus in Bethany by a female disciple may belong to this interval.[27]   On Thursday about noon a secret arrangement was put into operation and a meal prepared in the house of a trusted disciple in Jerusalem.[28] The silence of this period seems explicable only on the ground that Jesus was deliberately avoiding Jerusalem and waiting for "the feast". His absence may have suggested to his opponents that he would make no further move; and they held their hand, not being anxious to make a further issue of something that seemed to have been settled to their satisfaction. At least, the apparent haste with which preparation for the Trial was later made, following the message of Judas after the Last Supper, gives that impression. They were forced to act at the very time they had hoped to avoid, the time of the festival.

6. THE LAST SUPPER: THE NEW COVENANT

Returning to Jerusalem on the Thursday evening, Jesus shared with the twelve a Last Supper,[29] that in form resembled both the Passover feast, although that was traditionally a family observance, and ceremonial meals of a solemn character, probably eaten from time to time by Jesus' company as by pious Jewish brotherhoods. The familiarity of the ritual of sharing bread and wine may help to account for the inattention of the apostles until new and startling words were spoken.

"This is my body" was the startling new utterance, referring to the imminent self-offering of Jesus. It was reminiscent of ancient sacrifices, and particularly of the words, "This is the sacrifice of the Lord's passover", prescribed for the Passover ritual.[30]   The accompanying

mention of the "new covenant" made a deliberate connection also between his coming death and the promise
in Jeremiah.[31] Jesus evidently intended the twelve to
believe that his death would lead to a new kind of "exodus". Men were to be led out, not as by Moses from
enslaving circumstances like those of Egypt, but from
the inner slavery of sin and fear that is their real and continuing bondage.[32] Such a spiritual exodus is never as
readily desired by men as is a physical deliverance. It
is easier to get men out of Egypt than to get Egypt
out of men. The re-enactment of this meal has become
the central ritual act of Christian worship; but its frequency, the liturgy used, and the meaning read into the
re-enactment vary widely and controversially.

That this Last Supper was to symbolize a new kind
of Passover deliverance, a new exodus, seems certain. But
whether it coincided exactly in time with that year's Passover celebration is not certain. The synoptic evangelists
state that it did thus coincide with the Passover;[33] but
John quite definitely regards it as having anticipated the
Passover by a full day.[34] It seems that John was insisting
on the correction of an error. This is a problem for which
there is as yet no scholarly solution. According to the
Fourth Gospel, Jesus died at the time the lambs were
being slain, and therefore before the Passover was eaten.
That this was the case can be argued from the bearing of
arms by the apostles and by the Temple guard that night,
an action unlikely among the pious during the feast, and
from the ritual fastidiousness of those who avoided entering Pilate's hall the next morning, lest they be rendered
unclean for the approaching feast.[35] Increasing emphasis
is being laid by scholars on the Johannine tradition of the
betrayal and the Trial, and this is a case in point.

Subsequent words of encouragement to the apostles, and the only recorded lengthy prayer of Jesus, are absent from the Synoptics but recorded and interpreted in *John*.[36]

7. THE AGONY AND THE ARREST

Then came the mysterious Agony in Gethsemane,[37] the prolongation of which beyond any normal period of time[38] suggests that Judas had found the authorities unprepared for his news of Jesus' return to the city, and that hurried preparations had to be made.

The Agony is outstandingly difficult to interpret. No agony can be fully analyzed, and certainly not this one. It must not be traced to fear of death as such, since lesser men have faced equal physical pain quietly when sure of their cause. But being sure may be part of the problem. In this Agony there may be, among other elements, a last "temptation",[39] a haunting dread that he had misread God's will for the Messiah (hence the prayer for assurance that what lay ahead was "not my will but thine") by adopting a course that no one else believed to be the will of God. If that were so he would be causing men to be needlessly guilty of bloodshed and tragically substituting his own will for God's.[40] He would also be dooming his followers to pointless obloquy and pain. Suggestive as this idea of "temptation" may be, it is more usual to assert that the bitterness of "this cup" was there, not because God's will was not clear, but because the cup was embittered by all the sin of mankind that had led up to it and that Jesus was to taste to its dregs.

Thereafter, Jesus went quietly to the death he could still easily have avoided by flight. Whether the agonized cry on the Cross[41] was a later renewal of the Gethsemane struggle, a moment of disillusionment, or something more terrible still is a difficult question, often canvassed in theological thought but never satisfactorily settled. Peter's futile gesture of armed defiance was rebuked, and Jesus surrendered to his opponents; the Son of man was betrayed into the hands of sinful men.

8. THE TRIAL: THE ISSUE EVADED

The record of the Trial of Jesus[42] before both the Jewish and the Roman authorities is in substance familiar but at many points baffling. Our difficulty in reconstructing the Trial arises because of our imperfect knowledge of ancient Jewish legal procedure,[43] because the disciples were not legal reporters, and because in the Trial there appears to have been a deliberate and engineered confusion of the issue. To the end, no one wanted to face the question, "Who gave you this authority?"

The rich variety of subsidiary material may divert attention to character studies of the men who reacted so variously to the presence of Jesus. The cowardice of Peter—though less than that of all the other apostles save one[44]—the motives of Judas,[45] the ritual fastidiousness rather than spiritual sensitivity of Jesus' accusers,[46] the perversion of Pilate's judgment through fear and time-serving, the blood-lust of the mob, all have their places in our minds. But such memorable details must not be allowed to obscure what appears to have been a deliberate miscarriage of justice, a clever avoidance of the only issue that had led to the arrest.

In the first trial, before the Jewish Sanhedrin, the significant issue was postponed in the hope that some other charge would suffice. But witnesses could agree on no serious charge,[47] and therefore the Messianic claim was brought up. That Jesus had privately taught this to his disciples may have been the secret evidence that Judas supplied. But more than one witness was needed to establish a charge, and so Jesus was put under the oath of witness. He confirmed the charge.[48] After mockery, the case was held over until morning.

At this point a problem appears about which there is scholarly disagreement. Could Caiaphas have put Jesus to death, or could this only be done by the authority of Rome? The later stoning of Stephen[49] suggests that for proved blasphemy or other capital religious crimes Jewish authority could exact the death penalty. But if Caiaphas had this authority, he evidently did not choose to act on it in this case. This may be why the Sanhedrin hesitatingly took counsel.[50] They were in unanimous agreement that Jesus was worthy of death for blasphemy; but there must have been at least two difficulties: blasphemy is a difficult crime to pin down in any case;[51] and a claim to be Messiah need not clearly or automatically involve blasphemy.[52] Certainly it ought not to be considered blasphemy or apostasy to claim to be doing the will of God and to be fulfilling hopes everyone professed to hold. Instead of facing up to so difficult a legal decision, it would be surer and quicker if the embarrassing prisoner could be arraigned on a different capital charge that would justify a transfer of the case. Whether or not this is the reason for taking counsel, the result was that the Sanhedrin changed the charge from blasphemy to sedition, and the prisoner was hurried over to Pilate's court. A charge of blasphemy could not be officially heard there, but one of sedition could not be ignored. The charge being no longer a religious but a criminal one, Pilate had to preside. The Sanhedrin was thus not obliged to follow up its own decision.[53] Even if Caiaphas did have some power to execute offenders, he did not have to exercise it in this case.

No one appears to have been really serious about this

charge of sedition. The Jewish authorities are at one
point represented as counting on Pilate's natural anxiety
to preserve the peace at a most difficult time of year, and
so hoping not to have to formulate any specific charge at
all.[54] Pilate is reported to have regarded the charge as
false[55]—he knew a seditionist when he saw one, no doubt
—and to have tried to palm the case off onto Herod[56] and
to release Jesus as a festival favour.[57] Once his suspicions
were confirmed that this was really a religious case, he
tried to turn the prisoner back to Caiaphas;[58] but in the
end, cynically yet with some superstitious qualms,[59] he
capitulated in the face of mob insistence that he must
crucify Jesus or face being reported to Rome as a betrayer
of Caesar's interests.[60]

No one "esteemed"[61] the Servant seriously enough to
face squarely the issue he had raised. The Sadducees side-
stepped the question by charging sedition; the Pharisees,
though interested in the Messianic hope, went along with
the Sadducees; Pilate stifled his suspicion that there was
more involved than he would admit; and even the disciples were unnerved, as uneasy in their loyalty as Jesus'
enemies were uneasy in their opposition. The Servant
was rejected,[62] and the Cross was given its victim.

9. THE CRUCIFIXION

The Crucifixion is prominent in Christian worship and
art as a symbol of all human history and of God's mercy;
but the details of actual crucifixion are only symbolically
or sentimentally presented in art and oratory, never with
complete realism. Canons of taste permit the picturing
of the callousness of bystanders, the helplessness of friends,
the irresponsible gambling of soldiers and something of
the shame and degradation of being hung up for a slow
death without dignity or hope of swift release; but they

do not permit notice of the stark nakedness, the fever, the bloating, the flies, the ordure, or the sunscorching (in this case mercifully relieved by an overcast sky).

It is not such details that matter, although they forbid anyone to become sentimental about the Cross. What counts is the self-offering made to God in "an eternal spirit";[63] the revelation to men that the evil within them leads them to kill everything that makes life worth living;[64] and the revelation, to those with eyes to see, of the indefeasible love of God, who uses so strange a weapon to beat down man's guard. The sordid revelation to men of what they are doing with God's gifts is to lead them to "repentance";[65] the offering of the sinless on their behalf is to lead them to "faith".[66] The Cross is set to produce repentance, and to give assurance that true repentance will be accepted. The symbolism of the rending of the Temple veil remains as a sign that a way has been opened by God to God.[67]

CHAPTER XVII

THE EXALTATION OF THE SERVANT

God raised him from the dead, and gave him glory; so
that your faith and hope might be in God.—I Peter 1:21

I. THE FESTIVAL AND ITS REFERENCE

Modern paganism produces no real festivals. It takes
an uprush or remembrance of a religious joy to produce
them; otherwise holy days are only holidays. Easter, like
Christmas, is a mixed festival, a conflation of ancient cele-
brations of spring, involving eggs, rabbits, fresh meat and
new clothes, with the solemn remembrance of an event
in history. For the Jew, the season recalls the exodus from
Egypt; for the Christian, a second exodus and the rising
of Christ from the dead. As at Christmas, there are ethnic
overtones as well as the deep theological undertones that
are expressed in song more deeply theological than is
always realized. The overtones are those of the joy at
spring's renewal, the genial hope of immortality, and the
sense of the goodness of God in Nature; the undertones
are those of hope of man's inner renewal, of eternal life
through the deliverance of man from thralldom to evil
and death, and of the saving revelation of the Name of
God. The first, or ethnic, assertions make us comfortable;
the second, or Christian, assertions make us uncomfortable,
as all profound assertions do. But we would be much more
uncomfortable if they were not made.

203

2. INEVITABLE QUESTIONS

The thoughtful reader is conscious of at least four questions connected with the Resurrection of Christ: whether it happened, how it happened, why it took place, and what results can be traced to it.

Strictly, the term "happened" cannot be used here in the sense that applies to common events.[1] The Resurrection was not an event of history even in the way the Crucifixion was, since it was not evident to all and cannot be verified by historical research or common analogies. For that reason, it is sometimes called super-historical. A faint analogy can be drawn from our acknowledgement of the presence of atoms that cannot be seen but that are known to exist because of the effects they produce through their behaviour. These effects are not apparent to all; we accept them on the word of expert witnesses chosen by a process of intellectual elimination, but we all benefit by the results. The Resurrection is also known chiefly through its effects, and it was made known only to "witnesses",[2] not to all men indiscriminately. The analogy is admittedly faint, partly because physical analogies are unsatisfactory when one is dealing with spiritual matters, partly because atoms are recurrent phenomena whereas the Resurrection was unique. Christ died and rose only once, even though he is "alive for evermore" and the "power" of his Resurrection continues.[3]

That it was known only to "witnesses" does not necessarily weaken the evidence for Christ's Resurrection, or lay its witnesses helplessly open to the suspicion of hallucination. There could have been no universal demonstration that all men would have accepted. Even the witnesses doubted, and most of them showed at first an obstinate unwillingness to credit what they were shown.[4] The Jerusalem authorities are pictured as being alert to the possibility of deceit or self-deception on the part of the apostles.[5] But these men were in no mood for deceit; and their experience, judged by its results, lacks the usual marks of self-deception. Vision, a form of experience, is not necessarily hallucination or invention.

To the first question as to whether it happened, the answer must be sought in the fragmentary reports of Christ's post-resurrection appearances.[6] To the second, as to how, there can be no answer: the New Testament sheds no light on the subject, nor does it show any interest in it. But about the third and fourth, as to why and with what results, some considerations can be put forward.

3. THE VINDICATION OF GOD

It can be reverently suggested, in connection with the third question, that the reason for the Resurrection was not primarily to assure believing men of immortality, although that is also important.[7] Nor was it to put the seal of God's approval on the ethical demands of Jesus. The truly fundamental reason for the Resurrection seems to be the vindication of God Himself. No New Testament passage suggests that Jesus' moral teachings are any truer because he rose from the dead. But many passages speak of him as having become the Judge of all men;[8] it would be intolerable if the character of the Judge appeared nobler than that of the God whose will he executes.

We all recognize this, although we seldom put it into words. We are sure that we could "believe in Jesus" in any case, in the sense of holding that his character and example show what goodness ought to be. We could even accept him as the judge to whom we feel answerable within ourselves. But could we "believe in God", or take seriously the statement that Jesus is a God-appointed Judge, unless we were convinced that God is at least as "good" as Jesus? The character of Jesus is clear, never more so than on the Cross; the character of man is clear, never more tragically than at the Cross; but the character of God is not helpfully revealed in the Cross, unless something exists beyond it. The child's remark, "Mother, I love Jesus but I hate God", goes to the heart of this dilemma. "The silence of eternity" cannot be "interpreted by love" through the Cross alone; the Cross by itself might well forbid any such interpretation. It is one of the haunting suspicions of religious life that the good man may be morally superior to his God, as Prometheus was morally superior to Zeus, and as Habakkuk feared that he himself might be, when he questioned the ways of Yahweh.[9] That suspicion mattered a great deal and became a certainty, when the character of the Olympian gods was called in question; it matters vitally if one is considering "the God and Father of our Lord Jesus Christ".[10] Admittedly, God "moves in a mysterious way"; the important question is whether it is a mysteriously good way, whether His clouds are "big with mercy".

The New Testament does not put this as bluntly as we do, but the insistence that God himself is vindicated by the Resurrection is present in its pages. The Resurrection is never clearly spoken of as an act of Jesus; it is an act of God, who raised and glorified him.[11] This was not done to provide a happy ending for the familiar tragedy of the Hero facing an inscrutable Fate to which he was morally superior,[12] but to make it possible for men to believe that they are not facing an inscrutable and arbitrary Fate at all, but a God of love. Religiously, it is vital that men's "faith and hope" be in God.[13] This is illustrated in the Emmaus story, where the two disciples were not troubled about the goodness of Jesus but about God's apparent dereliction.[14] It is never asserted in the New

Testament that "Jesus commended his own love"—although that theme is sometimes sentimentally emphasized among us—but that "God commended his own love" in the Cross.[15] For the Christian, being "partakers of the divine nature"[16] is equivalent to being "in Christ", because the Resurrection has shown that the Name of God and that of Jesus are synonymous.

This insistence that the silence of eternity can be interpreted by love is found not only in such words as "that he might bring us to God" and "so that your faith and hope might be in God", but in the proclamation that God has ordained Jesus to be Judge of living and dead. In religion, it is not the inevitability of judgment that is in question, but the character of the Judge and the basis of judgment. The judgment-seat in the New Testament is the judgment-seat of Christ;[17] that is the only one we can fully respect, and also the only one before which we feel utterly naked and ashamed. Immortality itself would be unattractive or unbearable, if the purpose of the universe is not Christlike: mere everlastingness has little to commend it. Christ undoubtedly died to bring us to ourselves, that is, to repentance. But the New Testament asserts that he died to bring us to God, that is, to faith.[18]

4. THE RESULTANT REHABILITATION
   OF FAITH

The fourth question, that of results, usually leads to the assertion that the strongest argument for the reality of the Resurrection is the results that it produced. No hallucination, mass or individual, ever inspired the sustained moral and intellectual endeavour that became the mark of Christian men. Wishful thinking never brought such results, except as one may admit (and insist) that all thinking, positive or negative, is wishful. It appears that far from being merely wishful thinkers the apostles had to be almost bullied into belief.[19] Their transformation from men despairing and confused into men wiser and braver than they had ever shown themselves to be is remarkable,[20] as are the later change of Paul of Tarsus from a sincere persecutor into an advocate and leader,[21] and the conviction of quite ordinary people to this day that the face of the universe has been changed for them because in some undeserved and inexplicable way they have "risen with Christ".[22]

This argument from observed results to a sufficient cause is not proof in the mathematical sense, but at least we know that water rises no higher than its source and that the early Church had no adequate reason for its existence except the Resurrection. Moreover, Christians today who feel the power of the indwelling Christ are not usually fanatics and boasters, but men with an inner strength which they confess they did not derive from themselves. An acute awareness of the Resurrection may be only a rare or occasional experience in any individual; but it is a constant factor in the life of the Church. Christian worship has in consequence a content and an atmosphere that make it different from any other worship in the world.

5. THE RECORD AND ITS INTERPRETATION

The first question, as to whether Christ rose, involves the New Testament record. Some of its typical difficulties may be noted as follows:

(*a*) The record is hard to reduce to order. This is not surprising. Men are never able to reconstruct clearly an experience that has reconstructed them. There is something ineffable about any sublime moment. The record would be much more open to the suspicion of invention if it had been edited into an accepted uniformity.

It has to do with a unique and rather frightening experience[23] that came to confused people who had paid little attention to anything Jesus had said to them on the subject, except for a desultory argument.[24] They were bewildered, and some of that bewilderment lingers in the record. Clarity of conviction came after, not during, the few days and hours when they felt in direct touch with Jesus.

(b) The record in *Matthew* and *Mark* indicates that Jesus was expected to meet them in Galilee.[25] This raises some difficulty because *Luke* and *John* emphasize that the earliest and important contacts were in Jerusalem, and that Galilee was no more than a later and temporary centre before another more significant and longer tarrying in Jerusalem.[26] At the risk of an accusation of deliberately reconciling the facts so as to save the letter of the text, it can be suggested that this is not an insurmountable problem. The disciples were unlikely to desert Jerusalem for Galilee in headlong haste, particularly as the feast was still in progress. Galilee seems to have been intended as a temporary rallying place before a later return to Jerusalem.

(c) There is no way within our known experience of explaining the apparent mingling of sense-perception and vision-experience noted in the record.[27] The sensory perception of the original apostles is recorded as having ceased after "forty days", except that Paul, in listing his Damascus experience as being "last of all",[28] evidently regarded it as being of the same order and purpose as those of the original groups. Paul's experience involved sight and sound only, not touch. The phenomenon of tactual contact is not unknown in supersensory experiences, but most of us, who neither desire nor have such experiences, find this the most difficult to appreciate. Many Christians are content to ignore this part of the record.

(*d*) Whatever importance is attached to the emptiness of the tomb on Easter morning (referred to below), it must not be supposed that it presents difficulties, while some "spiritual resurrection" presents none. The latter is as peculiar to Christian belief as is the insistence that the tomb was empty. No one speaks of the "presence" of Moses or Plato with them, whereas Christian worship is instinct with the "Presence" of Christ.

(*e*) The paucity of Old Testament references, discoverable as one investigates Paul's claim that Jesus "was raised . . . in accordance with the [Old Testament] scriptures",[29] must be admitted. Moreover, the modern reader may feel that even these few passages do not very clearly anticipate the Resurrection. But this relative lack of frequent or plain Old Testament anticipation makes the doctrine all the more convincing: certainly no early Christian could have been driven to invent it in order to fulfil expectations. It can be more strongly urged that the doctrine of the Resurrection arose directly out of experience and that devout men, after accepting it, reverently sought for even the slightest hints of anticipation in their only Scriptures, the Old Testament.

(*f*) The difficulty presented by "three days and three nights", in view of the record that Jesus was in the tomb only about thirty-six hours by our time-reckoning, is more apparent than real. By the old Jewish reckoning, the day began at sunset, not midnight, and any portion of the twenty-four hours could be counted as a full day and night. From the death of Jesus about midafternoon on Friday, "the ninth hour", to some unspecified time before dawn on Sunday, involves one full day and portions of two others. Reference to "three days and three nights" and "after three days" occurs only once each on Christian lips in the gospels.[30] These expressions are seldom used now. The Apostles' Creed, for example, uses Paul's expression, "the third day", which is also found in *Luke* and *Matthew*.[31]

Notwithstanding what has been suggested above from (*a*) to (*f*), it is impossible to iron out satisfactorily all the records. But it is also impossible to discount the general effect of the testimony of those upon whose experiences it is based.

6. THE EMPTY TOMB AND THE APPEARANCES AS TEMPORARY SUPPORTS

To many devout Christians the physical emptiness of the garden tomb on Easter morning is all-important; to others, equally devout, it is a matter of difficulty or indifference. The first should not overestimate, or wrongly estimate, its importance; the second should not lose sight of its importance to the earliest "witnesses". It is as difficult to explain away as it is to explain.

The empty tomb is important, not because it was empty but because it had held the body of One upon whom religious trust is centred. There are records of other empty tombs. Herod had been superstitiously afraid that John the Baptist had left his grave, but he was none the better man for it.[32] The Old Testament tells of one tomb emptied, and of Elijah who had none,[33] but Hebrew ideas of God were not seriously affected by this. Matthew preserves (and he alone) a tradition that many tombs were emptied on Good Friday,[34] but nobody then or since seems to have paid much attention to this. Only the empty tomb of Jesus could have crucial importance, as his opponents recognized in their anxiety to circulate a neutralizing explanation.[35]   In spite of the relative disregard nowadays of a once favourite argument, it can still be pointed out that no opponent offered to produce the body and so puncture the balloon of the new faith once and for all, and that it is unthinkable that the apostles hid it and afterwards faced mortal risks to establish a profitless fancy.

No one, of course, can have an "experience" of the empty tomb now, and only a few people had even a puzzled sight of it then.[36]   It conveyed little to them by itself, and is never mentioned outside the gospels.   Paul could not claim to have seen it, and he bases no argument on it, but only on his own converting vision and sustaining experience.[37]   Men did and do have an "experience" of the Risen Christ.   That is the crucial thing.

But the emptiness of the tomb cannot be dismissed as though it never had any importance.   It can be argued that had certain of the apostles not seen that the tomb was inexplicably empty and believed that this had happened by the power of God, the larger faith that God had given "assurance" to men[38] would not have been born.   The tomb and the appearances may have been a kind of temporary ladder on which they climbed to a lofty faith in the Presence of Jesus;[39] but it is scarcely justifiable to kick that ladder down now and assert that because it soon ceased to be used it never was used and never existed.

The appearances are in their turn regarded in the gospels as temporary manifestations.   They ceased after an apostolic experience, the Ascension, that is described in figurative language as puzzling as it is satisfying.[40]   As to why they ceased, an analogy from bridge-building may be helpful. When a span is to be thrown across a forbidding gulf, to carry the confident traffic of man's life, there is need for temporary supports. The arch completed, the "false-work" is removed. That it has been removed and largely forgotten does not mean that it was never needed. No more forbidding gulf than that of death and "the silence of eternity" exists, and nothing has given man "faith and hope in God" as has the Resurrection of Christ. But analogies are of little use in discussing what is by definition unique, and reverent opinion is bound to differ over a number of points.

7. EVENT AND EXPERIENCE

The connection between the historical and mystical elements in the belief in, and the faith derived from, the Resurrection is indefinable. For that matter, the connection between any event and the experience to which it gives rise is inexplicable. Event and experience are both important.

In curious reversal of the feeling among early Christians, some would affirm that they find help and comfort in the sufferings of Christ, as the symbol of the problem of pain, but that they feel little interest in "the glory that should follow".[41] The first Christians certainly did not feel that way,[42] and those who feel that the gospel story could helpfully end at Calvary probably manage to do so only because they are subconsciously aware all the time that the Cross was not the end and is not the end. The Resurrection has cleared the Name of God. Not only professing Christians, but many who find difficulty in taking seriously this part of the faith, have a deep conviction that the Name of God and "the Name of Jesus"[43] can be thought of as one and the same.

Had the Cross been all, the conclusion could only be either that Jesus had been mistaken about God's will, in which case his death would be a grand example of self-sacrifice but would only add one more to the list of noble human tragedies;[44] or else that God had been and is either helpless or inactive.

What had happened, in the plain sense of "happen", is essentially as follows:

A Nazarene carpenter, in whose veins flowed some Davidic blood, had without formal rabbinical training become a wandering teacher dominated by a strange conviction of Messianic vocation. This young layman had set himself against religious and moral abuses, taught with unexampled perception, lived a blameless life, and won an unsought reputation as a wonder-worker, while conducting a ministry singularly free from high-pressure preaching, emotional appeal, advertisement, or the use of formal religious exercises such as stated meetings and public prayers. After months of selfless work, he had been deserted by the populace and by many who started out to be his disciples, and had become increasingly distasteful to the religious authorities. He had come to Jerusalem to claim an authority such as could be justified only in the Messiah, and had come to a death that he knew to be inevitable unless priests and people suffered a change of heart. He had been executed on a charge of sedition that had convinced no one. Thereupon, Pilate, the chief priests, and at first even the disciples had taken this to be the end of the matter.

In the face of death, Jesus had believed that he was accomplishing the mysterious will of God regarding the Servant-Messiah, and that the bitterness and blindness responsible for his rejection would bring destruction to

Jerusalem.[45] The record indicates also that he had faith that he would rise again, and that the Son of man would come with power at an unnamed and unknown time.[46]

The Crucifixion proved not to be an end of the matter. The city with its Temple, together with the national life of its people, were destroyed after 70 A.D., and a new religion was born, stemming from Judaism but capable of absorbing much of the highest Greek thought. Multitudes, predominantly non-Jewish, came to believe in him as their "Lord"—spiritual head as well as moral guide—and to claim that pardon and salvation had come to them through him and for his sake. They claimed to be the true heirs of Abraham, the new Israel, in which all lines of race and sex were to be obliterated.[47] A new law of love replaced the ancient law, at least as regards ceremonial requirements.[48] Their first expectation of an imminent "end" was disciplined, and changed into a conviction that they were to live on in the world but not to be "of the world",[49] living in the Presence of Christ through the Spirit.[50]

All this came to pass among people who at the first had been stunned by defeat and drained of hope. The renewal of their faith and hope, through the Resurrection of Christ, led them to make central in their preaching the very idea that had, during Jesus' lifetime, seemed to them incongruous and incredible, that it "was necessary that the Christ should suffer these things, and enter into his glory".[51] They preached a Messiah who had been crucified, and sounded a note of assurance, although Paul realized that the whole thing would sound as foolish to most people as it had once sounded to him.[52]

That this message stemmed from faith in the Risen Christ is evident. Their theological thinking led them to inquire how this experience of reconciliation, or "justification", could be intellectually as well as emotionally substantiated both for them and for others. Such thinking has never ceased or been completed. So far as they had any stated creed, it appears to have been "Jesus is Lord", which emphasized not only the dignity of their Master but the action of God in raising him from the dead.[53] This emphasis on "Jesus and the resurrection" still forms the heart of the Christian creeds.

CHAPTER XVIII

THE BACKGROUND OF ETERNITY

The true light that enlightens every man was coming into the world. . . . We beheld his glory, . . . full of grace and truth.—John 1:9, 14

I. A MYSTIC AMONG THE EVANGELISTS

A brief examination of the purpose and characteristics of the Fourth Gospel, *John*, fittingly closes this survey of the gospel story. That book is in certain ways the crowning glory of the New Testament. Many Christians feel for it a greater affection than for the other three gospels, because it speaks to their condition and brings Jesus closer to their hearts. It is for them, as Clement of Alexandria (about 200) called it, a "spiritual gospel". Their feeling is in part traceable to the fact that it was written for mature and spiritually-minded believers, and in part to its special form. Unlike the Synoptic Gospels, it was not written for catechumens, but to interpret a faith long held. In that interpretation, it uses a characteristic style and outlook.

The Fourth Gospel differs in many ways from the Synoptics, as the following notes of contrast will illustrate:

(*a*) It opens with an affirmation that the writer (and others) had beheld Christ's "glory", as though the whole life of Jesus could be seen, by those with eyes to see, to shine with an inner radiance, as a candle lights up alabaster. The Synoptics admit, on the other hand, that even the apostles had been blind, the veil having been lifted from their eyes only for an uncomfortable moment at the Transfiguration.[1]

(b) It was written by a mystic or prophet, who was acutely conscious of eternity and of God's condescension to man's needs. He therefore thinks of Jesus as making the invisible God known, rather than of his bitter human struggle; and he omits such subjects as the Temptation, the consorting with sinners, the crisis at Caesarea Philippi, the Last Supper, the Agony, and the reserve of Jesus about "the Messianic secret". The Synoptics, on the other hand, give prominence to these.

(c) It was written by one who was not concerned with the order of events in *Mark*. Either he had a different chronology in mind or he deliberately chose a symbolic or logical order rather than a time-sequence. At any rate, he bequeathed to us such questions as whether Jesus cleansed the Temple early or late, or twice;[2] whether Jesus clearly admitted to strangers early in his ministry the Messianic secret that he only hinted at according to the Synoptics and forbade his apostles to mention;[3] and whether he introduced the theme of the bread of life clearly and early to a crowd of hostile and materialistic Galileans, rather than, as the Synoptics state, later and privately at the Last Supper (which John does not record).[4] That his order of presentation is logical or symbolic seems to be the explanation. This is strongly suggested by the way this evangelist organized his "witness" around seven symbolic sentences. These are not unlike parabolic sayings but they are not found in this form in the Synoptics. Each begins with "I am"—the bread of life; the door; the good shepherd; the light of the world; the resurrection and the life; the way, the truth and the life; the true vine.[5]

(d) It was written by one who thought of believers as "friends" of God, in contrast to the slaves of a tyrant deity or the slaves of sin. He pictures Jesus as increasingly attentive to "his own", and at last as dying for "his friends". This is not necessarily a variance in doctrine from the Synoptic emphasis on seeking the lost, but it is a different emphasis, just as it is different from Paul's thesis that Christ had died for God's "enemies". Paul cannot forget the obstinate and alienated heart of man; John cannot forget the unfailing friendship of God.[6]

(e) It was written by one who practised the art of quotation in a way unfamiliar to anyone who knows few ancient books; and (f) by one who used "Word" or "Logos" to interpret the cosmic significance of Jesus. About these latter two, further brief statements appear necessary.

2. THE JOHANNINE DISCOURSES

The Johannine discourses of Jesus are so much of a piece with the narrative portions of this gospel, and so different in style from the apophthegmatic and parabolic teaching preserved by the Synoptists, that a literary problem arises. This becomes doubly clear if one tries to introduce the relatively modern device of quotation marks. The use of these was unknown to the ancients, but is so common today that it is hard for us to realize that many ancient writers did not distinguish between direct and indirect quotation, between verbatim and interpretative reporting.[7]

Exact preservation of the sayings of the wise was a practice in Jewish circles, and this is reflected in the Synoptics; but in Greek circles it was also usual to "quote" men by mingling report with interpretation and contemporary application. This is familiar in the "Socratic" dialogues of Plato and in the writings of Hellenistic Jews. The Fourth Gospel was almost certainly written in the Greek city of Ephesus for readers with Greek backgrounds. Its writer seems to have arranged his material mystically rather than by using completely literal quotation. As B. H. Streeter says about the seven symbolic sentences and other passages, "What he gives us is not the saying as it came to him but the saying along with an attempt to bring out all the fullness of meaning which years of meditation had found in it".[8]

If this should appear at first glance to be an unexpected or reprehensible way of reporting about Jesus, two considerations may be of help: (*a*) there is no escape from the literary problem, once one starts inserting quotation marks, and to decline to use them is to recognize the problem anyway; and (*b*) this method of mingling quotation and loving interpretation is practised among us still and regarded with affectionate trust.

(*a*) There is plainly a problem as to exactly where, if anywhere, quotation marks can be inserted.[9] The Authorized Version, of course, escapes the problem by never using quotation marks anywhere. An excellent example is John 3:10-36. The Revised Standard Version puts quotation marks around verses 10 to 15 only, and indicates that verses 16 to 21 and 31 to 36 are to be understood as the evangelist's comment. One could argue that verse 13 should also be regarded as an explanatory comment. In striking contrast, Moffatt in his New Testament translation puts all of verses 10 to 21 and 31 to 36 into continuous quotation marks as words of Jesus, and consolidates this material by transposing verses 22 to 30 to another position, following 2:12. Where doctors differ, who shall decide? The more one studies this and other passages the more one wonders whether quotation marks can be introduced with certainty into this type of writing.

(b) We know, from religious literature outside the New Testament, that interpretative quotation and re-arrangement can sometimes be more illuminating and permanently influential than exact verbal reproduction. Many people feel that they are closer to Samuel Rutherford (d. 1661) and his quiet religious trust through the lines of Mrs. A. R. Cousins' poem, *Last Words of Samuel Rutherford*, based on quotations from his life and his letters, than they are through reading the letters themselves.[10] Some, who find Paul's epistles forbidding, feel in sympathetic touch with that stormy apostle through the stanzas of F. W. H. Myers' poem, *Saint Paul*.[11] Still others appreciate the Fourth Gospel itself more clearly after reading Robert Browning's poem, *A Death in the Desert*, which purports to be a reflective utterance by the dying apostle John.

These may be only faint analogies but at least they suggest that we are not totally unused to the literary convention used with inspired effect by the Fourth Evangelist. We really do not feel any surprise at finding that whereas the synoptic evangelists approach the life of Jesus as a first-century historical incident illuminated by glimpses of eternal light, the Fourth Evangelist approaches it as a revelation of eternal light and truth caught in the momentary circumstances of a first-century incident. It is to be remembered, of course, that John on occasion is definitely interested in the historical side, supplying material that supplements or modifies what the other gospels report.[12]

3. THE CATEGORY OF "THE WORD"

All religions attempt to explain God and the world and man, and Christianity attempts this in terms of Jesus

Christ. It is not just God and man, but God and the world and man. Therefore, the two great New Testament interpreters of Jesus, Paul and John, both carried the significance of Jesus into the field of cosmic speculation, insisting (as it is religiously vital to insist) that the creative power that makes a new heart in a man is the same creative power that brought all things into being.[18] There is one God. Many people feel more at home with John's vocabulary and approach than with Paul's. They like his "darkness" and "light" better than Paul's "dead in sin" and "newness of life". John is more Greek in emphasizing the original creative light as being the light of every man, and the light to which he must come.[14]

This cosmic interest and confidence of John and of the Greek-speaking Ephesian Christians for whom he wrote is nowhere so evident as in his introduction, in the first sentence of his gospel, of the term "the Logos" or "the Word". The term "Christ" had had a slightly national sound, and had pointed to a hope rather than suggesting an explanation as to why Divine deliverance could come. "The Logos" was a universal term, and was an attempt to explain how the Infinite could or would aid the Finite. It is the most far-reaching word on ancient lips and in the New Testament. But it appears that at least one New Testament writer felt that even this word was not big enough. There is a passage in *Revelation* that declares that while "the Word of God" is the name by which the mysterious Deliverer is called, his true or real name is known only to himself.[15]

The Fourth Gospel opens by identifying Jesus with "the Word". Like Judaism before it, Christianity thus laid hold on the profoundest of Greek speculations. Hellenistic Judaism, to which tradition Philo belonged, had borrowed this term from the Greeks; but neither Greek nor Jew had ever suggested that the condescension of the Infinite would take the form of embodiment or incarnation in a human life. "The Word became flesh" is a peculiarly Christian affirmation. But "the Word" was an idea already known. It meant many things: Mind, Thought, Reason, Mind in action, the Agent of creation, the Spirit that is fragmentary in every man, and the Bridge between the Creator and creation as a spoken word is a bridge between a creating mind and the intelligent mind of a hearer. The Old Testament had used the idea in its simplest, most pictorial or anthropomorphic form as "God said", or "by the word of the Lord were the heavens made", and in more nearly philosophical form in the concept of Wisdom in *Proverbs*.[16] Paul used the idea of the Logos, without using the actual word, when he called Christ the "Power" and "Wisdom" of God.[17] But the Fourth Evangelist fits the very term into the Christian vocabulary, by coupling it with the condescension of God in Christ. The Word is the light of men, the source of all life, the secret hidden in the bosom of the Father and now declared. No wonder he thought of "glory" as the key word and of the life of Jesus in retrospect as radiant with an inner light.

Not all Christians, in Ephesus then or in churches now, can be interested in such vast speculations. Perhaps that is why this gospel does not obtrude the idea of "the Word", once it has been set down. But there were special reasons why cosmic speculation should have been included in a gospel for Ephesus. That city was the centre of speculation, and early Christianity could not be allowed to sink in a morass of theosophical "genealogies", Gnosticism or "the knowledge falsely so-called".[18] The Fourth Gospel is for this reason a rebuke to fantastic imaginings, as well as an affirmation concerning the "one Lord" that

Christians were to choose as they repudiated the polytheism and theosophy of that world.

4. BACKWARD AND FORWARD FROM THE GOSPELS

From the above paragraphs it is at least clear that although *John* appeals directly to the simple heart of the believer, it carries the mature inquirer into depths beyond his understanding. This is the case with the other three gospels also, which combine a surface simplicity with a hidden depth. This is of the essence of "the gospel" itself, which combines the plain invitation to respond to the love of God with the theological insistence that God in creation and God in redemption must be thought of as one and the same God—the scientist's "Maker of heaven and earth" and the saint's "Lover of my soul".

Christianity, as an historical religion, presents eternal truth as something revealed in the process of time and space, and preserved in an "old, old story". That story culminated in a supreme moment when eternal truth was with the fullest possible adequacy embodied in the historical Jesus, "the Word made flesh". That Word still strives to enlighten men, and drives them on to the appreciation of God and the world and man. The lines along which that understanding is to be pursued are to be found in the New Testament. To a special moment in time we are bidden to look back, not as to something over and done with, but as to something that can be equally vital in our brief moment of life and death. Each faithful soul is a member of Christ,[19] not just a student of his sayings.

The Bible, and particularly the New Testament, shows concern that men should honour God as God and give thanks.[20] These seem to be the two things that, left to themselves, men signally fail to do. There is much that is true and important about God's power and methods on which the Bible sheds no light and about which Jesus spoke no word. But they are things that can be left to man's discovery, provided he is made fit to live at all, through the power of God at work within him.

NOTES AND READING LISTS

RECOMMENDED READING FOR CHAPTER I

Christianity, Edwyn Bevan. (Home University Library.) Oxford University Press, London. 1932.

An Introduction to the Bible, Chap. II, S. Cook. Pelican Books, Harmondsworth. 1945.

Before Philosophy, Chap. VIII, H. Frankfort. Pelican Books, Harmondsworth. 1949.

The Greek Way to Western Civilization, Edith Hamilton. Mentor Press, New York. 1948.

Christian Theology (*For Faith and Freedom*, Vol. II; Gifford Lectures, 1956), L. Hodgson. Blackwell Religious Publications, Oxford. 1957.

God and the World Through Christian Eyes. Ed. L. Hodgson. 2 vols. Student Christian Movement Press, London. 1933-34.

Greek Ideals and Modern Life, R. W. Livingstone. Harvard University Press, Cambridge. 1935.

Christian Faith Today, Stephen Neill. Pelican Books, Harmondsworth. 1955.

Christian Apologetics, Alan Richardson. Student Christian Movement Press, London. 1947.

The Gospel and Modern Thought, Alan Richardson. Oxford University Press, London. 1950.

Many Creeds: One Cross, C. E. Storrs. Student Christian Movement Press, London. 1945.

The Christian Answer. Ed. H. P. Van Dusen. Allenson & Co., London. 1945.

In Relief of Doubt, R. E. Welsh (Revised Edition). Charles Scribner's Sons, New York. 1933.

Adventures of Ideas, A. N. Whitehead. Mentor Press, New York. 1955.

Man's Knowledge of God, William J. Wolf. Doubleday Inc., London. 1955.

NOTES FOR CHAPTER I

[1] "Above all [Elsmere] was beginning, in the tutor's opinion, to concern himself disastrously early with that most overwhelming and most brain-confusing of all human interests—the interest of religion." *Robert Elsmere*, Mrs. Humphry Ward (John Murray Ltd., London, 1888), Book I, Chap. V.

[2] "I will mail you a Bible before I go to the hospital. . . . Get acquainted with the words. You'll never regret it. I came to the Bible, as I did to everything in life, too late." *The Caine Mutiny*, Herman Wouk (New York: Bantam Books, 1951), p. 76.

[3] Eccles. 12:13.

[4] Cf. Amos 9:7; Acts 14:17; 17:28 ("your own poets").

[5] Phil. 4:7.

[6] I Cor. 2:9; 13:12; Heb. 11:13, 40.

[7] "The Priesthood of Unbelievers", Gordon Rapp, *The Listener*, March 20, 1958.

[8] *Greek Ideals and Modern Life*, Sir R. W. Livingstone (Cambridge: Harvard University Press, 1935), p. 11.

[9] Eccles. 12:13-14; Livingstone, *op. cit.*, pp. 124-28.

[10] The Greek was not alone in cosmological advance. "It would seem that the Hebrews, no less than the Greeks, broke with the mode of speculation which had prevailed up to their time." *Before Philosophy*, H. Frankfort (Harmondsworth: Penguin Books, 1949), Chap. VII, p. 237 *et passim.*

[11] Livingstone, *op. cit.*, Chap. VI.

[12] The Greek heritage of philosophy must not be identified with the Greek myths which, as in *Tanglewood Tales*, are told in bowdlerized form to the young, without any suggestion that they be taken seriously.

[13] Matt. 11:11b, 25-26; 21:16; Tennyson, *In Memoriam*, xxxvi.

[14] Acts 17:2; 18:4, 14; 24:25; Phil. 4:8; II Pet. 1:3-5; cf. Acts 6:2; 18:19.

[15] I Cor. 1:17-25; Rom. 8:3-4.

[16] Acts 9:15; II Cor. 4:7.

[17] Amos 9:7.

[18] John 15:16; Luke 6:13, cf. John 6:70.

[19] Matt. 12:18; Luke 23:35; Isa. 42:1-4.

[20] Jas. 1:18; Rom. 16:25-26.

[21] Gen. 12:2-3; Amos 3:2.

[22] Rom. 11:5; 3:24; Gal. 1:15; Eph. 1:7; 2:8, cf. "I was

turned from a Christian to a believer, from a lover of love to an object of grace." *Positive Preaching and the Modern Mind*, P. T. Forsyth (London: Hodder & Stoughton Ltd., 1907), p. 282.

[23] Rom. 4:1-8, cf. Luke 17:10; 18:9-14, and note the frequency in Christian prayers of such words as "no merit of ours preceding", or "through the merit of Christ our Advocate and Redeemer".

[24] Rom. 5:20-6:2, cf. I John 1:8-10.

[25] This does not mean that one should wish to be somebody else than himself. The dissatisfaction that leads people to wish for that is not the deliverance that comes from "let him deny himself" or being "in Christ". The Prodigal came to himself before he came to his father (Luke 15:17-18), and "wretched" Paul longed for deliverance, not for a change into anybody but Paul (Rom. 7:24).

[26] Cf. Rev. 5:9, "by thy blood didst ransom men for God", not "from".

[27] Gen. 15:18; Ps. 105:9, 42; Micah 7:20; Luke 13:28; Gal. 3:7, etc.

[28] Isa. 45:4; Deut. 7:6; 10:15; Ps. 147:19-20, etc.

[29] Micah 2:12; II Kings 19:30; Isa. 1:9; 6:13; 11:11; 37:4; 46:3; Jer. 6:9; 15:11; 23:3; 42:2; Ezek. 6:8; 11:13; Hag. 1:14, etc.

[30] Matt. 24:22; Col. 3:12; Titus 1:1; Rom. 11:5; I Pet. 2:9, etc.

[31] Amos 3:2; Rom. 11:1-5; Gal. 3:16-23; II Pet. 1:10; Matt. 11:22; 21:43, etc.

[32] Scientists are much more sensitive to the limitations of science than are laymen and adolescents who feed on journalistic accounts and science fiction. Among recent delicate and hopeful books by scientists, is, for example, *The Immense Journay*, Loren Eiseley (New York: Random House, 1957). It must, of course, be granted that an awareness of a Power beyond discovery or explanation, while it constitutes a religious outlook, does not necessarily involve such ideas as Incarnation and Redemption, which are central to Christian religion but not within the field of a scientist's special interest as a scientist.

[33] See *Christian Faith Today*, Stephen Neill (Harmondsworth: Penguin Books, 1955), Chap. V.

[34] Gen. 1:31; I Tim. 4:4; Rom. 14:14, etc.

[35] "The Spirit of Earth in Autumn", Stanza xi.

[36] Lev. 18:21; I Kings 14:23; Jer. 3:6; 44:17, etc.

RECOMMENDED READING FOR CHAPTER II

Christianity and History, H. Butterfield. Charles Scribner's Sons, Ltd., London. 1949.

"The Bible View of History", *Concise Bible Commentary*, W. K. L. Clarke. Society for Promoting Christian Knowledge, London. 1952.

God Confronts Man in History, H. S. Coffin. Charles Scribner's Sons Ltd., London. 1948.

The Bible and Its Background, C. H. Dodd. George Allen & Unwin, London. 1952.

The Bible Today, C. H. Dodd. Cambridge University Press, London. 1946.

Which Books Belong in the Bible? Floyd V. Filson. Westminster Press, Philadelphia. 1957.

The Story of the Bible, Sir Frederick Kenyon. E. P. Dutton & Co., New York. 1936.

The Christian Doctrine of History, John McIntyre. Oliver & Boyd, Edinburgh. 1958.

Preface to Bible Study, Alan Richardson. Westminster Press, Philadelphia. 1950.

How God Inspired the Bible, J. Paterson Smythe. Sampson Low, Marston & Co., London. 1892.

The Authority of the Scriptures, J. W. C. Wand. A. R. Mowbray, New York. 1949.

The Historical Element in Religion, C. C. J. Webb. George Allen & Unwin, London. 1934.

Man's Knowledge of God, William J. Wolf. Doubleday Inc., London. 1955.

Christianity and the Nature of History, H. G. Wood. Cambridge University Press, London. 1934.

NOTES FOR CHAPTER II

[1] See *An Introduction to the Bible*, S. Cook (Harmondsworth: Pelican Books, 1945), Chap. IX. Certain phenomena of the Bible, such as the marks of ancient editing, the dated morality (or immorality) of the patriarchs, the minatory psalms, the difficulty of interpreting chronological and numerical references, the ancient respectability of the literary device known as pseudepigraphy, and the startling similarities yet significant differences between Hebrew and Babylonian stories of the creation, sometimes lead readers to think that this is a queer sort of literature to be called holy. But the

approach should be humble, as though the reader were rather to say, "If this is the kind of sacred literature God inspired men to produce, then this is the kind of literature He inspired them to produce; and my business is to appreciate it as it is, not to demand that it live up to advance specifications laid down by me."

² I Pet. 1:12 emphasizes that the prophets were aware that the truth they were given was not for their generation only. It does not, however, speak of them as writing for a proposed canon of scriptures. That Paul disclaims indisputable authority and commends his best judgment (I Cor. 7:12, 25, 40) shows that he was not consciously writing with an eye on distant posterity. II Pet. (3:15) testifies to the authority of Paul's writings, but makes no similar claim for itself. This is more convincing than if the writers had demanded canonical status for themselves. See Note 5 below.

³ Eph. 4:21.

⁴ II Tim. 3:15.

⁵ With regard to the claim that the Scriptures are inspired and authoritative, the following must be kept in mind. To base such a claim entirely on the fact that books of the Bible claim such authority (as in II Tim. 3:16) is to argue in a circle, assuming what is to be proved. To base the claim on the past judgment of "the Church" is natural enough, since antiquity and the test of time are important; but to base it entirely on this is to assert that "the Church" once possessed special inspiration to recognize inspiration, which is as difficult to prove as inspiration itself. There is therefore, in addition to all historical and objective considerations, always a need for the subjective judgment of the reader, who acknowledges inspiration because the books inspire and judge him. Paul speaks of the inner certainty of the understanding heart (I Cor. 2:9-16), of "having the same spirit of faith" as those who once wrote (II Cor. 4:13), and of the gospel as something "revealed through faith for faith" (Rom. 1:16-17). Jesus rebuked those who searched the scriptures but were not inspired by them to a proper spirit of faith (John 5:39).

⁶ Heb. 11:39-40; II Cor. 4:13-15; Acts 2:25-28; I Cor. 10:11; Rom. 15:4.

⁷ Heb. 1:1-4; John 1:17.

⁸ II Pet. 1:21.

⁹ Moses felt unwilling (Exod. 3:11, 13; 4:10), and Jeremiah (Jer. 20:9), and Paul (Acts 9:4-5). Jonah disagreed with God over the mercy he had been sent to urge men to seek (Jonah 4:1-3). Peter at Joppa (Acts 10:13-15) was outraged by the new truth thrust upon him.

¹⁰ Isa. 55:8, cf. Ps. 50:21.

[11] Isa. 55:9, cf. Ps. 94:9.

[12] Isa. 45:15, cf. Ps. 119:105.

[13] Eph. 1:9; I Cor. 2:9, "What no eye has seen, . . . nor the heart of man conceived." In I Cor. 1:21-25, Paul is not asserting that the gospel really was foolish or necessarily an absurdity or offence to a discerning mind.

[14] Rom. 1:19-20, cf. the idea of a natural law in Rom. 2:14-15; Acts 14:17; 17:27. See also *Christian Faith Today*, S. Neill (Harmondsworth: Penguin Books, 1955), Chap. II.

[15] Acts 10:9-35.

[16] Rom. 8:28; 14:5, 14.

[17] Matt. 13:17; Exod. 6:2-3; Eph. 3:5; Gal. 4:4; 3:23-26.

[18] Deut. 29:29, "The secret things belong to the Lord our God; but the things that are revealed belong to us and to our children"; I Cor. 13:10-12, "Now I know in part"; John 14:8, "Show us the Father, and we shall be satisfied."

[19] John 16:13.

[20] Greek myths are really not concerned with history as such. They may be ritual myths enshrining history, but the characters are not pinpointed in time and place. It can be admitted that some Old Testament stories are not completely historical, without altering the fact that their characters are rooted in time and space.

[21] I Cor. 10:11, "Now these things happened unto them".

[22] Note how Stephen, in Acts 7:2-53, bases his case on a review of history; cf. also Heb. 11:1-12:2; Acts 13:16-41.

[23] John 1:29. Note how I Pet. 1:19 speaks of blood "as of" a lamb.

[24] Heb. 10:1, 4; 9:14.

[25] Ps. 19:1; Rom. 1:19-21; Ps. 24:1; Gen. 1:31.

[26] Col. 3:10; Gen. 1:26.

[27] Gal. 4:4, cf. Matt. 13:17.

[28] Jas. 4:17; I John 1:7; 2:9-10.

[29] Rom. 6:10; Heb. 9:26-28; I Pet. 3:18; Jude 3.

[30] Eccles. 1:7-11 illustrates how this pessimism laid hold on the Hebrew mind when it came into contact with Greece.

[31] What we call the historical books in the Old Testament are called "the former Prophets" in the Hebrew canon, indicating that *Judges, Joshua, Samuel, Kings* were the product of prophetic witness. The interpretation of history that sees God's judgments at work, in both the past and the future, is essentially "prophetic". See also *Before Philosophy*, H. Frankfort (Harmondsworth: Penguin Books, 1949), p. 245.

[32] Acts 3:15; II Cor. 5:19.

[33] John 21:25; 20:30 (cf. II Kings 10:34).

[34] II Cor. 3:14 is the first reference to the Old Testament as "the old covenant". The "new covenant" is mentioned in Matt. 26:28; II Cor. 3:6; Heb. 9:15. The books of the New Testament are not themselves the new covenant; they are only the written records (the scriptures of the new covenant) that describe and offer it. The apostles were ministers of the new covenant, the church is the church of the new covenant, believers are men of the new covenant, and Christ is the mediator of the new covenant. The covenant itself inheres in God's character and eternal purpose of grace. It was not newly invented or created in the New Testament, but was therein revealed because the proper time had come.

[35] Luke 1:72; II Tim. 1:1; I John 2:25.

[36] Acts 17:30; Matt. 19:8.

[37] Rom. 4:13-17.

[38] II Tim. 1:1; I John 2:25; 5:11; II Tim. 1:9.

[39] Gal. 4:5-7.

RECOMMENDED READING FOR CHAPTER III

"The Style of Holy Scripture" (Ed. Koenig), *Dictionary of the Bible*, Vol. V. Ed. James Hastings. Charles Scribner's Sons, London. 1898-1904.

Introduction to the Bible, Chap. VI, S. Cook. Pelican Books, Harmondsworth. 1945.

The English Bible as Literature, C. A. Dinsmore. Houghton Mifflin Co., New York. 1931.

A Theological Word Book of the Bible. Ed. A. Richardson. Student Christian Movement Press, London. 1950.

New Testament Wordbook, William Barclay. Student Christian Movement Press, London. 1955.

NOTES FOR CHAPTER III

[1] Frequent in the *Psalms*, e.g. Ps. 22:1; 74:1-11; 73:2-14.

[2] II Cor. 12:4 speaks of things a man may not utter, because speech fails. Cf. Hab. 2:20, "let all the earth keep silence".

[3] Ps. 39:1-2; Job 2:9.

[4] As in Ps. 150:1, 4. The great prophets used acted symbols, dramatic acts, e.g., Jer. 13:1-10; Ezek. 4:1-8; I Sam. 15:24-31; I Kings 11:29-38.

[5] Gal. 4:26.

[6] Rev. 7:14.

[7] John 6:55.

[8] Eph. 5:30.

[9] Gen. 2:17; 3:22; Rev. 2:7 (cf. Gen. 2:9); Rev. 22:2, 14.

[10] Ps. 114:4; Isa. 55:12.

[11] Matt. 24:29.

[12] Deut. 8:4.

[13] Rev. 7:14; 14:2; 4:10.

[14] Those who feel that "the finger of God" in Exod. 31:18 refers to physical writing cannot think of it literally in Exod. 8:19; Ps. 8:3; Luke 11:20 (cf. Matt. 12:28, where "finger" and "spirit" are equated).

[15] Rev. 6:10; 15:3; II Cor. 1:18.

[16] Eph. 4:21.

[17] A single writer may use one set of symbols consistently, but poetry and symbolism are not logical or uniform. The same symbol may have many uses in various places and times; for example, a cross may be the Cross of Christ or the cross-shaped hammer of Thor; the serpent may be associated with subtle evil (Gen. 3:1) or with healing (Num. 21:8) or with a secret wisdom (Matt. 10:16); a lion may stand for Satan (I Pet. 5:8) or for "the lion of Judah" (Rev. 5:5); an eagle may be the Mesopotamian thunderbird or one of the "four beasts" of Rev. 4:7. Symbols are older than the things they currently represent. Conversely, the same person or thing may have many symbols: Christ is the Sun, the Pearl, the Rose, the Root of Jesse, etc.; and sin is slavery, adultery, death, and the second-last "enemy" of I Cor. 15:26.

[18] As when "my tears have been my meat day and night" (Ps. 42:3, cf. 6:6), or "my bones wax old through my roaring" (Ps. 32:3).

[19] Exod. 34:15; Lev. 20:6; Jer. 3:8-9.

[20] Hos. 2:19-20; II Cor. 11:2; Jer. 3:13; Mal. 2:11; Matt. 9:15; Isa. 37:3; Jer. 3:8-9.

[21] Matt. 16:4.

[22] Rom. 4:9; Gal. 5:6; Col. 2:11.

[23] Rev. 19:7; 21:2, 9; 22:17; Eph. 5:25. The church is also called the body of Christ (I Cor. 12:27; Eph. 4:12), showing how the same thing can be variously symbolized.

[24] Isa. 30:26, cf. 60:20 (cf. Amos 8:9 for the reverse symbolism of darkening).

[25] Isa. 24:23; Joel 2:10.

[26] Luke 21:25; Rev. 8:12.

[27] Isa. 30:26.

[28] Acts 2:16-21.

29 Isa. 55:12; Ps. 114:4; 65:13.

30 Judg. 5:20.

31 For the prohibition of astrological worship, see Deut. 4:19; 17:3; II Kings 17:16; 21:3; Jer. 19:13; Ezek. 8:16; Acts 7:42, etc. For "he leads them out" see Ps. 147:4; Isa. 40:26.

32 Mark 9:37; John 12:44; I John 3:18; I Cor. 2:4.

33 Deut. 1:28. For other familiar examples of overstatement, see John 21:25; Matt. 10:30; Mark 10:25; 11:23; Luke 10:3; 15:7; 12:6; Deut. 9:1; Dan. 3:19; Isa. 40:15.

34 I Sam. 1:22; Isa. 32:14-15; Ps. 23:6.

35 Exod. 14:21, cf. Exod. 15:8; Ps. 78:13.

36 Jer. 15:20; Hos. 2:6; Exod. 14:22; Eph. 2:14; I Sam. 25:16.

37 Matt. 3:5; Mark 1:5; Luke 3:15. For such a use of "all", see also Nah. 3:1; Jer. 9:2; Isa. 40:5; Ps. 22:17.

38 Matt. 12:19-20.

39 Acts 21:39.

40 Ps. 51:17.

41 Matt. 2:6 (Mic. 5:2).

42 Ps. 50:10.

43 Rev. 7:5 ff.

44 Luke 12:7.

45 For this, almost the strangest of Hebrew idioms, see such passages as Matt. 11:25-26 ("hid"); 13:13-17 ("make dull"); Luke 11:50; 14:10; Rom. 11:7-9, 32; John 12:38-40; Isa. 6:10; Acts 28:27; II Thess. 2:11-12. God's purpose is always merciful, but just as the sun that melts wax hardens clay, God's grace may harden men's hearts. Note how Exod. 10:1 and 8:15 find the hardness of Pharaoh's heart caused now by God, now by the man himself.

46 Matt. 23:32-35.

47 Job 5:7.

48 I Sam. 20:31; 26:16.

49 Matt. 9:15.

50 Eph. 2:3; Luke 7:35; 16:8; 20:36; Gal. 3:26; I John 3:10; Ps. 103:7; Deut. 32:8.

51 I Kings 20:35; Prov. 31:5 (margin); Hos. 1:10; Mark 3:17.

52 John 17:12.

53 I Sam. 2:12.

54 Matt. 21:5.

55 Ps. 8:4; 146:3; Ezek. 6:1-2.

56 Dan. 7:13; Matt. 26:64; 8:20; 13:37.

57 Rom. 8:14; John 1:12; I John 3:2.

58 John 1:34; Gal. 2:20; Matt. 27:43, 54.

[59] Scientific explanations of creation carry the story back only so far, to a cloud of gas, or of dust, etc. It is the same problem as the ancient idea of the eternity of matter. We cannot really think of "nothing before" or "nothing after", and there is normally no need to try.

[60] Isa. 48:13; Heb. 1:12.

[61] Gen. 1–Gen. 2:4a and Gen. 2:4b–24 are two stories differing as to whether the creation took seven days or only one; whether man and woman were made together after the beasts, or man first, then beasts, then woman; whether man was made in God's image, or made from dust with the breath of life added, and forbidden to become "like one of us".

[62] Rom. 8:19-25.

[63] John 1:18; Heb. 11:27; I Tim. 1:17.

[64] Exod. 20:4-5; Lev. 26:1; Isa. 40:18.

[65] Ps. 50:21.

[66] Exod. 33:20.

[67] Gen. 5:1; 9:6; I Cor. 11:7; Col. 3:10, cf. Col. 1:15.

[68] Matt. 6:9; Isa. 64:8.

[69] Isa. 53:1; 66:1; Ps. 34:15-16; 18:13; Exod. 31:18; Luke 11:20; Acts 7:55; Rom. 1:18; I John 4:16; Job 12:10, etc.

[70] As in Ps. 18:10; 2:4; 78:65; Isa. 42:13; Gen. 3:8; 6:6.

[71] Rev. 15:2; Acts 2:3; John 16:25; I Cor. 4:6; Exod. 24:10.

[72] Ps. 42:2; II Cor. 6:16; Jer. 10:1-11, etc.

[73] Exod. 33:11.

[74] Exod. 32:4-20; I Kings 12:28-32; Ezek. 8:10-13.

[75] II Kings 18:4-5.

[76] Ezek. 1:4-13; Rev. 4:6-8.

[77] Ps. 17:8; 63:7; 91:4.

[78] Ezek. 21:5 (cf. Isa. 34:5-6); Rev. 1:16.

[79] I Cor. 13:9; Heb. 1:1-4.

[80] Judg. 11:24-40.

[81] I Sam. 15:33.

RECOMMENDED READING FOR CHAPTER IV

The English Bible and Its Story, James Baikie. Seeley Service & Co., London. 1928.

The History of the English Bible, John Brown. Cambridge University Press, London. 1912.

The Ancestry of the English Bible, I. M. Price. Harper & Bros., New York. 1949.

The Coming of the English Bible, H. J. Cowell. Epworth Press, London. 1944.

The English Bible: A Sketch of its History, George Milligan. (Guild Text Books.) A. & C. Black, London. 1911.

The New Testament and its Transmission, George Milligan. Hodder & Stoughton Ltd., London. 1932.

The Making of the English New Testament, E. J. Goodspeed. Chicago University Press, Chicago. 1925.

Trials of a Translator (or, *On Englishing the Bible*), Ronald A. Knox. Burns, Oates & Washbourne Ltd., London. 1949.

"The English Bible", *Concise Bible Commentary* (pp. 329 ff.), W. K. L. Clarke. Society for Promoting Christian Knowledge, London. 1952.

William Tyndale, J. F. Mozley. Macmillan & Co., New York. 1937.

NOTES FOR CHAPTER IV

[1] Since ancient manuscripts were all in capital letters, it is necessary to decide whether "Spirit" should have a capital or a small letter (see Rom. 8:14-16; I Cor. 2:10-13), and when "Son of man" should be capitalized (see Ps. 8:4; Ezek. 33:7; Matt. 12:8; Ps. 146:3). The use of quotation marks is usually simple; but what of the Fourth Gospel, where quotation and comment are intermingled? (See Chap. XVIII.)

[2] A. C. Bouquet (*Sacred Books of the World*; Harmondsworth: Penguin Books, 1954, p. 102) quotes two widely varying translations of the same ancient Chinese sacrificial ode. No such wide variation is possible in translating the Bible, and no basic biblical idea rests on an unintelligible passage.

[3] Article VI of the Thirty-Nine Articles expresses it thus: "Holy Scripture containeth all things necessary to salvation: so that whatsoever is not read therein, nor may be proved thereby, is not to be required of any man, that it should be believed as an article of the Faith, or be thought requisite or necessary to salvation."

[4] Rom. 14:5 demands that, regarding observance of special days, each man be "fully convinced in his own mind". Cf. also Rom. 14:22; Gal. 5:13; Phil. 1:10.

[5] The question as to whether Jesus spoke habitually in Aramaic, although we have his words recorded only in Greek, is clarified by such evidence as the quotation of Aramaic phrases by the gospel writers, for example, Mark 5:41, "Talitha cumi, which means, Little girl, I say to you arise"; Mark 15:22, 34; John 1:38, 41.

[6] The Roman Church did eventually authorize translation, but with the Latin Vulgate as the chief authority. The translation of

"repent" as "do penance" is justified only in translating from the Latin (cf. the Authorized Version and Douay at Matt. 3:2; Luke 3:3; Mark 6:12). This is a hallmark in translation to this day, and has important doctrinal implications.

[7] Luke 1:3 and Acts 1:1 show that Luke wrote first of all for an individual. Col. 4:16 and Rev. 2:1–3:21 indicate that other books were for churches. The wealthy Ethiopian treasurer of Acts 8:27 possessed Old Testament books, and Paul had books also (II Tim. 4:13).

[8] Col. 4:16; Matt. 24:15; Mark 13:14; Rev. 1:3.

[9] A striking example of this is in Lev. 19:18-19, where the great "second commandment" appears to be no more important than an obscure taboo regarding mixed fabrics. Jewish rabbis of Jesus' day were not all bound by minute or outdated details (see Luke 10:25-28); but Jesus was extremely radical in such matters as Sabbath observance (Matt. 12:1-12), as Peter and Paul were later about circumcision (Rom. 4:9-12; Acts 15:1-11). Paul's distinction that "the law" is intrinsically good, yet in many respects outworn (Rom. 7:6-12; Gal. 3:23-25), is basic.

[10] The variation in quoting even "the great commandment" in the New Testament suggests that verbatim reproduction was not always the rule (Deut. 6:5; cf. Matt. 22:34-40; Luke 10:26-28). Other examples are Rom. 9:33 from Isa. 28:16, and Matt. 1:23 from Isa. 7:14 (the latter a case where a Greek word is narrower in meaning than the Hebrew word it translates).

[11] Isa. 6:2 is our clearest hint about these winged messengers of God, but no one knows what mental picture was once evoked. Certainly cherubim were not childlike cherubs. Baptize is transliterated, partly because no English word carries the necessary dignity, partly because Christians are divided as to what single word, if any, would suffice.

[12] For "deliver" see Matt. 8:25; Luke 1:71; for "heal" or "make whole" see Matt. 9:22; Mark 10:52. The ambiguity is well illustrated by Isa. 53:4, "he took our infirmities", which in Matt. 8:17 is interpreted as meaning that he healed bodily sickness; but it usually suggests to us deliverance from sins, and is so understood in I Pet. 2:24. Health and salvation are interchangeable terms, and health is both bodily and spiritual.

[13] Rom. 4:3, cf. II Tim. 1:12.

[14] John 1:1; Rev. 19:12-13, see Chap. XVIII, Sec. III.

[15] I Cor. 13; Col. 3:14; I Tim. 1:5; Gal. 5:6.

[16] John 3:16; 10:28; 12:25; Gal. 6:8.

[17] Gen. 3:1-7. The apple of discord appears in Greek myths, but there is no good reason to call the biblical symbol anything but "fruit".

[18] Rom. 11:11, 22; Gal. 5:4; Heb. 4:11.

[19] The reference in Ps. 51:5 cannot be to the act of procreation as something intrinsically evil (Old Testament references to that subject suggest rather an awesome holiness), but to the fact that every man is born of sinful parents and, like Elijah in I Kings 19:4, is no better than they. Ps. 51:5, taken literally, would teach that the female alone is guilty, whereas Exod. 20:5; Matt. 23:31-33 literally refer only to the sin of the father. Ps. 22:9; 139:15-16; Gen. 29:31; 49:25; Isa. 44:2 must be read alongside of Ps. 51:5.

[20] Matt. 6:11.

[21] Mark 6:3.

[22] Isa. 42:1; 52:13.

[23] Acts 4:27, 30.

[24] John 5:4 (the angel troubling the spring), Acts 8:37 (Philip's catechizing of the eunuch), Matt. 6:13b (the ritual doxology often used to conclude prayers in early Christian worship), and "the lost ending" of *Mark* (see Chap. V).

[25] Matt. 9:17; I Sam. 25:18.

[26] I Cor. 13:12; Jas. 1:23.

[27] Rom. 14:1; Phil. 1:25.

[28] Matt. 2:4; Acts 17:3.

[29] Several are so well known as almost to be part of our language. Should "from the foundation of the world" go with "slain" (Authorized Version) or with "written" (Revised Standard Version) in Rev. 13:8? "Goodwill to men" should probably be "to men of goodwill" (Luke 2:14); "almost thou persuadest me" (Acts 26:28) should be "with a few words you expect to persuade me"; "though he slay me" should be "lo, he will slay me" (Job 13:15); "vile" body should be "lowly" (Phil. 3:21), and so on.

[30] Gen. 37:3 says that Joseph had a coat of many colours in the Authorized Version, but "a garment with sleeves" is surely what is meant; for thus Joseph would have superiority over sleeveless shepherds.

[31] Phil. 2:3.

[32] Deut. 21:4.

[33] Rom. 1:13; Isa. 43:13; II Thess. 2:7.

[34] I Thess. 4:15; Matt. 17:25; Ps. 79:8; Amos 9:10.

[35] I Kings 20:11; Exod. 13:18.

[36] I Kings 11:8; Acts 17:18; Judg. 10:16.

[37] Prov. 8:12.

[38] Matt. 13:21; Mark 6:25; Luke 17:7; 21:9.

[39] Acts 28:13.

[40] I Pet. 2:9; Deut. 14:2; Ps. 135:4.

[41] John 1:5.

[42] Ps. 55:15; Acts 10:42.

[43] Ps. 22:21; Isa. 34:7.

[44] Matt. 12:44.

[45] In the Great Bible Version, Ps. 25:4 is translated as "Lead me forth in thy truth, and learn me", cf. also Ps. 82:5 in the Book of Common Prayer.

[46] Where the Authorized Version (Mark 6:25) says, "I will that thou give me by and by in a charger the head of John the Baptist", we would say, "I desire that you give me at once the head on a platter". When Jesus says (John 5:6, Authorized Version) "Wilt thou be made whole?" we should understand it as "Have you the will to be healed?" See also Mark 14:7; Matt. 8:3; 20:32.

[47] I Pet. 2:25; Acts 20:28; 1:20.

[48] John 13:13; 3:10; Jas. 3:1.

[49] Phil. 2:1; Isa. 16:11; Jer. 4:19.

[50] In the Revised Standard Version, "Counsellor" is usually substituted for "Comforter", and "refresh" or "exhort" for "comfort"; see John 16:7; Ps. 23:4; Acts 16:40; Col. 2:2; I Thess. 5:14.

[51] Ps. 139:8; 9:17; 116:3; Prov. 5:5; Jonah 2:2; Isa. 5:14; Matt. 5:22; 11:23; 16:18; Rev. 6:8.

[52] Jas. 3:6; Mark 9:42-48; Matt. 23:15, 33.

[53] Rom. 5:11; cf. Acts 10:36; Rom. 5:1; Eph. 2:14.

[54] Exod. 29:33; Lev. 25:9.

[55] Some words for "God" or a "god" may mean what the Christian means by a "demon". Shall a translator choose a fairly neutral term, such as the word for the god of the open sky, and carry on from there? The words "God" and "Lord" have had a long history among us, but still the instinctive connotation of "God" in some minds is other than that of Christlikeness.

RECOMMENDED READING FOR CHAPTER V

About the Gospels, C. H. Dodd. Cambridge University Press, London. 1950.

Opening the New Testament, Chap. I-VI, F. V. Filson. Westminster Press, Philadelphia. 1952.

The Nature and Purpose of the Gospels, R. V. G. Tasker. Society for Promoting Christian Knowledge, London. 1944.

"Introduction to the Synoptic Gospels", *Concise Bible Commentary*, W. K. L. Clarke. Society for Promoting Christian Knowledge, London. 1952.

"The Growth of the Gospels", *The Interpreter's Bible*, Vol. VII. Ed. G. A. Buttrick *et al.* Abingdon Press, New York. 1951-56.

They Told About Jesus, E. Cutler. The Woman's Press, New York. 1943.

The Apocryphal New Testament. Ed. M. R. James. Oxford University Press, London. 1924.

Gospel Parallels. Prepared by a subcommittee of the American Standard Bible Committee. Thomas Nelson & Sons, New York. 1949.

A Harmony of the Synoptic Gospels for Historical and Critical Study. Ed. Ernest DeWitt Burton and Edgar J. Goodspeed. Charles Scribner's Sons, New York. 1917.

NOTES FOR CHAPTER V

[1] Mark 1:1; Matt. 24:14; Acts 15:7; Rom. 1:9, etc.

[2] The inclusions, omissions and emphases of the gospels are traceable in some degree to the felt needs or difficulties of the early churches. This idea of the influence of need or controversy on the form of the gospels has given rise to what is called "form criticism". The reader can sense the pressure exerted by new situations in the form of John 16:4-5, "I have said these things to you, that when their hour comes you may remember that I told you of them." The incident of the Temple tax is preserved only in Matt. 17:24-27, obviously because it could be important only to Jewish Christians, facing questions as to how they should regard ancestral customs. In the rest of the New Testament, questions as to the Sabbath (Rom. 14:5) and circumcision arose (see XII, Note 91). It is not necessary to suppose that new needs and situations caused the invention of material; but needs may well have altered the emphasis of presentation. Some scholars, of course, hold that adaptation was quite radical, involving addition of fresh or modifying material. This is frequently suggested, for example, regarding the passages on divorce. Those who insist that Jesus can have uttered only the stark prohibition of all divorce are bound to regard the adultery exception and the clause, "not all men can receive this saying", as later additions, the church having found that the austere (and perhaps hyperbolic) prohibition could not be obeyed (see Matt. 19:3-12; Mark 10:2-12; Luke 16:18).

[3] Luke 1:1-4; Acts 1:1. The training of catechumens may be illustrated by the improvement of Apollos' knowledge (Acts 18:24-

26), Paul's reference to remembering "the words of the Lord Jesus" (Acts 20:35, which preserves a saying not found in any of our gospels), and possibly the reference to "outsiders" (Authorized Version, "the unlearned") in I Cor. 14:16, 23. Philip acted as a teacher or catechist in Acts 8:30-39.

⁴ Acts 17:2-3 emphasizes the theme "This Jesus . . . is the Christ" (cf. Acts 18:5; I Cor. 1:23-24). Beroeans were commended for examining what was endorsed as relevant Old Testament evidence (Acts 17:11).

⁵ Luke 2:11; Matt. 22:43; Mark 1:1, cf. I Cor. 8:5-6; 12:3; Rom. 10:9.

⁶ Acts 20:35. For church "readers", see Matt. 24:15; Rev. 1:3; Eph. 3:4; Col. 4:16. Private reading is seen in the case of the Ethiopian (Acts 8:28), and of Theophilus (Luke 1:1-4).

⁷ Reference to "the scriptures" in the New Testament (with the exception of II Pet. 3:16) is always to the Old Testament scriptures, as in II Tim. 3:15-16; Acts 17:2, 11; 18:24; I Cor. 15:3. The relatively early date of some epistles can be gathered from such a reference as Acts 18:12, the date of Gallio's office being known to be A.D. 51-52. Paul's Corinthian letters follow close after this date.

⁸ Acts 1:21 shows that the earliest preachers had this qualification. Luke could not claim it (see Luke 1:1-4), nor Paul, but their contact with those who had "been with Jesus" (Acts 4:13) was early and intimate.

⁹ The oral tradition must have been closely related to "the traditions" handed down in the early churches (I Cor. 11:2; II Thess. 2:15; 3:6). The claim that there was a secret tradition, handed down apart from and possibly at variance with the written New Testament, cannot be substantiated. Hints of "reserve" in teaching, such as in Matt. 7:6; I Cor. 2:6; Rom. 14:1; Matt. 13:11, are not sufficient to suggest that there was any such overruling esoteric tradition. See II, Sec. IV.

¹⁰ The office of "teacher" is mentioned in Jas. 3:1; Rom. 12:7; I Cor. 12:28, etc.

¹¹ *The Four Gospels: a Study of Origins*, B. H. Streeter (London: Macmillan & Co., 1924), although now a generation old, is a good example of the meticulous scientific and linguistic labour involved.

¹² *Luke* (1:1-4) suggests a careful attention to "order", but Papias (see Note 15 below) is more cautious. In any case, *Matthew* and *Luke* use the chronological framework supplied by *Mark*.

[13] These are Mark 1:1; 2:27; 3:20-21; 4:26-29; 7:3-4; 7:32-37; 8:22-26; 9:29; 9:48-49; 13:33-37; 14:30 "twice"; 14:51-52.

[14] For example, Luke 10:21, cf. Matt. 11:25; Luke 11:9-13, cf. Matt. 7:7-11, etc.

[15] "The Elder used to say this also: Mark became the interpreter of Peter and he wrote down accurately, but not in order, as much as he remembered [or, as Peter related?] of the sayings and doings of Christ. For he was not a hearer or a follower of the Lord, but afterwards, as I said, of Peter, who adapted his teachings to the needs of the moment and did not make an ordered exposition of the sayings of the Lord. And so Mark made no mistake when he thus wrote down some things as he remembered [or, as Peter related?] them; for he made it his special care to omit nothing of what he heard, and to make no false statements therein."—Papias (from *Documents of the Christian Church*, ed. Henry Bettenson [World's Classics, No. 495; London: Oxford University Press, 1943], p. 39.)

[16] Mark 7:3.

[17] Mark 1:35; 3:20-21; 8:23-25; 14:34.

[18] Col. 4:14.

[19] Luke 10:1; 17:5, etc.

[20] It is sometimes held that a special emphasis on Jesus' work of healing reflects Luke's medical interest. But *Luke* makes no more informed use of medical terms: indeed, where *Matthew* (17:15) describes one case as epilepsy, *Luke* (9:39) uses the less professional term "spirit-seizure". *Luke* is the only gospel to mention Samaritans with high praise (10:33; 17:16-18), and to mention John the Baptist's influence on Gentile (?) soldiers (3:14).

[21] Luke 9:51-18:14.

[22] Luke 15:11-32; 10:30-37; 12:16-21.

[23] Matt. 2:15, 17-18; 8:17; 12:17; 13:35, etc. The reference for Matt. 2:23 cannot be found in any Old Testament book.

[24] Acts 12:17; 21:18; Gal. 1:19.

[25] Matt. 3:2, cf. Mark 1:15, etc. *Matthew* is not consistent in this usage, since 6:33; 12:28; 19:24; 21:31, 43 have "kingdom of God". The point is that *Mark*, *Luke* and *John* never say "kingdom of heaven".

[26] Matt. 10:5, "go nowhere among the Gentiles"; 15:24, "I was sent only to the lost sheep of the house of Israel." The other gospels do not trouble to preserve these sayings (see Note 2 above, concerning "form criticism").

[27] Matt. 5-7.

[28] Matt. 12.

[29] Matt. 23.

[30] Matt. 25:31-46; 20:1-16; 25:1-13.

[31] Matt. 8:28, cf. Mark 5:2; Matt. 20:30, cf. Mark 10:46; Matt. 21:2, cf. Mark 11:2.

[32] The quotation from Papias is: "Concerning Matthew it is said, So then Matthew recorded the oracles [prophetic discourses?] in the Hebrew tongue, and each interpreted them to the best of his ability." Some suggest that this compilation of "oracles" may be "Q".

[33] Matt. 9:9; 10:3.

[34] John 1:14.

[35] Passover is mentioned in John 2:13, 23; 11:55; 12:1; 18:28.

[36] Trusted Jerusalem disciples included Mary and Martha (Mark 14:3; John 11:2), the family of Mary of Jerusalem (Acts 12:12, owner of the house of the Upper Room, and possibly mother of the young man of Mark 14:51), the owner of the Garden (Luke 22:39; John 18:1-2), the owner of the Ass (Mark 11:3-6). The interest of Nicodemus (John 3:1; 7:50; 19:39), Joseph of Arimathea (Matt. 27:57-59; John 19:38), and the "many" (John 11:45) was felt only at Jerusalem.

[37] John 6:15-20, 60-71.

[38] For the dating of the gospels, an excellent brief presentation is in *About the Gospels*, C. H. Dodd (London: Cambridge University Press, 1950).

[39] Matt. 13:52.

[40] The so-called "Sermon on the Mount", which occupies three successive chapters in *Matthew* (5-7), cannot have all been uttered on one occasion. The same type of material is scattered throughout *Luke* (6:17-49; 14:34-35; 11:2-13; 12:22-30, etc.). Similarly, the denunciations of hypocrisy that are gathered into one chapter of *Matthew* (23) are found scattered in *Luke* (20:45-47; 11:37-54; 13:34-35).

RECOMMENDED READING FOR CHAPTERS VI AND VII

"The Jewish Background of the New Testament", "The Gentile Background of the New Testament", *Concise Bible Commentary*, W. K. L. Clarke. Society for Promoting Christian Knowledge, London. 1952.

"New Testament Times", *The Interpreter's Bible*. Vol. VII. Ed. G. A. Buttrick *et al*. Abingdon Press, New York. 1951-56.

The World in Which Jesus Lived, Basil Mathews. Oxford University Press, London. 1938.

The World Christ Knew, A. C. Deane. Mich gan State University Press, East Lansing. 1943.

The Background of the Gospels, William Fairweather. T. & T. Clark, Edinburgh. 1926.

Daily Life in Bible Times, A. E. Bailey. Charles Scribner's Sons, New York. 1943.

NOTES FOR CHAPTER VI

¹ The Authorized Version confuses the meaning of Heb. 4:8 by using "Jesus" where the Old Testament "Joshua" is meant.

² II Kings 24:10-17; 25: 11-12.

³ Mark 9:4.

⁴ Ezra 7:6; Neh. 8:4.

⁵ In the New Testament, the first two sections, "the law" (*Genesis* to *Deuteronomy*, 5 books), and "the prophets" (*Joshua, Judges, Samuel, Kings, Isaiah, Jeremiah, Ezekiel* and *"The Book of the Twelve"*—the minor prophets—8 books), are referred to in Matt. 5:17; 7:12; 22:40; Luke 16:16; but the third section, "the writings" (finally including *Ezra–Nehemiah, Psalms, Job, Proverbs, Daniel, Lamentations, Chronicles, Esther, Canticles, Ruth, Ecclesiastes*, altogether, 11 books), is only once referred to, and then as "the psalms", the most prominent of these books (Luke 24:44). Our Old Testament has 39 books, because of a different arrangement of the same canon.

⁶ For the first mention of the public reading of the law, see Neh. 8:3, 8, 18; 9:3; 13:1. Other sacred books, including *Jeremiah*, are referred to in Dan. 9:2.

⁷ Tradition, that is, explanatory comments on or later detailed applications of laws, is necessary in any society. Such "traditions" are mentioned with respect in Gal. 1:14. But the usual New Testament mention of traditional comments or requirements based on the Old Testament is condemnatory, because of the arid artificiality that literal-minded obedience easily suggests and requires, as in Matt. 15:2-6; Col. 2:8; Mark 7:9-13; Matt. 23:13-24.

⁸ These "godfearers" or "devout men" (proselytes of the gate) were converts to Jewish monotheism, but were not bound by dietary and other features of "the law". They became Christians in large numbers, Acts 8:27-31; 13:16; 10:2; 13:50; 17:4, 17. The devastating reference to certain proselytes who accepted the whole law (Matt. 23:15) has passed into common use as "the zeal of a proselyte", because a fanatical proselyte shows his insecurity and lack of

a sense of proportion by being as great a problem to those who have won him as to those who have lost him.

[9] For Ezra's reform, see Ezra 10:9-19. The thesis of *Ruth* is that even David had foreign blood (Ruth 4:16-17), and the chief point of *Jonah* is that God's mercy knows no racial limits (Jonah 1:2-3; 4:10-11). It is of interest that Timothy was half-Greek (Acts 16:1).

[10] Acts 6:1.

[11] Dan. 2:30-45; 7:13, cf. Matt. 24:30; Rev. 14:14. See Chap. XIII.

[12] John 10:22 refers to this relatively new feast.

[13] I Macc. 15:16-21.

[14] John 4:20-23.

[15] Matt. 17:11; Acts 1:6, cf. Matt. 20:21; John 18:36.

[16] Acts 25:13-14.

[17] John 2:20.

[18] Matt. 2:16.

[19] Matt. 2:22; Luke 19:12-15.

[20] Luke 3:1; 13:31; Matt. 14:3-12; Acts 12:1.

[21] Luke 3:1; Matt. 16:13.

[22] Matt. 4:25; Mark 7:31.

[23] Matt. 9:16-17; 25:1-13; 13:24-30; 5:40; Luke 11:5-8, etc.

[24] The policy of the Romans not to interfere with the legitimate practice of religion by their subjects is illustrated in the scrupulously correct action of Gallio in Corinth (Acts 18:12-17). The Jewish authorities had power to excommunicate, to punish, and apparently even to execute religious offenders: see John 9:22, 34; 16:2; Luke 21:12; Acts 9:1, 2; 22:19-20; 26:10.

[25] Matt. 27:65.

[26] Mark 14:70.

[27] John 19:20.

[28] Mark 5:41; Matt. 27:46.

[29] Luke 7:2 ff.; Matt. 15:22.

[30] Mark 15:22; John 1:38, 41; 9:7.

NOTES FOR CHAPTER VII

[1] Matt. 5:25, 41; Luke 7:2-10.

[2] Luke 23:5.

[3] Matt. 6:31-35.

[4] These themes are noted in the study of the Temptations in Chap. X.

[5] This is part of the theme of *Romans* (see 3:1-2).

[6] Ezra 10:16-18; Neh. 13:23-31.

[7] Matt. 22:23; Acts 23:6-8.

[8] Acts 6:7.

[9] Acts 15:1; Gal. 1:6, etc.

[10] Luke 13:31.

[11] Luke 10:25-28; Mark 12:28-34.

[12] Luke 6:15.

[13] Mark 3:17; Luke 9:54.

[14] Luke 23:18-19.

[15] Luke 23:5; John 19:12.

[16] Luke 9:55.

[17] Mark 14:49; Luke 20:1; John 7:14; 10:22-23.

[18] Matt. 5:23; Luke 18:10.

[19] Matt. 8:4; 23:1-3; Mark 12:41-44.

[20] Matt. 17:24-27.

[21] Luke 13:1-5; Matt. 23:37.

[22] Acts 2:46; 3:1; 5:12.

[23] Heb. 3:1-3; 5:1-4; 8:1; 9:28; I Pet. 1:18-19.

[24] John 8:7; Matt. 6:1; Luke 18:9-14, etc.

[25] Luke 14:26-33; Matt. 16:24.

[26] Matt. 12:2; Luke 14:1-6; John 5:9-10.

[27] Mark 12:34; Luke 10:28.

[28] Matt. 5:20; 23:5; 21:31; 7:22; 8:11, etc.

[29] Luke 2:25, 36.

[30] Rom. 4:16; 9:6; Matt. 21:43; Titus 2:14; I Pet. 2:9-10.

[31] This expectation of Deut. 18:15-19 appears often in the New Testament: John 6:14 (cf. 7:40); 5:45-47; Luke 24:27, 44; Acts 3:22-23; 7:37.

[32] Acts 17:24-25; John 4:21-24.

[33] Gal. 3:14, 23-24.

[34] Acts 7:2-54. In this early Christian document, note that circumcision followed (did not cause or guarantee) Abraham's acceptance (8), the law was a temporary requirement, to be superseded (37), and the temple was built by a spiritually tragic figure, Solomon (47).

[35] Dan. 7-12; Ezek. 9-10; Zeph. 1:14-18.

[36] Mark 13:5-37; Matt. 24:3-51; Luke 21:8-28 and see Chap. XVI.

[37] Rev. 4:1-8; 7:14-17; 3:5, 12; Dan. 2:33.

[38] Such imagery seems long and involved partly because it is in verbal, not pictorial, form. This will appear if one translates into words any skilful political cartoon, in which figures allude to nations or conditions that are instantly understood by contemporaries,

but that would be obscure to later generations. One World War II
cartoon from *Punch*, prior to the entry of the U.S.A. into the war,
could be put into words somewhat as follows: "I beheld and lo,
toward the sunrising, a lion in distress because of an eagle having
a body all black and a fylfot in its talons. And I looked, and it
was shown to me that a third of the ships were overwhelmed in
the sea, and great cities were burned with fire. I beheld again,
and from the sunsetting arose a second eagle, having its head white
as wool, and it held in its beak a great sheet in which were all
manner of implements of war. And there followed many ships,
carrying the merchandise of a new world for the healing of the
nations. And I heard a great voice like a trumpet sounding, saying,
'Lend and lease, lend and lease, until this calamity be overpast.'
And the lion was strengthened to withstand the first eagle." Apocalyptic imagery includes eagles, beasts with numerous horns, plagues
let loose, etc., and involves swift changes, that could not be caught
in a still picture. William Blake's poems and drawings are notably
apocalyptic in our English tradition. The works of Rabelais have
been called the apocalypse of free-thinking, because of their con-
cealed references.

[39] Acts 1:6-8; II Tim. 3:1; I John 2:18. In II Pet. 3:4 this
expectation has become definitely a problem. In non-apocalyptic
language, every hour may be any man's last hour, for which he
should be ready (Matt. 24:44). See Chap. XIII, Sec. I and II.

[40] Luke 1:71-74.

[41] Matt. 7:1; I Cor. 4:5; Rom. 14:4.

[42] Rom. 3:23; 5:6, 10; 11:32; Col. 1:21, etc.

[43] Luke 12:42-56; Mark 13:32, cf. Acts 1:7.

[44] Luke 3:14.

[45] John 7:49; 9:16, 24; Gal. 2:15.

[46] Matt. 9:10-13; 11:19, etc.

[47] Matt. 21:31-32; 8:11-12; 23:28. From the frequent use of
"the righteous" to mean "the self-righteous" it must not be concluded that "righteous" is always a term of contempt for "the unco'
guid". "Righteous man" often connotes the "honest and good
heart" of Luke 8:15, as in Luke 1:6; Matt. 10:41. It is not necessary to feel that "who need no repentance" in Luke 15:7 is ironical,
although in Luke 5:32 it probably is. "All that I have is yours"
(Luke 15:31) is a sincere tribute to a righteous man, even though
the Elder Brother had grave faults.

[48] Luke 19:8-10, cf. 18:13-14.

RECOMMENDED READING FOR CHAPTER VIII

"Virgin Birth", *A Theological Word Book of the Bible*. Ed. A. Richardson. Student Christian Movement Press, London. 1950.

Concise Bible Commentary, pp. 201, 294-95, W. K. L. Clarke. Society for Promoting Christian Knowledge, London. 1952.

Belief in God, Belief in Christ (bound together in *The Reconstruction of Belief*), Charles Gore. Charles Scribner's Sons, London. 1926.

The Significance of Jesus, W. R. Maltby. Doubleday, Inc., New York. 1929.

"Christological", *Foundations of Faith*, Vol. II, W. E. Orchard. 4 vols. G. H. Doran, New York. 1924-27.

Doctrines of the Creed, O. C. Quick. Charles Scribner's Sons, London. 1951.

Christian Belief, A. R. Vidler. Student Christian Movement Press, London. 1950.

The Creed of a Christian, N. Nicklem. Society for Promoting Christian Knowledge, London. 1940.

Christmas Traditions, W. M. Auld. Macmillan & Co., New York. 1931.

How Christmas Came to the Sunday Schools, Katherine L. Richards. Dodd Mead & Co., New York. 1934.

NOTES FOR CHAPTER VIII

[1] Luke 2:19.

[2] II Cor. 5:19.

[3] In the New Testament it is always "the Word made flesh" (John 1:14) or God "manifest in the flesh" (I Tim. 3:16; John 17:6; I John 1:2; 3:8), not "God" without any qualification. The throne of the universe was not vacated. It is striking that such a faith should have had its birth among such passionate monotheists as the Jews. The Christian faith was a cosmic idea, with Christ regarded as the agent of creation, which was accomplished "through" him (Col. 1:16 ff.) and which will be "united" in him (Eph. 1:9-10). See *Christian Faith Today*, Stephen Neill (Harmondsworth: Penguin Books, 1955), p. 260 and Chap. IV.

[4] Col. 2:9; John 8:23.

[5] I Cor. 3:16; Col. 1:27; Eph. 4:15; II Pet. 1:4.

[6] I Cor. 15:23-28; Phil. 3:21.

[7] The birth of Christ "for us" is not so much emphasized in the New Testament as one might expect from the prominence given it by certain schools of theologians. It is mentioned in John 10:10; Heb. 2:14-17; Rom. 8:3; Matt. 1:21. But much greater stress is laid on "died for us" in the New Testament: even Heb. 2:14-17 emphasizes "taste death for every man" more than "taste life". Nevertheless, the Incarnation is a doctrine that takes logical precedence over the Atonement, since it is its prerequisite.

[8] I Thess. 5:10; Rom. 4:25; 5:8; Heb. 6:20.

[9] Rom. 8:31; Matt. 1:23.

[10] I Cor. 13:13, and see Chap. XVII, Sec. III.

[11] Heb. 11:13-16.

[12] Rom. 1:19-20.

[13] John 17:3.

[14] John 1:14; II Cor. 3:18; cf. Exod. 33:18-20 (and I Tim. 6:13-16).

[15] I Tim. 2:5. Apart from the early gospel references (Luke 2:27, 40, 52), there is no mention of Jesus as a child. The use of "holy child" in Acts 4:27, 30, in the Authorized Version, is a bad translation for "servant". See Note 7, above.

[16] The winter solstice, when light is most threatened by darkness, is the most suitable time to celebrate the rising of the "Sun of Righteousness" (Ps. 84:11; Mal. 4:2). The expedience of the choice of the solstice lies in the fact that this season was already a time of pagan festivities, including that of the Mithraic "Unconquered Sun". Many of these had immoral or orgiastic features, and the Christian Church wisely substituted its own feast. Very old ethnic customs were carried over in the process of this conversion of a pagan festal season to Christian use.

[17] A different reckoning was used in Alexandria and Antioch. In Antioch the creation was reckoned as 5492 B.C., in Alexandria 5503 B.C. In Abyssinia time was long reckoned from Alexander, 323 B.C.

[18] For this, see the commentaries on Matt. 2:16-23; Luke 2:1-3; Matt. 2:2, 9. The "star" may have been a repeated conjunction of planets over a period of months, or the sudden blazing and dying out of a nova or supernova, or a combination of the two. That it "stood over" a house is obviously poetic, but that there was a celestial phenomenon is sure. But whether the Magi are to be regarded as arriving at the time of the birth or considerably later is not certain, since the child they are reported to have seen was in a house, not a manger.

[19] John 4:42.

[20] *Belief in God*, in *op. cit.*, Chap. XI, Sec. III. When W. K. Lowther Clarke (*op. cit.*, p. 201) says, "It has been said that belief in the Virgin Birth is not necessary to the individual, but is to the Church", he probably had in mind the fact that any church body that officially repudiates the Virgin Birth usually cuts itself adrift from many other features of New Testament faith. On the other hand, an individual is not required to accept explicitly and constantly all the doctrines that his church holds. Most individuals find that the common faith is a larger thing than their own individual faith. Many devout Christians who are silent on the Virgin Birth (in which they resemble Mark, Paul and John in the New Testament) would regret their church's silence on or repudiation of it.

[21] There is some medical opinion that parthenogenesis (virginal conception) is theoretically possible not only in low forms of life but in human beings. But any infant so conceived would likely be weak, whereas Jesus must be regarded as outstandingly strong.

[22] Sometimes, heathen parallels are taken to suggest that the New Testament idea is borrowed from or coloured by heathen sources. But that argument presents difficulty, since all the literary characteristics as well as the moral atmosphere of the Nativity narratives mark them as being Jewish in origin, not heathen. Elsewhere, the Bible insists that a special act of God was involved in certain important births (Heb. 11:12; Luke 1:17-20; I Sam. 1:19-2:10), but virginal conception is not claimed.

[23] It is obvious that the handicap of an inherited bias toward sin (original sin is not original guilt) can come as surely through one parent as through two. Ps. 51:5, taken literally, puts emphasis only on the female (see Chap. IV, Note 19; and Note 43 below).

[24] Matt. 1:18; Luke 1:34-35.

[25] Luke 2:41, 48.

[26] Matt. 1:1-17; Luke 3:23-28.

[27] Salathiel (Matt. 1:12) was not physically the son of childless Jechoniah (Jer. 22:28), but of Neri (Luke 3:27). It seems natural to suppose that Jesus became the legal son of Joseph (Luke 4:22).

[28] Gal. 4:4; Matt. 11:11.

[29] This is the point of the apparently pointless references in I John 4:2 and II John 7 to "in the flesh". The Docetic heresy (the doctrine that Jesus had been among men only in appearance) was a danger in the earliest days. The nineteenth century saw a good deal of discussion of the "Christ myth": hence such books as *Did Christ*

Really Live? H. G. Wood (London: Student Christian Movement Press, 1938).

[30] Heb. 6:19; 10:20; cf. Wesley's words, "Veil'd in flesh the Godhead see."

[31] Heb. 13:4. See Chap. IV, Note 19, and *What Christianity Says About Love and Marriage*, Roland H. Bainton (New York: Association Press, 1957).

[32] Heb. 2:17-18; 4:15; 5:8 forbid any such suggestion. Augustine made the point by repudiating the idea of *non posse peccare* in favour of *posse non peccare*. The same is true of Jesus' foreknowledge. He cannot have enjoyed complete foreknowledge (which he never claims in detail, John 13:3 being a general statement of conviction by the gospel writer) and at the same time have needed to pray and to exercise faith. Without the need to exercise faith (Heb. 12:2-3), his example is morally of little value, and his exhortations cannot ring true as the testimony of his own faith. The parallel drawn with "Adam" (see Sec. V) necessitates Christ's victory after struggle if this victory is to cancel the results of man's former defeat in the face of temptation.

[33] Isa. 7:14; 9:6-7; Mic. 5:2 (see Matt. 1:22-23; 2:6). In Matt. 2:23, "he shall be called a Nazarene" cannot be traced to any Old Testament source. It was probably introduced because the Hebrew for "branch" sounds like part of the word Nazareth (Jer. 23:5; 33:15; Isa. 11:1). *Luke* does not refer to any of these Old Testament passages. See also XV, Note 20, and XVII, Sec. V (*e*).

[34] The same may be the case with "called my son out of Egypt" (Hos. 11:1; Matt. 2:15), obviously referring primarily to Israel at the exodus. The claim that a Christian midrash must have grown out of the Hosea passage, so that the Egyptian flight is pure legend, need have no greater validity than the counterclaim that Hos. 11:1 was pressed into use as an exegetical ornament for a story that existed independently. Scholarly opinion differs. A curious thing, of course, is that no use is made of the Egyptian flight elsewhere in the New Testament.

[35] I Cor. 15:20-49; cf. II Cor. 5:17-21; John 5:24; I John 2:8; Rev. 1:4 ("is and was and is to come").

[36] Rom. 5:12-14; Col. 1:15.

[37] "Adam" is used generically of mankind, both male and female, in Gen. 5:2; 6:1. The name scarcely appears again in the Old Testament, except at Job 31:33 and possibly Deut. 32:8.

[38] Gen. 2:7; I Cor. 15:49.

[39] Rev. 2:11; 20:6, 14.

[40] Acts 4:12.

[41] Rom. 8:31; Matt. 1:23.

[42] John 1:14, cf. Col. 2:9.

[43] The Roman Church has created difficulty because it has supplemented the Birth narratives with two dogmas, both repudiated by Protestants, and both relatively recent as dogmas. The "Immaculate Conception" (changed from pious opinion to dogma in 1854) teaches that Mary was immaculately conceived in her own mother's womb, thus breaking the entail of original sin as it affected her. The dogma of the Bodily Assumption of Mary (1950), in turn, gives to Mary a place of at least semi-divine importance that non-Romans respectfully deny to her, since there is no New Testament evidence or accepted historical corroboration of the dogma. The New Testament evidence is that Mary appears but once outside the gospels, in Acts 1:14, and that in the gospels, apart from the salutations in Luke 1:28, 42-45 (and cf. 11:27-28), she is pictured only as an exemplary woman. She appears not to have been always in full sympathy with or to have shared the intimate confidence of her Son. See Luke 2:48-50; 8:19-21; 11:27-28; Mark 3:31-35; Matt. 12:46-50; John 2:4; 19:25-27. She is therefore honoured by Protestants as an example of piety and because of her high privilege in bearing her Son, but is never regarded as a mediatrix or heavenly advocate.

[44] Luke 2:46-51; 4:16.

[45] John 7:15.

[46] The view, strictly required in the Roman Church, that Mary remained perpetually virgin can be neither completely proved nor disproved by New Testament evidence. Those who hold the view of Helvidius that "the brethren of the Lord" (John 7:5; Matt. 13:55-56; Mark 6:3; Gal. 1:19) were children born to Joseph and Mary do so on the grounds that this is the natural inference from Matt. 1:18, 25, and that marriage is ordained of God for the union of man and woman, and that if any other supposition than that of normal married life had been important, this would surely have been clearly stated. But "brethren" is a loose term, not necessarily meaning children of the same two parents. Respect must therefore be paid to the view of Jerome that they were cousins of Jesus, and to the view of Epiphanius that they were his step-brothers, the children of Joseph by a former marriage. There is no incongruity in the "Helvidian" view. It is the normal one in Protestant circles, and dates from the earliest times.

[47] Rom. 1:4, cf. Phil. 2:9.

NOTES FOR CHAPTER IX

[1] Matt. 11:11-14. For the puzzling reference to the superiority of the "least in the kingdom", see the commentaries. It may be a declaration that the new age is divided, in hope and privilege, very sharply from the old.

[2] Luke 3:15; John 1:8, 20, 24-27; 3:28, cf. Mark 8:28.

[3] Acts 19:1-5; 18:24-26.

[4] I John 5:6 (cf. John 1:8).

[5] Mal. 4:5, see also Matt. 11:14; 16:14; 17:10-12; 27:47; Mark 9:13; Luke 1:17; John 1:21.

[6] Matt. 11:16-19.

[7] Matt. 9:15; 25:6; John 3:29.

[8] Num. 6; Luke 1:15, 80; 7:33.

[9] Of this the Rechabites of Jer. 35 are an example. It is a curious fact that one strand of the traditions preserved in Gen. 4:16-20 traces civilized arts to the evil line of Cain, in contrast to the idea of the Divine inspiration of craftsmen, stressed in Exod. 31:2-5.

[10] Matt. 3:4-6.

[11] Luke 1:5-13. Heb. 7:14 stresses the non-Levitical origin of Jesus, who was admittedly a layman by traditional reckoning. He is there presented as belonging to another type of priesthood, symbolized by Melchizedek, whom even the great ancestor of Levi had acknowledged and honoured (Gen. 14:18-20).

[12] Luke 3:7-9.

[13] Luke 5:33; 11:1.

[14] Matt. 3:7-12; John 3:25-30.

[15] Mark 1:4-5.

[16] Luke 3:15.

[17] John 1:35-37.

[18] Mark 1:14-15.

[19] Matt. 11:1-6.

[20] Luke 7:30; Matt. 21:24-26, 32.

[21] Luke 3:7-9, cf. John 8:33-42.

[22] John 1:26-31.

[23] Luke 3:14.

[24] Luke 3:10-18. Note that soldiers were to forgo looting and grumbling, two favourite activities.

[25] John 10:41.

[26] John 3:29; 10:41.

[27] Mark 7:4; John 9:7.

[28] Matt. 3:2. Heb. 6:5 refers to this, as a warning against retreat.

[29] John 3:22; 4:1-2 are the only references prior to Matt. 28:19. The references to baptism in Luke 12:50 and in Mark 10:39 are metaphors for overwhelming suffering.

[30] Luke 3:1.

[31] See Chap. XVI, Sec. VI.

RECOMMENDED READING FOR CHAPTER X

"The Servant of God", J. Jeremias, trans. H. Knight, *Studies in Biblical Theology*, No. 20, 1957.
The Screwtape Letters, C. S. Lewis. Macmillan & Co., New York. 1943.

NOTES FOR CHAPTER X

[1] Mark 1:9-13; Luke 3:21-22; 4:1-13; Matt. 3:13-4:11; John 1:31-34.

[2] Most readers instinctively follow Matt. 3:16 and Mark 1:10-11, which speak of the vision of the Spirit descending "like a dove" as being an experience of Jesus only. But in John 1:32 John the Baptist shares the vision but hears no voice, while Luke 3:22 uses the materialized term, "in bodily form", and could be understood to suggest that some sound and sight were evident to bystanders also, but without spiritual benefit to them. John 12:29 and Acts 22:9 show how bystanders can be conscious that something extraordinary is taking place, without understanding or being improved or inspired by it. Visionary experiences are often apprehended through current and apt symbols: Jesus' vision, that "I have put my spirit upon him" (Isa. 42:1; Ps. 2:7) was expressed through the dove, the symbol of a spirit of peace; Moses in desert country had his vision of a terrifying duty in the symbolic shape of a burning desert bush (Exod. 3:1-4); Isaiah's vision was mediated through the image of the familiar and awful Temple (Isa. 6:1-13); Peter the fisherman had a vision involving what seems to have been a sailcloth (Acts 10:10-16).

[3] Matt. 4:5, 8. In Ezek. 37:1 the same suggestion of physical transport occurs. This is always understood to refer to a vision, not a journey.

[4] Acts 4:27, 30 speaks of God's "holy servant" (Authorized Version misleadingly translates it as "child"). The extent to which "the Servant" influenced New Testament thought can be seen in

the following list of passages. For echoes of Song One (Isa. 42:1-4), see Matt. 12:18-21; 3:17; Phil. 2:7; of Song Two (Isa. 49:1-6), see Acts 13:47; Heb. 4:12; Rev. 1:16; of Song Three (Isa. 50:4-9), see Matt. 11:28; 26:67; 27:26; Mark 15:19; John 14:31; Phil. 2:8; Rom. 8:33-34; Heb. 5:8; 10:7; of Song Four (Isa. 52:13-53:12) see Matt. 8:17; Luke 22:37; Mark 9:12; 14:61; Matt. 26:63; 27:57, 60; John 1:10-11; 12:38; 19:9; I John 3:5; 2:1-2; Acts 13:36-39; 8:32; Rom. 15:21; 16:25; 10:16; 4:25; 5:18-19; 8:34 (margin); II Cor. 2:14-15; Phil. 2:9; Heb. 4:15; 7:25 (margin); I Pet. 2:22-25.

[5] Compare the Authorized Version and the Revised Standard Version at Isa. 53:3, 8. The four passages called "Servant-songs" are Isa. 42:1-4; 49:1-6; 50:4-9; 52:13-53:12.

[6] Matt. 8:17; 12:17-21; 11:28; 26:67, etc.

[7] Isa. 42:1; Ps. 2:7.

[8] Isa. 53:10.

[9] Matt. 3:13-17; Mark 1:9-11; Luke 3:21-22; John 1:31-34.

[10] Matt. 3:15.

[11] Luke 9:22; Matt. 8:20; 16:13; Mark 8:38.

[12] Matt. 4:1-13; Mark 1:12-13; Luke 4:13 (not in *John*).

[13] The Lord's Prayer (Matt. 6:13) shows this double sense, as does also Matt. 26:41, whereas Matt. 22:18 (Authorized Version); 22:35 (Authorized Version); Luke 10:25 (Authorized Version) mean primarily to test or examine. Jas. 1:12-14 uses the double sense, the Revised Standard Version distinguishing between "test" and "tempt". The idea of putting God to the test is in Luke 4:12; Matt. 4:7. "Put to the proof" would be clearer.

[14] Matt. 16:23 refers to Peter as "Satan"; Luke 22:28 indicates the recurrent experience of temptation; Luke 4:13 says ominously that the devil departed from him "until an opportune time".

[15] Ps. 72:4; 89:16-37; Isa. 30:19-26; 60:10-16; 66:20-24; Jer. 31:23-29. Many non-canonical books known to Jesus' contemporaries promised Messianic plenty.

[16] Matt. 16:22; Mark 9:32; Luke 18:34; John 12:16.

[17] The changing of stones is a figure used by John the Baptist (Matt. 3:9) to indicate God's power to disregard physical descent in the interests of spiritual affinity. Here the loaf-like stones are indicative of a hope that the earth would bring forth miraculous plenty without human toil.

[18] Rom. 14:17; John 6:26-27; Prov. 30:8-9 (Isa. 55:1-2 might be taken to suggest physical food, but it also symbolizes the satisfaction that comes from seeking God, since "that which is not bread" means what can never satisfy man's real hunger).

[19] Deut. 8:3 (cf. the warning in Deut. 6:10-15).

[20] The tempter's suggestion is met by reference to Deut. 6:13. The New Testament regards earthly power as necessary for the good of society, see Rom. 13:1-7; I Pet. 2:13-17, etc. The Old Testament everywhere holds to civil authority as a trust from God, Prov. 8:15; Judg. 11:29; I Kings 19:15-16, etc., whether the civil ruler be king or judge or soldier.

[21] John 18:36; Rom. 14:17.

[22] Luke 4:9-12. It is to be noted how Jesus later emphasizes precaution and planning in such parables as Luke 14:28-32. The need for planning is also emphasized in Luke 22:35-38.

[23] The promise of Jesus that his persecuted disciples would be tutored by the Spirit in their emergency (Matt. 10:19-20) must not be taken as encouraging presumptuous avoidance of stern educational discipline and organized thinking. These men had been under the strict discipline of Jesus and, like all who are ready in general, could count in an emergency on being made ready in particular. Jesus did not court needless danger (Luke 9:56; 13:31).

[24] Deut. 6:16. For the theme of presumptuous testing of God, see Exod. 17:7; Num. 14:22; Ps. 78:18, 41, 56; 95:9; 106:14; Acts 5:9; 15:10. The refusal by Ahaz in Isa. 7:12 was not from motives of reverence, but because he had already decided what he was going to do, and wanted no advice from any prophet. Ps. 42:3; 79:10; 73:2, illustrate the strain involved in a patient waiting for God. II Pet. 3:4 shows this in the New Testament, and Paul, in II Thess. 3:6-13, rebukes presumption in those who set a date for the Second Advent.

[25] Mark 8:12, and see Chap. XIV.

[26] John 18:1-11; 10:17-18; Matt. 26:53. The mocking "come down" and "let us see" (Matt. 27:40, 49) show how people expected personal safety for the Messiah.

[27] Luke 19:7; 7:37-39; Matt. 9:11; 11:19.

[28] There is evidence that some Palestinian rabbis regarded certain of the Servant passages as Messianic, and the Dead Sea Scrolls contain similar hints. But the evidence is slight and the teaching seems to have had little influence.

[29] It is not clear whether Jer. 31:31-34 means that the "new covenant" would come only after the need for teaching had been met. The Messiah was not expected to do as humble work as teaching.

[30] C. H. Dodd, in *The Apostolic Preaching and its Developments* (New York: Harper & Bros., 1936), shows how "the preaching" in the New Testament was not based on new moral conventions

but on the proclamation of "the time is fulfilled", and insists that "the kingdom" was thought of not only as approaching, but as actually present through the presence of the Christ. This he calls "realized eschatology". See Chap. XIII below.

[31] II Kings 3:27. There is also no parallel with the Greek myth of Prometheus, who suffered because he had helped deserving men, defying and deceiving the gods on man's behalf. Neither the idea of the placation of the gods' irrational fury nor Prometheus' punishment for outwitting the gods bears any resemblance to "God commendeth his own love toward us", etc., Rom. 5:8. Jesus did not defy the gods for the sake of men who deserved what they were prevented by the gods from having: he sought to bring to men, on behalf of a loving and seeking God, what men did not deserve.

[32] It is noteworthy that, whereas Jesus sometimes makes it clear that the "Son of man" is himself, as in Matt. 8:20; 16:13; 17:22, there are passages that are almost impersonal: Matt. 12:8, 32; 24:30; 25:31; Mark 13:34; Luke 12:8. For his veiling of himself, see John 2:23-24; 16:12; Matt. 7:6 (see also Chap. XIV, Sec. V).

[33] Mark 1:35; Matt. 14:23; Luke 6:12.

[34] Matt. 15:16; 16:11; Mark 4:33; John 16:12.

[35] Matt. 16:13-27; 17:1-9; 26:36-46; 11:27-30; John 17; 7:1-9, etc.

[36] The extraordinary variety of metaphors should be noted. For example, not only is Satan "the father of lies" (John 8:44); he is the "father" of evil men (John 8:44; I John 3:8, 10); he may "enter" or "possess" men (John 13:27), so that even an apostle may be called "Satan" (Matt. 16:23).

[37] Jas. 1:17.

[38] I Cor. 15:26; Rom. 7:17; Prov. 1:20; 7:4; 8:12-31.

[39] Rev. 6:2-8.

[40] Job 2:1-7, cf. Rev. 12:10.

[41] Matt. 13:25, 39; Luke 10:19; Acts 13:10; cf. 5:3.

[42] John 14:30; Eph. 6:12; II Cor. 4:4.

[43] Rev. 20:2.

[44] II Cor. 11:14.

[45] Matt. 5:28; 5:22.

[46] Luke 4:6.

[47] Isa. 45:7 mentions "evil" in this sense.

[48] Gen. 1:31; Ps. 24:1; John 3:16; Rom. 14:14, 20; I Tim. 4:1-5.

[49] Eph. 6:12.

[50] Isa. 26:3; I John 3:8.

[51] Rom. 7:13-18; Heb. 12:1; Matt. 6:13.

RECOMMENDED READING FOR CHAPTER XI

Life of Christ, R. J. Campbell. (Benn's Sixpenny Library.) Ernest Benn Ltd., London. 1928.

"The Life and Ministry of Jesus", *The Interpreter's Bible*, Vol. VII. Ed. G. A. Buttrick *et al.* Abingdon Press, New York. 1951-56.

Did Christ Really Live? H. G. Wood. Student Christian Movement Press, London. 1938.

The Men Whom Jesus Made, W. M. MacKay. R. R. Smith Inc., New York. 1930.

St. Mark's Life of Jesus, T. H. Robinson. Allenson & Co. Ltd., London. 1949.

"The Life of Jesus", *Concise Bible Commentary*, W. K. L. Clarke. Society for Promoting Christian Knowledge, London. 1952.

NOTES FOR CHAPTER XI

[1] Papias (see Note 15, Chap. V) appears to suggest that Mark did not arrange his material in order, but Luke claims to have prepared an orderly account (1:3). Definite chronological interest does not appear until the Passion narrative. See Chap. XV, Sec. I.

[2] Mark 1:14; 10:32; Matt. 20:18.

[3] Luke 4:16.

[4] Mark 3:7; Matt. 12:15; 15:21.

[5] Heb. 5:8, cf. 2:17-18; 4:15.

[6] The earliest hint is the taking away of the bridegroom (Mark 2:19; Matt. 9:15; Luke 5:35). The clear anticipation of suffering begins at Mark 8:31; Matt. 16:21; Luke 9:22, but at this early point crucifixion and delivery to the Gentiles are not mentioned, as they are later in Matt. 20:19; Mark 10:33; Luke 20:20.

[7] Matt. 14:23; 26:36; Luke 9:18; 11:1.

[8] Matt. 15:16-18.

[9] John 2:23-25.

[10] Mark 7:1-8.

[11] Luke 17:17-18.

[12] Mark 1:15.

[13] To "speak comfortably to Jerusalem" (Isa. 40:2), to be "comforted" by rod and staff (Ps. 23:4), and to be left "comfortless" (John 14:18) are examples of this use. We use it still in "aid and comfort to the enemy".

[14] Mark 1:14; Matt. 4:12; Luke 4:14; John 4:3.

[15] John 2:13-4:3.

[16] Mark 1:14; 6:17.

[17] Mark 1:39; Matt. 6:2; Matt. 4:23-25; 9:35; 12:9; Luke 4:16; 4:44; John 18:20.

[18] Luke 13:6-9.

[19] Mark 2:21-22.

[20] Mark 2:7-10; 2:27-28; Matt. 7:21.

[21] John 10:20; 7:20; 8:48 suggest that some opponents thought him mad; Matt. 9:3; John 10:36, and possibly Luke 4:29; John 8:59; 10:31; 11:8, suggest that they thought him a blasphemer; others entertained the possibility that he was the expected "great prophet": Luke 7:16, cf. Matt. 16:14.

[22] Matt. 12:15; Mark 3:1-8; John 6:59, cf. John 18:20; Luke 13:10.

[23] Luke 4:28-30.

[24] John 7:48-49; Matt. 9:11, 36; Luke 18:13; Mark 2: 1-2; 3:7-10; 4:1; 6:56.

[25] Mark 8:2; Matt. 15:32; 9:36.

[26] Luke 10:26; Mark 2:25.

[27] Mark 4:33.

[28] Mark 3:20-21. For the opinion of his opponents concerning his sanity, see Note 21 above.

[29] Mark 4:1-20.

[30] Matt. 10:1-4; Mark 3:13-19, but see XIII, Sec. IV below.

[31] Mark 1:16-20; John 1:35-42.

[32] Mark 6:7-14, 30-32.

[33] Matt. 13:52.

[34] The "rich young ruler" (Matt. 19:20-22) was invited but declined; the three hot enthusiasts (Luke 9:57-62) were rebuffed; the healed demoniac was definitely refused (Mark 5:18-19).

[35] Matt. 5:1 ff., puts an emphasis on "*you* [that is, the disciples] are the salt". But Matt. 7:5, 21 suggest unfriendly hearers, and 7:28-29 speaks of crowds of listeners, who compared his note of authority with the appeal to precedent usual among scribes.

[36] Luke 6:17-49 reports sayings "on a level place" addressed to disciples and crowds outdoors in Galilee.

[37] Matt. 14:13-21; Mark 6:32-44; Luke 9:10-17; John 6:1-69, esp. 15, 66.

[38] Mark 7:24, 31; 9:30; cf. 8:10-13.

[39] Matt. 15:21.

[40] Matt. 15:21-39.

[41] It is not possible to know whether "his disciples" always, or even often, refers to a larger circle, but such passages as Mark 4:34; Matt. 18:1, 21; Luke 17:1 show that he was at least not addressing

the public.   Sometimes, as in Matt. 19:28; Mark 6:30; Luke 17:5, the twelve apostles are exclusively mentioned.   On a few occasions, three of the twelve form a special inner circle: Mark 5:37; 9:2; 14:33.

⁴² Teaching characteristic of this period is found at Luke 9: 46-50; 17:1-4; Matt. 18:1-35; 13:12-20; 19:1-12; Mark 10:23-31.

⁴³ Matt. 18:1 ff.   The hyperbole is interesting in that, far from exhorting children to act like adults, Jesus demanded that adults recover something of childhood.

⁴⁴ Matt. 18:21-35; Luke 17:3-4.   The hyperbole of "seven times in a day" (an unthinkable frequency if sincere repentance is being exercised) is destroyed by "seven times" without "in a day". Jesus restores the hyperbole by making it "seventy times seven" and leaving out "in a day".

⁴⁵ Matt. 19:3-12 (cf. Mark 10:2-12; Luke 16:18) includes the admission that not all are capable of "receiving" this saying. Actually, few people can fully receive any of Jesus' sayings, and no one has been able to "receive" them all.   The disciples were not prepared to accept everything, but their loyalty was fixed (cf. John 6:60).

⁴⁶ Matt. 15:24 suggests that Jesus hesitated to work outside his ancestral community.   That this limitation may have been to a geographical area, not a racial group, is suggested by his helping the centurion earlier, Matt. 8:5-13.   The cleverness as well as the faith of the Syro-Phoenician woman is noteworthy, and obviously pleased Jesus.

⁴⁷ Mark 8:27-33; Matt. 16:13-23; Luke 9:18-22.

⁴⁸ He had spoken of fulfilment in Luke 4:21, and of men who did work "in my name" being rebuffed in the judgment: Matt. 7:21-23.   See also Note 6 above.

⁴⁹ Matt. 16:20, cf. Luke 9:36.

⁵⁰ Luke 9:28-36; Matt. 17:1-8; Mark 9:2-8.   The theme is the exodus (departure) that he was to accomplish.

⁵¹ This most difficult problem involves such considerations as: (1) the widely varying interpretations of Matt. 16:18-19 by early Christian Fathers; (2) the absence here of any statement that power is to be passed on to Peter's or the apostles' successors; (3) the fact that the insufflation of the Spirit (John 20:19-23) occurred when at least one apostle was absent and when probably others besides the twelve were present; (4) that Paul regarded his own authority as equal to that of Peter or any apostle (Gal. 1:15-2:10; II Cor. 11:5); (5) that "apostle" in the New Testament is not a term confined to the twelve; (6) that "the Rock" may have been (a) Christ himself, the

"one foundation" of I Cor. 3:11 (cf. Eph. 2:20), (b) Peter's confession, or (c) people of like faith with Peter; (7) that it is highly unlikely that Jesus would have authorized an overriding Petrine primacy by using an obscure play on words, that is never elucidated elsewhere in the New Testament; (8) that in any case Jesus makes no mention of Peter having successors in office with unique authority; (9) that *Mark, Luke* and *John* make no mention of any Petrine commission. See the commentaries for a more complete study.

[52] Luke 9:58.
[53] Matt. 16:21; 20:18; Mark 10:32.
[54] Luke 13:31.
[55] Luke 9:51-62; 10:8-12; 12:4-7, 49-53, etc.
[56] Luke 17:25, etc., but cf. Luke 13:5, 9, "unless ye repent".
[57] Luke 9:51-19:28; Matt. 20:17-34; Mark 10:32-52.
[58] Mark 8:30; 9:9-10.
[59] Luke 10:1-20.
[60] Luke 9:57-62.
[61] Luke 19:1-10.
[62] Luke 10:25-37; 15:11-32; 18:9-14.
[63] Mark 10:32-34.
[64] Luke 12:50; Matt. 16:21.
[65] Luke 18:35; 19:1, 11.
[66] John 1:26.
[67] Luke 23:34.
[68] John 17:4, 26.

RECOMMENDED READING FOR CHAPTERS XII AND XIII

The Faith of the Bible, Chap. III, J. E. Fison. Pelican Books, Harmondsworth. 1957.

"The Teaching of Jesus", *The Interpreter's Bible*, Vol. VII, pp. 145 ff. Ed. G. A. Buttrick *et al.* Abingdon Press, New York. 1951-56.

The Life and Teaching of Jesus Christ, J. S. Stewart. Student Christian Movement Press, London. 1933.

The Life and Teaching of Jesus Christ, C. E. and E. Raven. Cambridge University Press, London. 1933.

New Testament Ethics, C. A. A. Scott. Cambridge University Press, London. 1930.

The Challenge of New Testament Ethics, L. H. Marshall. St. Martin's Press, New York. 1948.

The Jesus of History, T. R. Glover. Harper & Bros., New York. 1916.

The Parables of the Gospels, H. Martin. Allenson & Co., London. 1954.

The Heart of Christ's Religion, E. E. Raven. Longmans, Green, New York. 1933.

Christ, W. R. Matthews. (What Did They Teach? Series). Blackie & Sons Ltd., London. 1939.

Jesus and Civil Government, A. T. Cadoux. G. H. Doran, New York. 1923.

Jesus Christ the Teacher, W. A. Curtis. Oxford University Press, London. 1943.

Christians in a World at War, Chap. IV, V, VII, VIII, Edwyn Bevan. Student Christian Movement Press, London. 1940.

Ecce Homo, Sir J. Seeley. (Everyman's Library.) J. M. Dent & Sons, London. 1868.

NOTES FOR CHAPTER XII

[1] It is unlikely that, had Jesus been only a sayer of ideal sayings, any "church" would have been formed or any gospels written. The world did not lack moral advice: it lacked spiritual power and "assurance". *Mark* and *Acts* indicate that the earliest preaching was not on moral themes, but on "the time is fulfilled". The *kerygma* (preaching) was "foolish" (I Cor. 1:21), if men really are able to raise themselves by their own moral bootstraps, whether through "the law" or "the wisdom of men". See *The Apostolic Preaching and its Developments*, C. H. Dodd. (New York: Harper & Bros., 1936).

[2] *Adventures of Ideas*, A. N. Whitehead (New York: Mentor Press, 1948) pp. 23-25.

[3] Mark 10:26; Matt. 19:10; John 6:60; Luke 8:9; Matt. 13:10; Mark 4:10.

[4] John 6:63.

[5] I Tim. 6:10.

[6] Luke 6:20, referring to the disciples. Matt. 5:3 says "the poor in spirit".

[7] The difference vigorous words make is illustrated by Richard D. Fay's translation of Lincoln's "Gettysburg Address" into gobbledygook (*Reader's Digest*, January, 1957). "Now we are engaged in a great civil war, testing whether that nation, or any nation so conceived, and so dedicated, can long endure. We are met on a great battlefield of that war . . . ", becomes: "We are now engaged in an over-all evaluation of conflicting factors in order to determine

whether or not the life-expectancy of this group or of any group operating under the stated conditions is significant. We are met in an area of maximum activity among the conflicting factors . . . ."

⁸ The argument as to whether there is humour in the sayings of Jesus would be better changed to the question of wit. Ancient humour was not like ours. Laughter in the Bible is usually derisive or boastful (Gen. 18:12; Job 5:22; Ps. 2:4; 22:7; 37:13; Prov. 1:26; Neh. 2:19). Happy laughter is seldom associated with wit (Job 8:21; Luke 6:21; Eccles. 3:4; Ps. 126:2; Jas. 4:9). But the rapier thrust of wit is important if teaching is to be memorable, with power to disarm opponents. Wit is less "dated" than is humour. It is frequent in the gospels, the ludicrous often being pictured, as in Matt. 23:24; 19:24; 7:3, etc.

⁹ Matt. 7:3-5; Matt. 19:24 (the needle's eye being by some identified with a small gate of the city, although Jesus said the feat was impossible); Matt. 17:20 (as though a tidal wave were desirable!) It is to be noted that removing mountains, mentioned by Paul in I Cor. 13:2, was sometimes used to describe the ironing out of legal difficulties by highly trained rabbis, whereas Jesus promises this kind of wisdom to people with only the merest seed of sound faith.

¹⁰ Matt. 15:15-20; Mark 4:10-20; Matt. 13:12-13; John 13:7; 16:12.

¹¹ Matt. 11:15; 26:75; Luke 24:8; John 2:17; 15:20; 16:4; 13:7.

¹² But see Mark 7:11b, 19b; John 2:21; 21:13; 12:33.

¹³ John 10:8, cf. Acts 5:34-39.

¹⁴ Matt. 23:8, 10, cf. Jas. 3:1.

¹⁵ Luke 22:21-30; Matt. 23:2-3 (cf. I Pet. 5:1-5).

¹⁶ Luke 14:26, cf. Matt. 10:34-39; Luke 12:51-53; 18:29-30; Mark 7:9-13; Matt. 15:3-6; John 19:26-27.

¹⁷ John 2:4; Mark 3:31-35; Matt. 12:46-50; Luke 8:19-21; 11:27-28.

¹⁸ Matt. 5:34; 26:63.

¹⁹ Matt. 5:39; 26:67.

²⁰ Luke 16:31.

²¹ Matt. 5:44; John 11:5; 19:26; Mark 10:21.

²² "It is possible to be moral without being virtuous. You can be ostentatiously hospitable without being generous, financially scrupulous without being honest, continent without being chaste, just because you can go through all those visible actions for motives of prudence, and because mere compliance with obligations is no index to character or intention."—"Morals and the Sceptic", Bertram

Henson, *The Listener*, June 13, 1957, p. 959. This is manifestly compiled from the hyperbolic statements in Luke 14:12; Matt. 5:37; 6:24; 5:28; 15:11 (Mark 7:14-23); Matt. 25:25; 23:23.

[23] Mark 7:18; 9:32.

[24] Matt. 5:39; 5:42 (cf. 5:46); 7:1-2.

[25] Matt. 18:6.

[26] The priest and the Levite may have stood aside because of scruples, and not wholly because of hard-heartedness. They may well have been on the way to take up duties in Jerusalem, for which they would have been rendered unclean by touching a corpse (Lev. 21:11, etc.); and they did not care to risk touching a man apparently dead.

[27] Matt. 5:46; Rom. 13:5-10.

[28] Matt. 7:1, cf. John 7:24; Matt. 18:15-17; Rom. 12:18.

[29] Matt. 19:3-12; Mark 10:2-12; Luke 16:18.

[30] John 7:46; Mark 1:27.

[31] Matt. 5:5 quotes Ps. 37:11 (cf. Ps. 76:9; Isa. 11:4), but "meek" has a new sound on Jesus' lips (it never meant "spineless", but he made it mean "free of self-seeking"). Matt. 5:6 echoes Isa. 55:1-2. Matt. 5:8 echoes Ps. 24:4. Matt. 5:4 refers back to Isa. 61:2; Matt. 6:7 to Eccles. 5:2; Matt. 6:27 to Ps. 39:5; Matt. 7:13-14 to Jer. 21:8. With Matt. 24:28 cf. Job 39:30.

[32] An illustration is A. N. Whitehead's remark (*op. cit.*, p. 57) that the parable of the wheat and the tares is "the first important pronouncement in which tolerance is associated with moral fervour", a significant advance on the moral fervour of the Old Testament prophets.

[33] Rabbi Hillel said, "What is hateful to thyself, that do not thou to another. This is the whole law, the rest is commentary." Tobias (Tob. 4:15) said, "What thou hatest, do thou to no man." Confucius said, "Do not to others what you would not wish done to yourself." Aristotle is credited with saying, but about the treatment of friends only, that we should act "as we would they act towards us". Cf. Matt. 7:12; Luke 6:31. This is ably discussed by H. H. Rowley, in *Submission in Suffering* (Cardiff: University of Wales Press, 1951), pp. 74-108.

[34] Matt. 5:13; 6:25-34; 23:9; Luke 9:23-27; 11:9-13; Mark 6:4.

[35] "A little philosophy inclineth the mind to atheism, but depth in philosophy bringeth men's minds about to religion."

[36] II Cor. 13:8. For other Pauline aphorisms see Rom. 11:32; 12:20-21; Gal. 3:22; Rom. 2:12; I Cor. 13:13; 15:33; II Tim. 2:12-13.

[37] In the Talmud, "It is not upon thee to finish the work; neither art thou free to desist from it."

[38] Matt. 15:13-15; Luke 12:35-48; 14:5.

[39] Judg. 9:6-21; II Kings 14:8-10.

[40] I Cor. 10:1-4; Jude 9.

[41] Luke 16:22-31.

[42] Zech. 4:11-12; 11:7-14.

[43] Gal. 4:22-26; I Cor. 9:9-10.

[44] Ps. 103:5b; 74:13-15; Isa. 27:1; 51:9.

[45] Matt. 25:31-46.

[46] Luke 14:16; Matt. 20:1; 13:44.

[47] Luke 19:12. The reference is to Archelaus.

[48] Mark 4:26; Matt. 13:31.

[49] Matt. 6:26; Mark 4:27-29.

[50] II Sam. 12:1-7; 14:4-13.

[51] This may be the case in Matt. 20:1-16; 25:31-46, for example.

[52] Matt. 13:1-53; 11:16-19; Mark 4:26-33.

[53] Luke 12:41-48; Matt. 18:21-35; 20:1-16; 25 (see 24:3).

[54] Luke 7:40-50; 14:7-11; 15:2-32; 16:14, 19-31; 10:29-37.

[55] Matt. 21:23, 28-46; 22:1-15.

[56] Luke 10:25-37.

[57] Matt. 13:37 ff. (also John 15:1-11).

[58] Matt. 25:9.

[59] Luke 14:23.

[60] Matt. 20:9-15.

[61] Luke 16:1-9.

[62] Luke 18:1-8.

[63] Matt. 12:29.

[64] Matt. 15:21-28; 8:5-13; Luke 7:1-10; 12:13-15; John 7:53-8:11; Mark 5:25-34.

[65] Matt. 15:26.

[66] Luke 10:41.

[67] Matt. 19:16-22; Mark 10:17-22; Luke 18:18-23.

[68] Matt. 18:8-9.

[69] Luke 7:36; 22:11-13; Matt. 27:57.

[70] Luke 8:3.

[71] Mark 1:20; 2:14-16; John 21:1-3.

[72] Luke 6:20; Matt. 5:3.

[73] John 6:15, 26; Matt. 4:3-4.

[74] Luke 12:13-21.

[75] Luke 12:33, cf. 11:41.

[76] Mark 10:24; Luke 12:13-31.

[77] Luke 12:42, cf. I Cor. 4:2. The well-intentioned but short-lived experiment of dissipating wealth, introduced to meet an emergency in the Jerusalem church (Acts 2:44; 4:34), had no relation to a community of productive measures. It was morally unsuccessful (Acts 5:1; 6:1), and economically only a stopgap. The Jerusalem Christians remained poverty-stricken (II Cor. 8-9), possibly because of unemployment.

[78] Matt. 5:41.

[79] Mark 2:24-27; 3:2; Luke 13:16.

[80] Matt. 17:27; 5:17.

[81] Luke 6:35.

[82] Matt. 18:6; Luke 17:1-2; 12:41-48.

[83] Matt. 5:37, cf. Matt. 7:6; John 2:24; 7:8-10; 16:12; Mark 4:33; Matt. 13:9-12.

[84] Matt. 19:28-30, cf. Luke 22:25-30; Mark 10:35-45.

[85] Matt. 5:25.

[86] Matt. 5:39, cf. John 2:15; Rom. 12:17.

[87] Gen. 3:24.

[88] Matt. 5:33, 38, 27; 6:1-18; 5:45; Luke 13:4; 12:57; 17:17; Matt. 19:23; 13:22; Luke 12:15; Matt. 6:34.

[89] John 21:25 literally states that a full account would fill innumerable volumes, but this can scarcely mean that Jesus spoke on a great many subjects about which his followers recorded nothing.

[90] Eph. 6:4; Col. 3:21; II Cor. 12:14.

[91] I Cor. 2:16. The problem of circumcision of Gentiles is an example. There is no record of any saying of Jesus on this subject, but the churches, guided by Peter's experience, agreed that it should not be required, despite bitter opposition from one Christian group (see Acts 15:1, 7-11, 27-29; Gal. 2:3-10, etc.). Paul felt less certain about marriage problems, as in I Cor. 7:12, 25, 40 (cf. verse 10), on which there was no Dominical word. The problem of eating meat that had been offered in heathen temples was at first solved by requiring abstention as a courtesy to Jewish Christians, but later by permitting Christians to eat it, lest superstitious fears seem justified (see Acts 15:29, and cf. I Cor. 8:8; 11:25-27).

NOTES FOR CHAPTER XIII

[1] Heb. 3:1-6 draws the distinction between Moses as "a servant" and Christ as "a son".

[2] Matt. 15:2-6; 23:23-26.

[3] I Pet. 2:8; I Cor. 1:21.

[4] Matt. 7:1-2, 5; 5:47.

[5] Matt. 5:23-24; 6:1; 12:3-6, cf. 12:11-12.

[6] Matt. 24:35; 11:27; 7:21-23; 9:6; Mark 8:38; Luke 22:29.

[7] Mark 2:7; 14:64; Luke 22:70; John 10:33; Matt. 13:44.

[8] "Church" became more frequent than "kingdom", and "the Son of man" gave place to "the Son" or "the Son of God". See Notes 9, 39, 42.

[9] Dan. 7:13-14, cf. Rev. 1:13; 14:14; Matt. 3:2. Outside the gospels, "Son of man" appears only once (Acts 7:56), "kingdom of God" only about fourteen times, and "the kingdom" about nine times, whereas they are met at every turn in the gospels.

[10] Mark 4:30; Matt. 13:31, 33, 44, 45, 47, 52; Luke 13:18, etc.

[11] Matt. 5:35.

[12] Matt. 8:11-12; 21:43; 23:13.

[13] John 8:33-39, cf. Matt. 3:9.

[14] Ps. 89:26; 103:13; Prov. 3:12; Mal. 1:6; 2:10; Isa. 63:16; 64:8.

[15] Mark 2:17; Matt. 9:13; Luke 19:10; 15:4, 8; Matt. 18:12-14.

[16] Isa. 55:6; 65:1 (Revised Standard Version), but cf. Isa. 65:2.

[17] Lev. 18:5; Ezek. 20:11; Ps. 125:4-5.

[18] Rom. 11:32; Eph. 2:5, cf. Luke 13:2-5; 17:10; 18:14.

[19] Phil. 3:4-7.

[20] Prov. 3:34; Jas. 4:6.

[21] Matt. 18:3; John 3:3, 5.

[22] Luke 12:32.

[23] Matt. 20:21; Mark 10:37-40.

[24] Matt. 25:41 ff., 34 ff.; 8:11-12.

[25] Mark 4:26; Matt. 13:38, 33.

[26] Luke 17:21 (margin).

[27] Matt. 12:28.

[28] Luke 19:12; Matt. 25:26, 10; Luke 13:25; Matt. 22:7, 12.

[29] Matt. 12:28; Luke 17:20-21.

[30] Luke 12:32; 22:29-30.

[31] Matt. 6:10; 25:34; Luke 17:20.

[32] Matt. 6:33.

[33] Matt. 16:28; Luke 9:27; 21:31; John 16:33. For the theme of the Fall of Jerusalem, see Chap. XVI.

[34] Acts 1:6-8, cf. Mark 13:32.

[35] Acts 3:21; I Pet. 4:7; I Cor. 7:29, etc.

[36] John 14:18, 26; 16:7, etc.

[37] John 3:15; 4:36; 6:54; 10:28; 17:3; I John 5:11, etc.

[38] Dan. 7:13.

[39] Acts 7:56 is the only New Testament use of "Son of man" outside the Gospels. "Son of God" is a title often attributed to Jesus by others, as in Mark 1:1; 3:11; Luke 1:35; 4:41; 22:70; John 1:34; 3:18; 19:7; 20:31. It is recorded on Jesus' lips in John 9:35; 10:36; 11:4. "One like a son of man" (Rev. 1:13) should not be translated as "the Son of man" as it is in the Authorized Version.

[40] Matt. 16:13-16.

[41] Phil. 2:7; Luke 19:10; John 3:17.

[42] Matt. 11:27, cf. John 14:9. It is stated that, while men may know the Father, the mystery of "the Son" is known only to God. If this phrasing is deliberate, it adds to the feeling of "incognito" that Jesus gives. He is a Being who shares both human and Divine "natures", as Christian orthodoxy has striven to express in the Nicene Creed; cf. John 1:14, "the only Son". See also Chap. XVIII, Note 15, and VIII, Sec. I.

[43] II Pet. 1:4; Isa. 59:2; Rom. 4:17; Col. 2:13.

[44] I Tim. 2:5; Job 9:33.

[45] II Cor. 4:4.

[46] Matt. 8:20; Luke 9:58; Matt. 11:19; 12:8; 13:37; Luke 22:48; Mark 2:10; 8:38.

[47] Mark 8:38; Matt. 24:30, 44; 25:31; 13:41, etc.

[48] I Cor. 15:24-28.

[49] Matt. 18:15-20; 16:18.

[50] Matt. 19:28; 18:20; Luke 12:52; 22:24-26; 22:15.

[51] John 16:2; Matt. 10:18; 10:16; 21:43.

[52] Luke 15:31-32; John 10:16; Luke 9:49-50; Matt. 12:30.

[53] John 10:15; 15:13.

[54] John 7:5 shows that Jesus' own relatives were divided from him; but the family was not split, and was later united. I Cor. 7:12-16 shows that Paul, although lacking a "command" of Jesus, strongly urged Christians not to break up their families.

[55] John 17:15.

[56] Matt. 26:11; Gal. 6:10; Rom. 13:2-7; I Tim. 3:7.

RECOMMENDED READING FOR CHAPTER XIV

The Miracle-stories of the Gospels, A. Richardson. Allenson & Co., London. 1941.

"Miracles", *Concise Bible Commentary*, pp. 284 ff., W. K. L. Clarke. Society for Promoting Christian Knowledge, London. 1952.

The Problem of Pain, C. S. Lewis. G. Bles Ltd., London. 1942.

The Faith that Rebels, D. S. Cairns. Harper & Bros., New York. 1928.

The Wonders of the Kingdom, G. R. H. Shafto. Student Christian Movement Press, London. 1924.

The Case for Miracle, C. F. Rogers. Society for Promoting Christian Knowledge, London. 1936.

Christ and Human Suffering, E. Stanley Jones. Abingdon Press, Nashville. 1933.

Belief in God, Chap. X (*The Reconstruction of Belief*), Charles Gore. Charles Scribner's Sons, London. 1926.

The Faith of a Moralist, A. E. Taylor. (Gifford Lectures, Series 1 & 2.) Macmillan & Co., London. 1926-28.

"The Physical Sciences", *Religious Perspectives in College Teaching*, Hugh S. Taylor. The Ronald Press, New York. 1952.

NOTES FOR CHAPTER XIV

[1] Titus 3:4.

[2] Acts 10:38.

[3] Mark 2:3; 1:32; 8:22; but cf. Mark 10:46 ff.

[4] Acts 2:22.

[5] Luke 5:17; Mark 3:22.

[6] Mark 8:12; John 2:18; Luke 2:34.

[7] Acts 2:22 is almost the only use of this argument, and here it is used to attest to the authority of Jesus by citing what the audience would regard as corroborating general evidence. No specific miracle of Jesus is cited in the New Testament outside the gospels.

[8] Matt. 24:24; 7:22.

[9] In Luke 7:16, for example, the raising of the widow's son moves the people only to the acknowledgement that "a great prophet" had arisen, after the model of Elijah in I Kings 17:21. They took it fairly calmly, and there is no evidence that it resulted in their permanent spiritual improvement, or that it produced conviction.

[10] John 10:41.

[11] Devout readers will, for example, differ over whether Jairus's daughter was in suspended animation or finally dead (Luke 8:52-53), whether the Four Thousand story is a variant of the Five Thousand or a separate incident (Matt. 16:9-10; 15:32-39; 14:17-21), whether John 6:21 involves an effortless speeding of the boat, and over many other details.

[12] Luke 11:20; John 10:38; 14:10.

[13] Matt. 5:45; Luke 13:2-4; 12:4.

[14] Matt. 5:45; 6:26 ff.; 7:24 ff.; Luke 12:54.

[15] Mark 2:3-12; 5:25-29.

[16] Matt. 10:1; Mark 3:15; Luke 9:1, 49-50; 10:1, 9, and cf. Matt. 12:27; 7:22-23; 24:24.

[17] Matt. 11:20; Luke 17:17.

[18] Mark 1:44; 5:43; 7:36; 8:26; Luke 5:14.

[19] Mark 8:22-26; Mark 7:33, cf. John 9:6.

[20] Acts 5:1-11.

[21] Acts 3:1-10.

[22] II Cor. 12:1-10.

[23] Matt. 8:27; Mark 7:37; John 6:69.

[24] Luke 10:17; Matt. 12:27.

[25] John 10:38; 14:11.

[26] Mark 16:9; Luke 8:2; Matt. 27:56.

[27] Mark 5:17-20. He was told to explain to his *friends*, and he took it upon himself to make a public proclamation.

[28] Matt. 12:43-45; John 5:14. This question of the failure of men to achieve true responsibility after cure is analogous to the salvaging of a ship. A ship stranded on the rocks cannot be ordered to sail anywhere at all. But after it has been refloated and repaired, its captain may disobey orders and sail on a pirate voyage or to a vicious port or back on the rocks, rather than engage in lawful commerce. A pirate ship is worse than a ship on a reef; so the last state is worse than the first. Cf. Matt. 12:43-45.

[29] Mark 8:22-26.

[30] Mark 6:5.

[31] Mark 9:28, cf. 6:13.

[32] Not all demons were labelled "unclean": Luke 4:33; Mark 1:27; 3:11, etc. Biblical leprosy was probably the dry tetter. It made a man only ceremonially unclean; no one is spoken of as "a moral leper". Epilepsy is called by that name in Matt. 17:15 (Authorized Version, "lunatick"). Mark 1:32 says, "those who were sick or possessed", also see verse 34.

[33] Mark 1:34; 3:11-12.

[34] Acts 16:16-18.

[35] I Cor. 14; II Tim. 1:7.

[36] For the interesting story of the "second sight" of Kruger, see *Against These Three*, S. Cloete (Boston: Houghton Mifflin Co., 1957).

[37] John 1:48-50.

³⁸ Matt. 15:28; John 4:46-54; Luke 7:1-10.

³⁹ Mark 11:2; 14:13-15.

⁴⁰ As in such general statements as Mark 1:33-34, 39.

⁴¹ I Cor. 13:12.

⁴² Matt. 9:8.

⁴³ Matt. 14:28-31; Mark 4:38; 6:48. For "nature miracles" see Mark 4:37 ff.; 6:41, 48; Luke 5:4-7; John 21:6-8; Mark 8:1-10; John 2:1-11.

⁴⁴ John 6:14-16, 26, 66.

⁴⁵ Mark 1:35-39; 8:12.

⁴⁶ Matt. 26:53.

⁴⁷ Luke 8:55; John 11:44.

⁴⁸ Matt. 12:29; Luke 10:17-20; John 12:31; 14:30; 16:11.

⁴⁹ Mark 7:31.

⁵⁰ As also in the "far country" of Luke 15:15.

⁵¹ Mark 10:17; Luke 10:25.

⁵² Mark 5:13; Luke 8:32.

⁵³ Mark 5:18-20; 8:30; 9:9.

⁵⁴ Mark 1:40-45.

⁵⁵ Other examples of Peter's headstrong ways are in Mark 9:5; Matt. 14:28-31; 26:33-35; John 18:10.

⁵⁶ Matt. 22:15-22.

⁵⁷ See the warning in Luke 13:1-5, 34-35. For the theme of the Fall of Jerusalem, see Chap. XVI.

⁵⁸ Jesus appears to have often used the figure of a tree to refer to contemporary Judaism. There are four "tree sayings", and they seem to occur in a series, of which this incident is the second. All appear to refer to Judaism or to Jerusalem's fall. (1) Luke 13: 6-9 may mean that Jesus for some time hoped that his message would fertilize a barren system into renewal. (2) Mark 11:12-14 must mean that, because of the rejection he was experiencing in Holy Week, he had come to despair of any such fruitfulness, and foresaw only the city's doom (see also Matt. 23:37; Luke 13:34), that came to Sadducism in 70 A.D. (3) Luke 23:27-31 tells of his rebuke to the hysterical women of Jerusalem, who are bidden to reserve their pity for themselves, in view of what would happen when the green tree had died. (4) Mark 13:28-30 refers to the Fall of Jerusalem "before this generation pass away", in terms of a fig-tree, but in this case the new age of the Christian faith is likened to the budding of a living tree, not the dying of a doomed one.

⁵⁹ I Peter 4:19.

RECOMMENDED READING FOR CHAPTERS XV AND XVI

Who Moved the Stone? Frank Morison. Faber & Faber Ltd., London. 1938.

And Pilate Said, Frank Morison. Rich & Cowan Ltd., London. 1939.

No Cross, No Crown, William J. Wolf. Doubleday Inc., London. 1957.

Doctrines of the Creed, Their Basis in Scripture and Their Meaning Today, O. C. Quick. James Nisbet & Co., London. 1938.

The Gospel of the New World: a Study in the Christian Doctrine of Atonement, O. C. Quick. James Nisbet & Co., London. 1944.

"Atonement", *A Theological Word Book of the Bible*. Ed. A. Richardson. Student Christian Movement Press, London. 1950.

The Significance of the Cross, F. W. Dillistone. Westminster Press, Philadelphia. 1944.

The Renewal of Man, Alex Miller. Ed. Reinhold Niebuhr. Doubleday & Co., London. 1955.

Benefits of His Passion, C. H. Dodd. Abingdon Press, Nashville. 1956.

Christ and His Cross, W. R. Maltby. Abingdon Press, New York. 1936.

Ultimate Questions, N. Micklem. Abingdon Press, New York. 1955.

The Atonement in Literature and Life, C. A. Dinsmore. Houghton Mifflin Co., Boston. 1906.

Christians in a World at War, Edwyn Bevan. Student Christian Movement Press, London. 1940.

NOTES FOR CHAPTER XV

[1] I Cor. 1:21-25.

[2] See the remark of the centurion in Luke 23:47, and the exhortations to heroic endurance in I Pet. 2:19-23; Heb. 12:2-4.

[3] This is essentially the attitude of the man "who feared not God or regarded man", Luke 18:2; or of Paul in Acts 26:9; or of the high priest in Acts 5:28 (4:17-18), or of the Athenians in Acts 17:32.

[4] Zeph. 1:12b; Job 34:9; Ps. 42:10; I Cor. 15:15, 19.

[5] Rom. 7:24; Acts 2:37; 16:30; 20:21, etc.

[6] Heb. 10:22; I Pet. 2:24; Acts 15:11; II Cor. 4:13.

[7] (1) The earliest preaching is "you crucified" (Acts 2:23, 36; 4:10); (2) the extenuating plea of ignorance, used by Jesus on the Cross (Luke 23:34), appears again in Acts 3:17; I Cor. 2:8; (3) the emphasis on "for me" rather than "by you" comes in Gal.

2:20; (4) it is not "your sin" (that of the rulers) but "our sins" in I Cor. 15:3; Gal. 1:4; Heb. 1:3; I Pet. 2:24; I John 2:2.

[8] Jer. 31:31-34; Gal. 2:20; II Cor. 5:18-20; Rom. 5:1; Eph. 2:14, 17; Phil. 4:7.

[9] See "The Servant of God", J. Jeremias, trans. H. Knight, *Studies in Theology*, No. 20, 1957, for a discussion of Isa. 52:13 ff.; 42:1 ff.; Mark 14:24.

[10] Matt. 13:35; Luke 11:50; John 17:24. Mark 14:35; Matt. 26:45; John 12:27; 18:37. Luke 19:44; 13:34; 22:53; John 14:30; 16:33.

[11] Luke 24:7.

[12] Mark 10:45; Matt. 20:28; (Rev. 5:9; I Tim. 2:6) Matt. 26:28.

[13] Luke 24:26; Heb. 10:7-9; John 14:31.

[14] Heb. 12:2; 3:2; 5:8; John 13:1; 18:4.

[15] Matt. 26:24.

[16] Matt. 26:54-56; Luke 18:31; 22:22; John 13:11; Acts 2:23; 3:18; 4:27-28; 13:27.

[17] Matt. 18:7; 26:24; Luke 17:1; John 19:11.

[18] John 12:16; 18:9, 31-32; 19:28.

[19] Acts 2:23.

[20] Isa. 50:6; cf. Matt. 26:68; Mark 14:65; Luke 22:64. This illustration of how the devout reader still follows the method of ancient exegetes, by seizing on what a passage suggests rather than what it says, can be supplemented by noting that many people, if asked what "thee" means in Phillip Brooks's line, "The hopes and fears of all the years are met in thee tonight", would answer that it means the Christ-child, whereas the hymn writer referred to the town of Bethlehem. They are technically wrong but spiritually right. See also VIII, Notes 33 and 34, and XVII, Sec. V (*e*).

[21] John 2:4; 7:6, 30; Matt. 17:27; 26:18.

[22] John 11:8, 16, 45-57.

[23] Luke 10:1 ff., cf. John 11:55; 12:9.

[24] Matt. 21:9-11, 15.

[25] Luke 19:40, cf. John 1:19-23, for John the Baptist's refusal to let any such report be circulated about himself.

[26] John 11:50.

[27] Cf. Isa. 53:8-9.

[28] John 18:40; Matt. 27:15-21.

[29] Matt. 19:27-30; Mark 10:35-45; Matt. 18:1; Luke 9:46.

[30] Luke 22:24; Mark 14:37, 50, 66-67, cf. John 16:32; Mark 14:27-31.

[31] Matt. 27:3-5.

[32] Mark 12:41-44; John 12:20.

[33] Matt. 23:1 ff.

[34] Luke 21:29-33; Matt. 21:43, cf. Luke 13:22-30; 14:15-29.

[35] Matt. 6:26-29; 10:31.

[36] Matt. 16:1.

[37] Mark 14:1, cf. Acts 4:1.

[38] Matt. 14:1-2; Luke 9:7-9; 13:31.

[39] Luke 15:11; Matt. 21:33, 45.

[40] See Chap. XVI, Sec. IV.

[41] John 10:17-18, see also Chap. X, Sec. VI; and Sec. III above.

[42] Col. 1:20; Eph. 1:7; 2:13; Heb. 13:20; I Pet. 1:2; I John 1:7; Rev. 5:9, etc.

[43] See *Conversion*, A. D. Nock (London: Oxford University Press, 1933), for the thesis that the assured forgiveness of past sins was one of the chief reasons for the swift growth of Christian faith.

[44] John 15:22, cf. Rom. 1:22.

[45] These include: the two servants (Matt. 18:23-35); the two debtors (Luke 7:40-43); the impenitent one-talent slacker (Luke 19:19; Matt. 25:24-25); unlimited forgiveness of penitent offenders (Matt. 18:22; Luke 17:4); the repentant Prodigal (Luke 15:20-24). See also Matt. 6:15; 18:35; Luke 6:37; 7:47; 23:34.

[46] That forgiveness, if it is to be truly forgiveness, must be free to the one pardoned (John 8:36; Rom. 3:24; 5:15; 8:32; Rev. 21:6, etc.), does not alter the fact that a "price of sin" exists and is met by the pardoner. The father of the Prodigal not only had to see the family resources squandered (as the king absorbed the loss in Matt. 18:27, 32) but had to live with the fact of the boy's sinfulness. The bringing back of sinners (Jas. 5:19-20) is a costly business, even though love does not count the cost.

[47] Suffering for sins and being punished are radically different things. The Servant suffered, as the innocent can and often must; but he was not punished, since only the guilty can be punished (Matt. 25:46; Heb. 10:29, etc.). Christ is always said to have suffered, never to have been punished (Luke 24:26; Matt. 16:21; Acts 17:3; I Pet. 2:21; 3:18; 4:1, etc.). Jesus was not made guilty when he "bore our sins" (I Pet. 2:24), any more than he became diseased through his healing work, when he "bore our diseases" (Matt. 8:17).

NOTES FOR CHAPTER XVI

[1] Mark 11:12, 19-20, 27, cf. Matt. 21:10-17; Luke 19:37-20:2.

² Mark 11:1-11; Matt. 21:1-9; Luke 19:29-38.

³ Mark 11:15-19; Matt. 21:12-16; Luke 19:45-48, cf. John 2:13-16.

⁴ Zech. 9:9, cf. Isa. 62:11. The importance of the act in Jesus' eyes can be gathered from "the stones would cry out" (Luke 19:40), as though the whole history of the city testified to what was happening.

⁵ Mal. 3:1-3; Isa. 56:7; Jer. 7:11; Ps. 69:9.

⁶ Mark 11:27.

⁷ Matt. 21:45-46; 26:3-4, 14-16; Mark 11:18; 14:1-2; Luke 19:47; 22:1-6.

⁸ Matt. 21:33-23:39; Mark 11:27-12:38; Luke 19:47-20:47.

⁹ Matt. 21:23-27; Mark 11:27-33; Luke 20:1-8.

¹⁰ Matt. 21:28-22:14; Mark 12:1-12; Luke 20:9-19, cf. Isa. 5:1-7.

¹¹ I Pet. 2:4-9; Phil. 3:3; Gal. 6:15; Acts 2:39; Matt. 21:43.

¹² Matt. 22:15-22; Mark 12:13-17; Luke 20:20-26.

¹³ Matt. 22:23-33; Mark 12:18-27; Luke 20:27-38. There is no reason to think of this woman as any more an actual individual than the Prodigal Son. For levirate marriage, see Deut. 25:5; Gen. 38:9; Ruth 4:5.

¹⁴ I Cor. 15:50; II Cor. 5:4.

¹⁵ Exod. 3:6.

¹⁶ Matt. 22:34-40; Mark 12:28-34; Luke 20:39-40, cf. 10:25-28.

¹⁷ Matt. 22:41-46; Mark 12:35-37; Luke 20:41-44.

¹⁸ Mark 12:37.

¹⁹ Matt. 23:1-36; Mark 12:38-40; Luke 20:45-47, cf. Luke 11:37-52; 13:34-35; 20:45-47.

²⁰ Isa. 42:1-3.

²¹ But cf. John 11:57 for emphasis not in Synoptics.

²² Mark 12:41-44; John 12:20.

²³ Mark 13:1-2.

²⁴ Mark 13:3-37; Luke 21:5-36; Matt. 24:3-51.

²⁵ Matt. 25:1-46.

²⁶ The parable of the pounds in Luke 19:11-27 closely resembles Matt. 25:14-30 in framework.

²⁷ Mark 14:3-10 may belong to Tuesday (Mark 14:1, 10) or may have occurred earlier (cf. John 12:1-8; Luke 7:37-38).

²⁸ Mark 14:12-16; Matt. 26:17-19; Luke 22:7-13.

²⁹ Mark 14:17-31; Matt. 26:20-35; Luke 22:14-38.

³⁰ Mark 14:22-25, cf. Exod. 12:27.

[31] Jer. 31:31-34. (The "departure" mentioned in Luke 9:31 is the same word as "exodus", and suggests the contrast between the ancient deliverance and the new one.)

[32] Heb. 2:15; II Tim. 1:7; John 8:34-36.

[33] Mark 14:12; Matt. 26:19; Luke 22:7.

[34] John 13:1; 18:28. For Paul's apparent agreement, see I Cor. 5:7-8.

[35] Matt. 26:51; Luke 22:38; Matt. 26:47; John 18:3, 28.

[36] John 14-17.

[37] Mark 14:32-42; Matt. 26:36-46; Luke 22:40-46, cf. Heb. 5:7.

[38] The return of Jesus from his solitude (Mark 14:35-37), the thrice-repeated agony, and the disciples' sleep, all suggest an unexpectedly long period. It was but a few minutes' walk from the Temple to the Garden.

[39] Luke 22:28.

[40] Matt. 16:22-23.

[41] Mark 15:34; Matt. 27:46.

[42] Mark 14:53-15:20; Matt. 26:57-27:31; Luke 22:54-23:25; John 18:12-19:6.

[43] No British court can require a man to accuse himself or plead guilty when his life is at stake, but one cannot expect this exemption in ancient legal procedure. Many supposed points in Jewish legal procedure in the first century are misleading, being drawn from the *Tractate Sanhedrin*, which dates from long after the Fall of Jerusalem. It is probably an ideal statement of procedure after the court had ceased to exist. Christians should hesitate to denounce those who tried Jesus, as though they deliberately jettisoned their own rules and acted illegally. The real tragedy is that injustice can come amid strictly legal procedure.

[44] Mark 14:50; John 18:15-16.

[45] The complexity of motives in betrayal is convincingly portrayed in Graham Greene's novel, *The Power and the Glory* (New York: Viking Press, 1946). The theory of De Quincey, that Judas only intended to force Jesus to exercise his power and abandon his unacceptable plan, is of interest because of Judas's swift repentance (Matt. 27:4).

[46] John 18:28.

[47] Mark 14:55-60; John 18:19-21.

[48] Matt. 16:20; 17:9; 26:63-66; Mark 14:61-65; Luke 22:67-71, cf. Deut. 17:6.

[49] Acts 7:58. Pilate's mocking suggestion in John 19:6 may not prove anything, but there are suggestions that the Jewish authorities

had not only the power to excommunicate and imprison (John 16:2; 9:22, 34; Luke 21:12; Acts 9:12), but to put to death for blasphemy or apostasy (Acts 22:19-20). See also Chap. VI, Note 24.

[50] Matt. 27:1.

[51] The sin of blasphemy is not defined in the Old Testament, beyond "cursing the name" of God (Lev. 24:16; Job 2:9); and only two executions are recorded (Lev. 24:10 and the trumped-up case of Naboth, I Kings 21:10). Blasphemy was, however, acknowledged to occur frequently (Isa. 65:7; Ezek. 20:27). John 10:31-34 indicates that Jesus had earlier been suspected of this crime, as also does Matt. 9:3. Paul is said to have tried to trap Christians into blasphemy (Acts 26:11). John 19:7 refers to the existing law, but the Jews wished Pilate to take the initiative through a criminal charge.

[52] Gamaliel's great caution on this point is of interest: Acts 5:33-39. He recalled that the political power had dealt with awkward cases.

[53] Some have averred that the Fourth Gospel is anti-Semitic, that its writer blames "the Jews" (as in John 5:16-18; 18:35) and suggests that Pilate was only an unwilling tool in their hands. It should at least be remembered that the evangelist was himself a Jew, and that no statement in the gospels is as violently condemnatory of Jews as are many of the charges made by the Hebrew prophets in the Old Testament. John, however, blames the Pharisees in a way the other gospel writers do not (John 3:1; 7:32; 11:47, 57).

[54] John 18:30.

[55] Luke 23:1-5.

[56] Luke 23:7.

[57] Matt. 27:15 ff.

[58] John 19:6.

[59] John 18:38; 19:7-9; Matt. 27:19.

[60] John 19:12. Pilate put his foot down only once, in refusing to be badgered into changing the superscription on the Cross: John 19:19-22.

[61] Isa. 53:3.

[62] Isa. 53:8-9.

[63] Heb. 9:14.

[64] "Each man kills the thing he loves": "The Ballad of Reading Gaol", Oscar Wilde.

[65] Luke 24:47, cf. Acts 5:31; II Tim. 2:25.

[66] Acts 20:21, etc.

[67] Matt. 27:51. Whether this was a physical fact or is a symbolic statement, the meaning is the same; see also Heb. 9:1-26;

10:19-20. Similarly, Paul's fighting with beasts at Ephesus (I Cor. 15:32) may be taken as either figurative or literal without essential change of meaning.

RECOMMENDED READING FOR CHAPTER XVII

Resurrection and Historical Reason, Richard R. Niebuhr. Charles Scribner's Sons, New York. 1957.
Christians in a World at War, Chap. VI, Edwyn Bevan. Student Christian Movement Press, London. 1940.
Ultimate Questions, N. Micklem. Abingdon Press, New York. 1955.
"Resurrection", *A Theological Word Book of the Bible*. Ed. A. Richardson. Society for Promoting Christian Knowledge, London. 1950.
Good News of God, C. E. Raven. Harper & Bros., New York. 1943.
The Gospel of the New World, O. C. Quick. James Nisbet & Co., London. 1944.
The Right to Believe, J. S. Whale. Charles Scribner's Sons, New York. 1938.
And the Life Everlasting, John Baillie. Charles Scribner's Sons, New York. 1933.
The Christian Hope of Immortality, A. E. Taylor. Macmillan & Co., London. 1939.

NOTES FOR CHAPTER XVII

1 As in I Cor. 10:11.
2 Acts 10:39-43; 13:29-32; 1:22; Luke 24:28.
3 Rev. 1:18; Phil. 3:10.
4 Luke 24:11; John 20:25; Mark 16:11; Matt. 28:17.
5 Matt. 27:62-66; 28:11-15.
6 Matt. 28; Mark 16:1-8; Luke 24; John 20-21; Acts 1:1-11; I Cor. 15:3-8.
7 Phil. 3:10-11; John 14:19; I Cor. 15:20 ff.
8 Matt. 25:31 ff.; Acts 10:42; 17:13; Rom. 14:10; Heb. 12:18-24.
9 Hab. 1:13.
10 Eph. 1:3.
11 Acts 2:24; 13:30; Rom. 4:24; 6:4; I Cor. 15:15; Col. 2:12.
12 This is the theme of Sophocles' *Antigone*, Henley's "Invictus", and of *The Rubaiyat*. (In this latter, Fate is amoral. In Greek mythology, Fate was mysteriously stronger than the gods, and not

necessarily governed by moral laws. But the idea of some immutable moral law was not absent from the vague concept of Fate.)

[13] I Pet. 1:21; 3:18.

[14] Luke 24:21.

[15] Rom. 5:8; II Cor. 5:19. Neither is Jesus ever recorded to have said, "I love you", or "I love everybody; so I am going to die for them." John 15:13 approaches it, but may refer to the duty of discipleship. John 16:27 stresses God's love for men; John 14:31 stresses Jesus' love of the Father. Jesus is always portrayed as following the will of God, as in John 5:30; 6:38-40, etc.

[16] II Cor. 5:17; II Pet. 1:4.

[17] Rom. 14:10; II Cor. 5:10; cf. John 12:48.

[18] Acts 5:31; 11:18; 20:21; Rom. 2:4; II Tim. 2:25; II Pet. 3:9; Rom. 4:5; 14:22, etc.

[19] Luke 24:11; John 20:25; Matt. 28:17.

[20] This is not to suggest that the transformation was instantaneous and complete. John 21 shows their hesitation.

[21] Gal. 1:12-17.

[22] Col. 3:1.

[23] Mark 16:8; Luke 24:37.

[24] Luke 18:34; Mark 9:10, 32.

[25] Matt. 26:32; 28:7, 10, 16-20; Mark 16:7.

[26] Luke 24:33-52; John 20:18-28; 21; Acts 1:1-11.

[27] John 20:27; Luke 24:39.

[28] I Cor. 15:3-8; Acts 26:12-15; 22:9.

[29] I Cor. 15:4. The New Testament repeatedly emphasizes that the Rising accorded with ancient hopes (Luke 24:25 ff., 44 ff.; 18:31; John 3:14; Acts 2:25; 13:33; 24:14; 26:22; I Cor. 15:3). But the Old Testament references turn out to be very few (Ps. 16: 10-11; Isa. 53:10, with some possibility of Hos. 6:2; Ps. 22:24-31; Gen. 3:15). The "third day" of Hos. 6:2 can be made to refer to Christ only by what we would today call exegetical violence, but it was customary in New Testament days to extract meanings by inference as well as by direct meaning. While this method has little appeal now, such ancient exegesis is evidence of passionate convictions. The Old Testament passages could not have produced the conviction they were used to illustrate. The very paucity of Old Testament references therefore suggests that New Testament Christians, holding to the Resurrection on apostolic evidence, found added comfort in discovering that what they held was nowhere contradicted by the Old Testament. See also Chap. XV, Sec. IV, and VIII, Note 34.

[30] Matt. 27:40; 28:1; 12:40; 27:63 (cf. Matt. 26:61; 27:40). Luke 9:22 and Matt. 16:21 have "the third day", but the parallel passage in Mark 8:31 says "after three days".

[31] I Cor. 15:4; Luke 9:22; Matt. 16:21.

[32] Mark 6:14.

[33] II Kings 13:20-21; II Kings 2:11.

[34] Matt. 27:52-53.

[35] Matt. 28:11-15.

[36] John 20:2-9; Matt. 28:11-15; Luke 24:1-11; Mark 16:1-8.

[37] I Cor. 15:8; Gal. 1:15-17; 2:20.

[38] Acts 17:31.

[39] John 14:23.

[40] Acts 1:9-11, cf. Luke 24:50-53.

[41] I Pet. 1:11.

[42] Paul puts "the power of his resurrection" first, and "share his sufferings" second (Phil. 3:10). In II Cor. 5:16-21 the "new creation" is the basis for the invitation to be reconciled, etc.

[43] Phil. 2:9-10; I Cor. 6:11.

[44] This is part of the point of the words "we are of all men most to be pitied" (I Cor. 15:19). The "pitiable" condition of Christians in I Cor. 15:9 would arise because nothing had been changed. If Christ's death had been the end, no acquitting judgment had been pronounced. Hopeless repentance or remorse is common in human experience (the theme of "I cannot forgive myself" or "it is useless to repent"): the gospel deals with hopeful repentance. Paul writes of Jesus as having been "put to death for our trespasses" (the evil in men being clearly the cause of his death), but also as having been "raised for our justification" (Rom. 4:25). This puzzling use of "for" (because of, on account of, or for this cause) in connection with "justification" (acquittal) cannot be examined here, but the passage at least shows that Paul was not thinking of our immortality but of our forgiveness as an important result of the Resurrection.

[45] Luke 12:54-13:5; 13:3-5, 34-35, etc., see Chap. XVI.

[46] Mark 9:9, 31; Luke 18:33, and see Chap. XIII.

[47] Gal. 3:28-29.

[48] I John 2:7-11; Gal. 3:5-14; 5:19-26; Jas. 1:25; Rom. 12:2.

[49] I Cor. 7:31; II Thess. 2:1-2; 3:11-13.

[50] II Cor. 3:17; Gal. 5:16; John 15:25-26, etc.

[51] Luke 24:26.

[52] I Cor. 1:21-25; 2:1-2; Acts 26:9, cf. I Pet. 2:2-8.

[53] I Cor. 12:3; Rom. 10:9; 14:9; Phil. 2:9-10; I Cor. 4:4; 8:5-6; I Tim. 2:5; Acts 2:36; 9:15; 10:36; 17:18.

RECOMMENDED READING FOR CHAPTER XVIII

The Faith of the Bible, pp. 255-64, J. E. Fison. Pelican Books, Harmondsworth. 1957.

The Gospel of John, William Barclay. 2 vols. Daily Study Bible Series, Edinburgh. 1955.

The Incarnate Glory, William Manson. James Clarke & Co. Ltd., London. 1928.

The Four Gospels: a Study of Origins, Chap. XIII-XVI, B. H. Streeter. Macmillan & Co., London. 1924.

"A Death in the Desert", Robert Browning.

NOTES FOR CHAPTER XVIII

[1] Luke 9:33-34 (II Pet. 1:16-18).

[2] John 2:13-22, cf. Mark 11:15-19. Most readers instinctively feel that Jesus cleansed the Temple only once, and then in Holy Week. Mark 14:58 (cf. John 2:19) seems to suggest that these words were spoken by Jesus during Holy Week, not three years before. But it is symbolically proper to think of the cleansing as representing the immediate effect of Jesus' appearance.

[3] John 4:25-26, cf. Matt. 16:20.

[4] John 6:27-64. The problem here is that the discourse emphasizes the eucharistic theme, although identifying the "flesh" of the Son of man as a matter of his words (verse 63) or spirit. The fact that this gospel does not record the Last Supper makes it natural to think that the symbolism of bread was suggested by the Feeding of the Five Thousand, and that the resultant discourse introduces the eucharistic theme at this first opportunity.

[5] John 6:35; 8:12; 9:5; 10:7; 10:14; 11:25; 14:6; 15:1 (cf. 8:58). The term "witness" is not used in the Synoptics in the sense it frequently bears in *John* (1:7; 3:11; 5:31-37; 21:24, etc.). This appears to mean an interpretative witness rather than merely a factual account. A man who witnesses (the word martyr comes from "witness" in Greek) to his faith is not quite the same as a man who reports a series of sayings.

[6] For the theme of "his own" and "my friends", see John 1:11; 13:1; 15:13-15; 17:6, 9. For that of "we were enemies", see Rom. 5:6, 10; Col. 1:21, etc.

[7] See B. H. Streeter, *op. cit.*, pp. 369-74.

[8] *Ibid.*, p. 372.

[9] The question is not whether Jesus could have spoken in such startlingly different styles as are recorded in the Synoptic and Johan-

nine Gospels respectively. No one would venture to limit Jesus to the Synoptic epigrammatic style and no other. The point is that the narrative and discourse sections of the Fourth Gospel are uniform in style, indicating that comment has been united with report in many cases. The familiar third chapter of John is the clearest illustration of this, the alternation or combination of sayings and comment being unmistakably present.

[10] This nineteenth-century poem, from which the hymn "The sands of time are sinking" is taken, is often printed at the close of *The Letters of Samuel Rutherford*, much as the Scottish Paraphrases are bound with the Bible.

[11] First published 1867, and frequently corrected by the author and reprinted, this poem is written in the first person. It draws on Paul's epistles, his discourses in *Acts*, and some words of Jesus that he can be assumed to have thought about often.

[12] See Chap. V, Sec. V; Chap. XVI, Sec. VI.

[13] For John, see John 1:1-14; 5:26; 9:5; 17:5, etc. For Paul, see Col. 1:13-20, etc. (cf. Prov. 8:22-31, for the concept of Wisdom being present at creation). The God of creation and the God of redemption must be seen to be the same God. This was more of a problem in early Christian preaching than it is now.

[14] By John the gospel is often expressed as a matter of enlightenment (John 3:19), by Paul as free forgiveness (Col. 1:13-14). Paul speaks of being "dead in sin" and needing "life"; John speaks of "loving darkness rather than light" (Col. 2:13; John 3:19). This does not mean that they disagree. Darkness and light, death and life, disobedience and obedience, all refer to the same problem of redemption. Jesus used all three, speaking of "children of light" and "seeing the light" (Luke 16:8; 8:16), and about fulfilling the law and practising righteousness (Matt. 5:17-20). He makes the father of the Prodigal say, "This my son was dead and is alive again; he was lost and is found" (Luke 15:24, 32). Being lost, dead, or in darkness are the same; being found, born again, or brought to the light are the same. (Luke 15:4; John 3:3; I John 1:7).

[15] Rev. 19:12-13. Paul, in Phil. 2:9-10, appears to feel the same humility. Believers worship in "the name of Jesus", but Jesus has been given "the name which is above every name". This name is not defined, presumably because there are no human words to use for the ineffable. See Chap. XIII, Note 42.

[16] Gen. 1:3; Ps. 33:6; Prov. 8:22-36.

[17] John 1:14; I Cor. 1:24.

[18] I Tim. 1:3-5; 6:20, etc. Against this is the insistence that it is from the Logos only that fullness comes (John 1:16), that the Logos alone has made the Father known (1:18), and that Christians have "one Lord" in contrast to the "many gods and many lords" of the heathen (I Cor. 8:5).

[19] Eph. 1:23; 5:30; 4:13-16.

[20] Rom. 1:19-21.

THE TOOLS OF LEARNING

The people in the Bible were real people, with passions like ours, and scholars engaged in biblical and allied fields are real scholars, with passions like those of other scholars. They use tools of scholarship, and records of scholarly investigation conducted in many nations and languages. The present generation can enjoy the fruits of scholarly work in the form of popular yet accurate writing to an extent unknown to earlier generations.

Among the types of book available in English for the non-technical reader are the following:

1. *English Translations (or Versions) of the Bible*

Translations exist in hundreds of languages. From the Hebrew and Greek documents of the biblical books, supplemented by the use of Latin Vulgate and other sources, many English translations have been made. There is no final or perfect translation. In common use are:

(*a*) Translations that have been carried out at the request or with the approval of the great Christian churches, usually through large committees of scholars:

The King James (Authorized) Version, 1611
The Douay Version (Roman Catholic), 1582-1609
The English Revised Version, 1881-5
The American Standard Version, 1901
The Revised Standard Version, 1946-52

(*b*) Translations by individual scholars, useful and illuminating, but not generally used for reading in public worship:

New Testament. Trans. R. F. Weymouth. James Clarke & Co. Ltd., London. 1902.
A New Translation of the Bible. Trans. James Moffatt. 2 vols. Hodder & Stoughton Ltd., London. New Testament, 1913; Old Testament, 1924.
The Bible: An American Translation. Ed. Edgar J. Goodspeed. University of Chicago Press, Chicago. 1923-24.

New Testament. Trans. Ronald A. Knox. Burns, Oates & Washbourne, London. 1945.

Old Testament. Trans. Ronald A. Knox. Sheed & Ward, New
York. 1952.

The Four Gospels. Trans. E. V. Rieu. Penguin Books, Harmondsworth. 1952.

The New Testament in Basic English. Cambridge University
Press, London. 1941.

(*c*) A freer translation by J. B. Phillips, that is in part a para-
phrase, not following the exact text but illuminating in its phrasing
is

The New Testament in Modern English. Trans. J. B. Phillips.
William Collins Sons & Co., London. 1958.

2. *Concordances*

These are elaborate indexes, useful for tracing any passage
through key words, and valuable in any study of the use of a given
term in the Old Testament and the New (for example, "holiness",
"law", "kingdom"), to show its changing meaning or frame of
reference. Since the same English word may represent several
different words in Hebrew or Greek, there is need, in the exact
study of words, for a more elaborate concordance, listing the various
words behind each English term. (The reverse process, whereby the
same Greek or Hebrew word may be translated by several different
English words, cannot be readily discerned through a concordance
in English.)

(*a*) The commonest concordances are simply indexes, built on
the admittedly imperfect model of Alexander Cruden's *Complete
Concordance*, first published in 1737. These volumes are most
commonly based on the Authorized Version, but the Revised Standard Version now has a mathematically complete, and therefore bulky,
concordance:

Nelson's Complete Concordance to the Revised Standard Version.
Ed. John W. Ellison. Thomas Nelson & Sons, New York.
1957.

(*b*) For more exact study based on the different words translated by a single English word (for example, the English word "for"
translates five different Greek words in the New Testament) there
is need for such a work as

An Analytical Concordance to the Bible, Robert Young. 1881.

3. *Dictionaries, Encyclopedias and Word Books*

Reference volumes with such titles supply articles of historical, biblical or anthropological interest, indispensable for an introductory study of such various topics as sacrifice, Christmas, circumcision, the calendar, etc. They include:

The Westminster Dictionary of the Bible, J. D. Davis. Revised by Henry S. Gehman. Westminster Press, Philadelphia. 1944.

Dictionary of the Bible. Ed. James Hastings. 5 vols. Charles Scribner's Sons, London. 1898-1904.

Dictionary of the Bible. Ed. James Hastings. 1 vol. Charles Scribner's Sons, London. 1909.

Dictionary of Christ and the Gospels. Ed. James Hastings. 2 vols. Charles Scribner's Sons, London. 1906.

Encyclopaedia of Religion and Ethics. Ed. James Hastings. 13 vols. Charles Scribner's Sons, London. 1910-27.

International Standard Bible Encyclopaedia. Ed. James Orr. 5 vols. William B. Eerdmans, Grand Rapids. 1915.

Catholic Biblical Encyclopaedia, New Testament Volume, J. E. Steinmüller & Kathryn Sullivan. J. F. Wagner, New York. 1949.

Oxford Dictionary of the Christian Church. Ed. F. L. Cross. Oxford University Press, London. 1957.

Books that enlarge on important words as they are used in the Bible (for example, "justification", "love", "faith", etc.), include:

A Theological Word Book of the Bible. Ed. Alan Richardson. Student Christian Movement Press, London. 1950.

New Testament Wordbook, William Barclay. Student Christian Movement Press, London. 1956.

More New Testament Words, William Barclay. Student Christian Movement Press, London. 1957.

Words, C. A. Anderson Scott. Student Christian Movement Press, London. 1939.

4. *Commentaries*

As the name implies, these supply comments on the text of the biblical books, sometimes scholarly, sometimes devotional, along with relatively brief articles on background, chronology, etc. They exist in one-volume brief commentaries, and longer multi-volume series.

(*a*) One-volume commentaries include:

Concise Bible Commentary, W. K. L. Clarke. Society for Promoting Christian Knowledge, London. 1952.

A New Commentary on Holy Scripture, Charles Gore *et al*. Macmillan & Co., London, 1928.

Commentary on the Bible. Ed. A. S. Peake (Second Edition). T. C. & E. C. Jack, London. 1929.

The One-Volume Bible Commentary. Ed. J. R. Dummelow. Macmillan & Co., London. 1909.

The Teachers' Commentary. Ed. Alan Richardson (Seventh Edition). Student Christian Movement Press, London. 1955.

(*b*) More elaborate commentaries appear in a number of volumes published over a period of years. These series include:

The Daily Study Bible. Published by St. Andrew Press, Edinburgh. 1955.

The Interpreter's Bible. Published by The Abingdon Press, New York.

A New Testament Commentary for English Readers, Ronald A. Knox. 3 vols. Burns, Oates & Washbourne, London. 1953-56.

The Torch Bible Commentaries. Published by the Student Christian Movement Press, London.

There are series, useful chiefly to scholars and ministers, such as the Westminster, Moffatt, and International Critical Commentaries, together with the smaller volumes of the Clarendon Bible and the Century Bible.

5. *Atlases*

A brief, recent atlas is

Westminster Atlas to the Bible. Ed. G. Ernest Wright & Floyd V. Filson (Revised Edition). Westminster Press, Philadelphia. 1956.

Larger, and containing much explanatory and descriptive material, is

Rand McNally Bible Atlas. Ed. Emil G. Kraeling. Rand McNally & Co., Chicago. 1956.

6. *"Reference Bibles"*

Most editions of the Bible contain some marginal cross-references, but not doctrinal notes and comments as footnotes to the text. Several editions, however, have been published in an attempt to give the reader theological or schematic guidance page by page. Such

"Reference Bibles" can seldom be recommended, since their editors are too often protagonists of views not representative of stable church bodies, or of the scholarly world. If notes and comments are desired, it is better to use commentaries. The Bible is a big book, and no system of comment can be adequately included with it in a single volume. The Bible Societies publish without note or comment, allowing the text to speak for itself.

7. Anthologies of Documents from Christian History

Certain documents and decisions have such importance in Christian history that convenient reference to them is of interest. Several recent anthologies put the main documents within reach. These include:

Documents of the Christian Church. Ed. H. Bettensen. (World's Classics No. 495.) Oxford University Press, London. 1943.

The New Testament Background: Selected Documents. Ed. C. K. Barrett. Macmillan & Co., London. 1957.

The Wisdom of the Fathers. Ed. Erik Routley. Student Christian Movement Press, London. 1958.

A New Eusebius. Ed. J. Stevenson. Society for Promoting Christian Knowledge, London. 1957.

8. Anthologies of Sacred Literature

Many readers of the Bible desire some knowledge of the sacred books of other religions. As an introduction to this limitless field, there is now available, among others,

Sacred Books of the World. Ed. & trans. A. C. Bouquet. Pelican Books, Harmondsworth. 1954.

9. General Books

The output of scholarly yet popular books on biblical, historical and theological topics is probably larger today than in any preceding generation, and any list must be fragmentary. Many are issued in the good paperbound series, and others in relatively cheap editions. These include:

Christian Faith Today, Stephen Neill. Pelican Books, Harmondsworth. 1955.

Christianity, S. C. Carpenter. Pelican Books, Harmondsworth. 1952.

An Introduction to the Bible, Stanley Cook. Pelican Books, Harmondsworth. 1945.

Christianity, Edwyn Bevan. (Home University Library.) Oxford University Press, London. 1932.

The Faith of the Bible, J. E. Fison. Pelican Books, Harmondsworth. 1957.

Understanding the New Testament, H. C. Kee & F. W. Young. Prentice-Hall Inc., Inglewood Cliffs, New Jersey. 1957.

Preface to Bible Study, Alan Richardson. Westminster Press, Philadelphia. 1944.

The Bible and the Common Reader, Mary E. Chase. Macmillan & Co., London. 1944.

The Church of Our Fathers, Roland H. Bainton (Revised Edition). Charles Scribner's Sons, New York. 1941.

England's Churches, Their Rise and Witness, H. A. L. Jefferson. Rockcliffe Publishing Corp., London. 1948.

Several series of books, designed for the general reader, are available. These include:

(*a*) *Ecumenical Biblical Studies*. Published by Student Christian Movement Press, London.

(*b*) *Religion and Life Books*. Published by Student Christian Movement Press, London.

(*c*) *The Christian Faith Series*. Ed. Reinhold Niebuhr. Published by Doubleday Inc., London.

(*d*) *Reflection Books*. Published by the Association Press, New York.

(*e*) *Harper Torchlight Books*. Published by Harper & Bros., New York.

As an introduction to the Christian faith in its doctrinal expression, the following are among many available:

Christian Commitment, E. J. Carnell. Macmillan & Co., New York. 1957.

Christian Belief, A. R. Vidler. Student Christian Movement Press, London. 1950.

The Truth of the Gospel, G. B. Caird. Oxford University Press, London. 1950.

The Gospel and Modern Thought (or *Science, History and Faith*), Alan Richardson. Oxford University Press, London. 1950.

Christian Apologetics, Alan Richardson. Student Christian Movement Press, London. 1947.

Many Creeds: One Cross, C. E. Storr. Student Christian Move-
The Problem of Pain, C. S. Lewis. G. Bles Ltd., London. 1942.
Christian Counter-Attack, H. Martin *et al.* Student Christian
Movement Press, London. 1943.
The Padre's Question Box. Ed. L. F. Church. Epworth Press,
London. 1945.
Asking Them Questions. Ed. R. S. Wright. 3 vols. Oxford
University Press, London. 1936-50.
Soldiers Also Asked. Ed. R. S. Wright. Oxford University
Press, London. 1944.
Many Creeds: One Cross, C. E. Storr. Student Christian Move-
ment Press, London. 1945.
God and the World Through Christian Eyes. Ed. L. Hodgson.
2 vols. Student Christian Movement Press, London. 1933-34.
The Reconstruction of Belief, Charles Gore. Containing in one
volume *Belief in God, Belief in Christ*, and *The Holy Spirit
and the Church.* Charles Scribner's Sons, London. 1926.

10. *Journals*

Too few families subscribe to religious periodicals other than
denominational newspapers. It is important to cultivate acquaintance
with some of the many learned journals in the field. Some are
highly technical, but among those more easily read are:

> *The Expository Times.* Edinburgh.
> *The Journal of Religion.* Chicago.
> *The Ecumenical Review.* Geneva.
> *Canadian Journal of Theology.* Toronto.

There are also journals the purpose of which is to discuss current movements and political principles in the light of Christian
ideas. These include:

> *The Christian Herald.* New York.
> *The British Weekly.* Edinburgh.
> *The Christian Century.* Chicago.
> *Christianity and Crisis.* New York.
> *Christianity Today.* Washington.

11. *Religious Fiction*

Much of our literature contains references to the essential problems of religion, morals, and philosophy, as do, for example, the
novels of Aldous Huxley. Other novels are imaginative develop-

ments of biblical or theological themes. These must always be taken for what they are, imaginative reconstructions and not factual or documented works of research.

(*a*) Valuable for recreating the atmosphere and issues of a period, and available in various paperbound series, are such novels as:

> *The Galileans*, F. G. Slaughter. Doubleday Inc., London. 1953.
> *The Road to Bithynia*, F. G. Slaughter. Doubleday Inc., London. 1951.
> *Confessors of the Name*, Gladys Schmitt. Signet Books, New York. 1952.

(*b*) Less successful, because of the vastness of the central figure, are novels based on the life of Christ, such as:

> *The Man Born to be King*, Dorothy Sayers. Victor Gollancz Ltd., London. 1945.
> *The Hidden Years*, John Oxenham. Longmans, Green, New York. 1925.
> *Bold Galilean*, Legette Blythe. University of North Carolina Press, Chapel Hill. 1948.

(*c*) Fiction of a different kind, more nearly comparable to Dante's *Divine Comedy*, Milton's *Paradise Lost*, or Bunyan's *Pilgrim's Progress*, deals with such problems as the origin of evil and the experience of redemption. Among many modern examples are:

C. S. Lewis,
> *The Screwtape Letters*. Macmillan & Co., New York. 1943.
> *Out of the Silent Planet*. Macmillan & Co., London. 1943.
> *Voyage to Venus*. Macmillan & Co., London. 1944.
> *The Pilgrim's Regress.* G. Bles Ltd., London. 1943.

Charles Williams,
> *War in Heaven*. Pellegrini & Cudahy, New York. 1949.
> *The Place of the Lion*. Pellegrini & Cudahy, New York. 1951.
> *Descent into Hell*. Pellegrini & Cudahy, New York. 1949.
> *Many Dimensions*. Pellegrini & Cudahy, New York. 1949.
> *The Descent of the Dove*. Pellegrini & Cudahy, New York. 1950.
> *He Came Down From Heaven*. Faber & Faber Ltd., London. 1950.

(*d*) Stories of contemporary religious life, complete with the foibles of the godly, need not be cynical. An example of the joy of godliness can be seen in:

Bruce Marshall,
> *All Glorious Within* (or, *The World, the Flesh and Father Smith*). Constable & Co. Ltd., London. 1944.
> *Father Malachy's Miracle*. (Revised Edition.) Constable & Co. Ltd., London. 1944.

Works by G. K. Chesterton, Dorothy Sayers, T. S. Eliot, and Graham Greene often fall into the category of religious fiction, or fiction with an underlying religious theme. Notable also are the introductions by Dorothy Sayers to her translation of Dante in the Pelican Book edition. Such works of fiction often illuminate the meaning and relevance of scripture more tellingly than do the commentaries. One can hardly appreciate the subtle cogency of the treatment, however, without some prior knowledge of the Bible and of theological thought.

INDEX